D1450851

# MODERN ITALIAN SOCIAL THEORY

# MODERN ITALIAN SOCIAL THEORY

*Ideology and Politics from Pareto to the Present*

RICHARD BELLAMY

Stanford University Press
Stanford, California
1987

Stanford University Press
Stanford, California
© 1987 Richard Bellamy
Originating publisher: Polity Press, Cambridge,
  in association with Basil Blackwell, Oxford
First published in the U.S.A. by
  Stanford University Press, 1987
Printed in Great Britain
ISBN 0-8047-1393-6
LC 86-63257

*For my parents*

# CONTENTS

# PREFACE AND ACKNOWLEDGEMENTS

The present book originated from my Cambridge doctoral dissertation on the origins and political influence of the historical philosophy of Benedetto Croce. I am very grateful to those who helped with the original project and encouraged its expansion into the present form: namely my examiners Jonathan Steinberg and Maurice Cranston, and my supervisors Vittorio Sainati and Quentin Skinner. Professor Skinner has been particularly encouraging, giving me much invaluable advice at the planning stage, and his ideas have clearly influenced the form this study has taken.

Cambridge and Oxford are often portrayed as advocating incompatible approaches to the history of political thought. I have never accepted the implied distinction between historical and conceptual types of analysis, believing rather that the one requires the other. The Warden and Fellows of Nuffield College, by generously accepting me as a Research Fellow, enabled me to test my view that Oxford destinations are best arrived at by the Cambridge road. I have greatly benefited from my residence here, and trust that my debts to Oxford political theorists are as conspicuous as the influence of Cambridge intellectual historians.

Both style and content would have been a great deal more obscure than they actually are, but for Jon Brooks and Louise Dominian's careful reading of the whole manuscript. Without their support, together with the rest of the 'Charles Street Gang', I would never have completed it. John Thompson at Polity Press provided the right balance of enthusiasm and advice to encourage a first-time author and get me to write a book which I hope more than my immediate colleagues and friends will read. Finally, Katie Draper and Elaine Herman valiantly word-processed my manuscript through all its various stages with admirable speed and accuracy. The dedication requires no explanation, but I am indebted to my Dad for taking time off from teaching and research in physics at Pisa University and CERN to search out a number of references and texts unobtainable in England.

# 1

# INTRODUCTION

## *The unification of Italy – making the ideal real*

The Italian state existed as a theoretical ideal long before it became a practical reality. Nineteenth-century Italian social and political theorists concentrated on constructing and agitating for an ideal Italian state united more by a shared culture than by common political institutions. They blamed the social and economic differences between classes and regions on the largely foreign-backed regimes which governed the various parts of the peninsula. When unification was achieved finally in 1861, it seemed to many intellectuals that, in the words of Carducci, 'the epoch of the infinitely great had been followed by the farce of the infinitely small . . .'[1] Disillusionment and dissatisfaction with the reality of the political settlement linked thinkers of all ideological and methodological persuasions. For the earlier ideal continued to inspire the ideas and actions of Italian social theorists, although they had to turn their attention to finding new explanations to account for its failure to materialize. Thus fifty years later, when the editor of the Florentine journal *La Voce* sought a phrase representative of the diverse aspirations of his contributors,[2] he chose the words of Giovanni Amendola – 'The Italy of today does not please us' (*L'Italia com'è oggi non ci piace*).[3] As I shall show below, the divergence between 'the higher concept of life and individual morality' of the intellectual elite and the values governing Italian political life[4] formed a constant theme in the culture of modern Italy, and the tension between theory and practice became the main preoccupation of political thinkers from the Risorgimento to the Second World War.

I

This book provides an outline of the principal texts of the six main social and political theorists of this period: Pareto, Mosca, Labriola,

Croce, Gentile and Gramsci, and a chapter on a discussion between
two philosophers writing after 1945, della Volpe and Bobbio,
concerning the policies of the Italian Communist Party. As such, I
cannot pretend to offer a complete history of modern Italian social
theory.[5] However, I have not restricted myself simply to giving an
account of the major works of the thinkers under consideration
either. Some people conceive social theory as timeless ruminations
on the eternal problems of political organization. Others, whilst
acknowledging recurrent themes in the history of social thought,
regard it as addressing a particular set of issues arising out of a given
society at such-and-such a time.[6] In adopting this latter approach, I
consider two factors which served to place a range of problems on
the agenda of Italian social theorists. The first is the social and
economic condition of contemporary Italy, and the development of
political institutions since 1870. The second is the intellectual
tradition in which they thought and wrote. The questions they posed
themselves were constrained and in part constituted by the norms of
current political discourse. As a result, issues and difficulties which
seem central to us today often did not arise for them, whilst they
concentrated on many areas peripheral to or ignored by current
social theorists. Reconstructing the political and intellectual contexts
of the principal writings examined here has made it necessary to
advert to more ephemeral literature, both by the chief protagonists
and other, lesser, figures. A more complex history of Italian politics
and ideology, therefore, underpins the analysis of the classic texts.

This dual perspective will, I hope, help in the examination of the
key issue of the Italian political tradition – namely the relations
between theory and action. The methodology outlined above is
particularly relevant here, since the political intent of a given work
can be inferred from the manner in which the author manipulated
prevailing ideological assumptions concerning a particular practical
context.[7] Thus for some writers, notably Pareto, the connection
between ideology and political behaviour was purely instrumental,
presenting an *ex post facto* justification of action performed for quite
different, usually irrational, motives. Others, like Gramsci, regarded
the relationship between the two less cynically – they specifically
sought to develop a critique of erroneous forms of thought and to
elaborate an alternative political culture as the basis for a new
politics. Both projects exploited similar ideological conventions to
different political purposes – in Gramsci's case with Pareto's work
and that of similarly-minded thinkers, such as Michels, in mind. In
spite of their differences, both Gramsci and Pareto shared a common
concern with a certain set of problems: the relationship of elites to

masses, the role of ideology in legitimating political power, the organization of parties, the rational arrangement of productive forces; and divided a similar lack of interest in other problems, such as constitutional and institutional questions. Thus whilst they challenged conventional wisdom on these issues, they were also subtly constrained by contemporary definitions of the political sphere. Understanding either theorist, therefore, involves an appreciation of the interrelationship between shifting political relations and alterations in intellectual conventions, not just to explain one by the other, but because of the mutual dependence and internal dynamics of both.

Finally, this method may shed light on the kind of political and intellectual environments which have generated some of the concepts and approaches of current social thought, revealing their contingent and necessary elements.[8] The historical approach to social and political theory had often been charged with foreclosing the possibility of investigating the theoretical or conceptual validity of past bodies of thought, and thus of advocating antiquarianism.[9] This characterization trivializes and misrepresents the relationship of social theory to its past. When we turn to the history of thought it is naturally and inevitably with our present concerns in mind. However, to learn from any thinker one must first try as far as possible to understand what they are saying in a historical context, and only then decide which issues we find relevant and reject others with little bearing on our own societies. Thus the ideas of the Levellers on liberty, property and democracy are still believed pertinent by some people today, but nobody, as far as I know, wants us to return to the framework of ancient constitutionalism within which they were originally developed. Yet it is because salient aspects of these theories only make sense within their original context that they have a limited application for us today – a fact revealed by an historical approach rather than a conceptual analysis which applies anachronistic and parochial standards.

Whilst knowledge of the origins of these ideas aids our understanding of their true force and limitations, to base our criteria of relevance solely on whether or not they echo our own beliefs and judgements would prevent our learning from the past. History renders an important service because it makes us aware both of the varieties of political discourse and of the evaluative assumptions implicit in our own. We can locate, for example, the different social and linguistic contexts to which political terms such as justice, liberty or democracy have referred in earlier times, perhaps forcing us to change or expand our ideas on the subject. The relevance of a previous body of thought not infrequently derives from its *dissimilarity* to contemporary theories, helping us avoid incarceration within a present school of philosophy. The study of social and political concepts, in sum, is not a self-sufficient study, but requires history as its natural accompaniment. For these concepts change as social life changes; the two processes are inextricably linked. Thus in providing a historical survey of these thinkers, I wish neither to immure them in a museum, nor to provide a parentage for some pet theory of my own concerning the ills of modern society or their cure. Rather it is an investigation of a particular tradition of social and political thought, which by presenting familiar ideas on unfamiliar terrain will perhaps make us less confident to pronounce on the 'invariant' and 'omnipresent . . . *central* features of our social experience'. Herein lies the 'important *educative* task of intellectual history.'[10]


## II

The above discussion risks becoming over-generalized and too programmatic. I shall therefore briefly describe the main elements of the socio-political and ideological contexts prevailing in 1860, and highlight a number of the core themes which recur in the six main thinkers explored in the rest of this book.

The social and political problems facing the new state were twofold. They consisted essentially of cultural and economic divisiveness between both the educated classes and the unschooled masses, and between the different Italian territories, particularly the developing north and the underdeveloped south.[11] In 1861, 75% of the population were illiterate, and barely 8 per thousand head of population spoke the national language. Only 418,696, 1.9% of the population, had the right to vote, and of those just 57.2% exercised it in the elections. Provincial differences provided a further source of difficulty. The growing industrial zones of the north, around Turin and Milan, contrasted sharply with the declining peasant communities of the south, and the very different urban development of Naples and Palermo. This situation placed grave obstacles in the way of a unified and participatory political system. Regional interests inevitably prevailed over national ones, with the bulk of the population tied by tradition, language and economic necessity to the local sources of political power. This was especially true of the south, where landlords controlled the livelihood of the peasants so completely that few could afford to take an independent stance. The 'southern question' came to epitomize these problems, and, with the exception of Pareto, it is significant that all the thinkers examined here came from the peripheral, mainly agricultural, areas of the *mezzogiorno* and Sardinia. As a group of writers, known as the *meredionalisti* or 'southernists', were at pains to show, unification had simply legalized the local oppression of the peasants by landowners and mafia bosses, and extended their ominous influence into national politics into the bargain. Indeed, more Italian troops died suppressing the groups of 'brigands' formed amongst southern peasants than in expelling the Austrians from the north.

Although the Italian parliament contained two broad groupings of deputies, the 'Right' and the 'Left', neither constituted real parties with the ideological and bureaucratic structures we expect today. The Right tended to come from amongst the aristocratic, land-owning class, who formed the liberal establishment and had engineered Italian unification. Principally from the north, with a traditional allegiance to the Savoy monarchy, they also had many prominent spokesmen amongst southern thinkers – not least the Neapolitan Hegelians De Sanctis and Silvio Spaventa, and sub-sequently Mosca and Croce. Their wealth and background gave them a reputation for disinterested service to the community, which contrasted strongly with the common view of the Left, as 'unscrupu-lous manipulators and common fixers, with no personal convictions and no dignity.'[12] Lawyers rather than landowners, the Left's foremost concerns were local and personal. Thus, whilst the Right favoured a more centralized government, somewhat inconsistently combined with a commitment to free trade and balanced budgets, the Left devised schemes which, by channelling central funds through to their friends in the municipalities, increased their local power base. Given the lack of party organization and the relations between national and local politics, the descent into clientalism seemed inevitable. In 1876 the parliamentary majority grouped around the Right finally broke down. Thereafter, governments rose and fell by the manipulation of state patronage to gain the support of different factions, whose only allegiance was to the highest bidder. The policy of *trasformismo*, as it came to be known (transforming an erstwhile opponent into a supporter by bribery and corruption), dominated the contemporary political scene, having its heyday under Giolitti, who effectively held office from 1900 to 1914 by means of this procedure.

All the theorists under discussion condemned this system, although Mosca and Croce revised their opinion following the rise of fascism. However the problem appeared insoluble. The two most frequently canvassed reforms were to widen the suffrage and decentralize local government. But, as the Left's frequent support for such measures suggests, in the Italian context these schemes merely exacerbated the problem. Until the rise of organized labour, which many of these thinkers saw as just another interest group subjugating the rights of the individual, the electorate hardly had a will of its own. For they remained economically dependent on the only groups with the resources to seek office – the landowners and businessmen. Since no clash of interests or ideologies around which rival parties could form divided them, they remained what Gramsci termed 'an historical block' constituted of the dominant economic and social classes, which no extension of the vote could shift.[13] Economically, the rural south provided a cheap source of materials and labour, and a market for the industrialized north. Politically the peasantry were in the pockets of the landowners, who traded their votes to the northern businessmen to maintain their respective power bases. As long as this system remained mutually beneficial, democratic procedures were little more than a facade behind which the dominant groups exploited the mass of the population.

The Risorgimento – the nineteenth-century movement for national unity – bequeathed a distinct intellectual legacy to the thinkers confronting this situation. Both the Giobertian catholic-liberal school and the republican democrats inspired by Mazzini had professed essentially eschatological ideologies, in which the unification of Italy was conceived as the realization of a national destiny. Both movements had placed great emphasis on the role of the people as carriers of this national consciousness – they constituted the 'real' nation in contrast with the largely foreign-backed regimes then governing various parts of the country. Whilst effective as a means of legitimizing the revolt against the de facto governments of the time, it had profound drawbacks once unity was achieved. As we have seen, the cultural and social cohesiveness such theories required was plainly lacking. They had attempted to gain the people's allegiance to the new state by invoking nationalism as a quasi-secular religion. Yet the vast majority of the populace remained faithful to the Catholic Church, which did not recognize the united Italy until after the First World War, and forbade participation in elections. In D'Azeglio's famous phrase, the Risorgimento had made Italy, but it had not made Italians. The intellectuals found themselves an isolated group, politically conscious yet rarely holding power, so that the divide between social theory and action seemed unbridgeable.

Basically two strategies developed for analysing society, reflecting the two main schools of nineteenth-century Italian thought –

Positivism and Idealism. The latter seemed particularly compromised by the reality of the new state, since they had explicitly adopted the Hegelian theory of the 'national spirit', or *Volkgeist*, as the basis of their political demands. 'The ideal of nationality', according to Silvio Spaventa, 'has been either the express subject or the intimate and vital material of the Italian movement.' It constituted the 'living consciousness of the state, because it is the intimate reflection of its own material in which human association is brought about, that is to say, the complex of the universal and distinctive characteristics of the people.'[14] Once in government, as a member of the Right, Spaventa was confronted with the awesome task of 'making Italians', thereby reversing the original Hegelian formula of the nation creating the state.[15] The 'heroic age' had passed, and a 'realist idealism' was called for, which would give practical content to the Hegelian's ideas by recognizing the 'limits' of the present. Machiavelli joined Hegel as a patron saint of their creed.[16] The ideologues of the idealist school saw their chief task as residing in the creation of a native cultural tradition, believing 'political unity is not possible where there is no ethnic and linguistic homogeneity.'[17] The chief products of this project were Bertrando Spaventa's studies on Italian philosophy,[18] and Francesco De Sanctis' magisterial *History of Italian Literature*.[19] Both works sought to prove that the ideals of modern philosophy formed part of the real development of history. Their political role as an intellectual elite lay in educating the rest of the population, principally through a national secular school and university system. As Silvio Spaventa wrote

> We would not be fulfilling our duties if first of all we did not strive with all possible effort and expense, so that the culture, which illuminates the peaks of the social classes and was the principle of our Risorgimento, penetrates slowly into all the valleys and lower strata; and illuminates them with its light, germinating the seeds of intelligence, morality and human activity, which in large part are contained within them, so as to reap the fruits necessary for a healthy and robust national life.[20]

They accepted that education alone would not transform the condition of the people. Silvio argued that the state must interfere in social and economic life 'to make the general interest triumph over the particular interests which fight it . . . It must promote universal well-being.' The masses 'desired to participate in the goods of life . . . And the civility of a people consists precisely in this . . . Civility is the unity of culture and well-being. One cannot call a people civilized, where only a few [have the capacity for] knowledge and enjoyment, but a people amongst whom the majority know and enjoy is truely civilised.'[21] In Hegelian fashion, they regarded the state as an ethical unity, transcending and rendering possible the life of contracting individuals in civil society. 'The state', wrote Bertrando Spaventa, 'must draw and concentrate within itself, in its universal substance, the dispersed and diverse individuals, unite in a single and common end the souls and wills of everyone.' A common national spirit, inherent in the particular goal of each citizen, was the pre-requisite of a politically united Italian state. In the absence of a common culture its guardians, the intellectual elite, were justified in governing over the rest to secure those universal goods upon which the pursuit of all individual projects on an equitable basis depended.[22]

This ambitious political programme later inspired, albeit in different ways, Labriola, Croce, Gentile and Gramsci. Cultural politics – the ethical transformation of society on the part of an intellectual elite – was an essential element of all four social theorists. Yet the project was compromised from the outset by the paradox that both aspects of their strategy – cultural and political reform – presupposed the other. The legitimacy of their social policies assumed the existence of a popular national culture, which in turn was unlikely to flourish without drastic changes in the political system – a fact discovered too late by Silvio Spaventa, whose party was indecorously ousted from office in 1876. Finding a real basis for their ideals proved an intractable problem.

Turning to the positivist school, one might hope to encounter a little more of the 'clear thinking' and 'attention to reality' which De Sanctis had urged upon his fellow idealists.[23] However, despite differences in method and approach, the positivists shared remarkably similar beliefs about the difficulties attendant upon unification and their solution. Pasquale Villari, whose *Southern Letters* provided the spur for the empirical study of the 'social question', remained convinced that the chief problem was a lack of patriotic sentiment. He surmised that

> If the Italian revolution had lasted half a century, without the need of outside help, it would certainly have created, through misfortunes, sacrifices, defeats and victories, a new generation; [which would have received] the great education which the sorrows suffered in a noble cause give to a people. But, instead, our patriotism was supported by diplomatic intrigue, outside help, and good luck, such that, in a very short time, with comparatively few sacrifices, we obtained the independence and political unity we'd so desired. And the old generation found itself faced with the colossal task of creating a new society within this new political form.[24]

Villari similarly turned to Machiavelli and Vico for inspiration, and discovered therein a cultural political role for the intellectual class.[25] Positivism, no less than idealism, took on the character of a surrogate religion, an attempt to 'make Italians'. A younger generation than the idealists, and predominantly a northern movement, the theme of 'modernising' Italy replaced the search for national unity *per se*. They believed that by industrializing the country, particularly the south, they could solve the 'social question' of the exploited peasantry and indigent urban masses. A political harmony would gradually evolve, mirroring the interdependence of economic interests governed by free market relations. Once again it was a tradition with eighteenth- and early nineteenth-century forebears, reaching back to the political economists Antonio Genovesi and Carlo Cattaneo respectively.

As a result, they were less concerned with building up a native cultural tradition, identifying instead with European writers – particularly Mill, Spencer, Darwin, Comte and Taine. Yet the problem of social cohesion, and in particular of developing a common identity, remained the chief issue. Like the Hegelians they assumed the inner rationality of reality as the basis for linking the development of a unified civic consciousness with the creation of a united modern state. If the Hegelians interpreted this dual process in terms of the progressive unfolding of a metaphysical entity, *Geist* or Spirit, inherent in both the individual and society, the positivists believed the whole of reality could be interpreted in terms of certain basic physical laws.

Roberto Ardigò, the principal figure of Italian positivism was, like the idealist Bertrando Spaventa, an ex-priest, who transferred his allegiance to a new creed. He adapted Spencer's theory of an evolutionary development from a primordial homogeneity to greater heterogeneity within the social organism. He argued that all 'natural formations', including the solar system and human society, evolve from a single inchoate 'indistinct' unity, to a plurality of 'distinct' spheres. He believed

> The major wonder of the orderliness of nature . . . consists in the fact that the prodigious diversity of the objects which compose it, and the inexhaustible variety of forms it takes, is the result of a simple mechanism, that is of nothing more than attractions and collisions: and that . . . each smallest part . . . working alone and on its own account . . . , or as the blind force which moves it dictates, . . . finishes by harmonising with the small whole of which it forms a part, and this with all the others; and not once but always and in every moment . . . a faultless order, an intelligent rationality of the whole

always succeeds in being present, even when one believes there to be disorder amongst the parts.[26]

He applied this theistic Newtonianism, in true enlightenment fashion, to the understanding of human psychology. The choice is significant, since it reflects the Italian preoccupation with educating its citizens, rather than studying social and economic processes directly, in order to tackle the issue of political organization. He held that the mind (ego) and natural objects were both constituted of sensations, and differed only according to the nature of the synthesis established between them. Consciousness, he believed, created the links between sensations itself, as 'autosynthesis'; natural objects were formed by external action, in the 'heterosynthesis' which gave rise to things. Morality derived from our increasingly internalizing the connections between our acts and their consequences.[27] Ardigò advocated a quasi-behaviourist system of education to aid this process, already implicit in the rational development of modern industrial society, since the technology and complexity of the productive process encouraged increasingly instrumental forms of reasoning on the part of its members.[28] His ideas influenced the Italian school of criminology, particularly Cesare Lombroso and Enrico Ferri, who argued that penalties should aim at preventing crime by being relative to the psychological type of the delinquent, rather than providing a set punishment for a particular category of offence.[29]

The positivists maintained that social injustice would cease once individuals had acquired the altruistic morality attendant upon a progressive evolution of human sentiments – a development facilitated by the introduction of an enlightened system of education and a reformed criminal code. Yet the practical implementation of their proposals confronted the identical dilemma facing the idealist school. The postivists argued that the intellectual transformation of the people would produce concomitant changes in the political and social organization of the country, yet unless they had already established a political base the reforms they desired were unlikely to occur. This became evident, as we shall see, when Ferri attempted to apply these ideas to the formation of an Italian socialist movement.[30]

Ardigò died in 1920, but the influence of his school began to decline around 1900. Pareto and Mosca dropped the metaphysical overtones of positivism, though the study of human psychology and the faith in a crude empiricism remained basic to their understanding of political institutions. Labriola, a former pupil of Bertrando Spaventa, began the criticism of positivism and the return to the thinking of the Hegelian school. Croce and Gentile republished the works of De Sanctis and of Silvio and Bertrando Spaventa, and worked a remarkable renaissance of the idealists' cultural project. Both men were influential ministers of education and successful popularizers of the Italian literary and philosophical tradition. Finally, Gramsci directly confronted the central difficulty of their political isolation, carving out a practical role for intellectuals in the changing of society.

Although each of the following chapters can be read independently of the others, a number of common themes concerning the relation of social theory to political action are developed throughout. I pay particular attention to the relationship each thinker established between consciousness and economic and social conditions, both as a theoretical and a political tool. The different views of Marxism of these thinkers naturally form a sub-theme of the book. Each chapter was roughly three main sections: a brief biographical note; a discussion of methodology, and especially the theory of action of each thinker; and an examination of the application they made of their respective theories to the analysis of Italian society. Since all these theorists commented at one time or another on each other's work, reference to their differences will be made throughout – a comparison aided by the chronological arrangement of the authors. The concluding chapters reflect on the relationship between political theory, ideology and action within the Italian tradition, chapter 8 centring on the post-war debates between Bobbio, della Volpe and Togliatti aroused by Bobbio's book *Politics and Culture* (1955), and chapter 9 offering a number of more general remarks.

# 2

# VILFREDO PARETO

Pareto, when studied at all, is generally interpreted in two apparently mutually exclusive ways. Economists regard him as a classical liberal, who made important contributions to the theory of rational choice underlying the defence and analysis of market mechanisms. Sociologists and political theorists, by contrast, tend to dismiss his ideas as crude and illiberal – as attacking the role of reason and democracy in politics, and exalting the use of force by an elite to impose its will on the populace.[1] The two images are said to correspond to different periods of his life. The first belongs to the early phase when, as an engineer and later a captain of industry, he threw himself into the movement for free trade. The second resulted from disillusionment at the frustration of his early hopes. An exile and recluse in Switzerland, he became the bitter and cynical commentator and dissector of contemporary events. The two divergent views are thereby reconciled by the thesis of an historical break between the early and the late Pareto.[2]

This chapter challenges this view by exploring the development of his sociology in the context of his political opinions and involvements.[3] If disappointment with Italian politics is indeed the key to his sociological thought, then the ideals of the early period repay study by providing the background to his later criticisms. This constitutes the first section of this chapter. I then turn, in section two, to the examination of his system to show how the principles of his economic liberalism governed those of his sociology. Finally, in section three, I demonstrate the continuity between the supposed two Paretos, revealing how his use of the insights of the *Trattato* to describe political developments from the First World War to his death in 1923, echoes his analysis of events before the war.

I claim that the similarity between Pareto's earlier and later views derives from the conceptual scheme he employed to interpret human behaviour. Pareto's liberal principles led him to shrink the political spectrum drastically, reducing all human activity to certain sharply-defined and contestable types – essentially 'rational' or 'irrational'. These categories were then enshrined within his sociology. This, in turn, had the effect of legitimizing a particular form of political practice – namely fascism. Pareto's development thereby illustrates the central issue of this book – namely, the nature of the relationship between social theory and political action.

### THE POLITICS OF PARETO'S SOCIOLOGY

Pareto was born in Paris in the year of liberal revolutions, 1848. His father, the Marquis Raffaello Pareto, had been exiled from Genoa to France in 1835 or 1836 for his Mazzinian opinions, and had taken a French wife. An amnesty enabled him to return in 1855. A civil engineer, he rose to high rank in the service of the Piedmontese (later Italian) government. Pareto followed his father's career, graduating in engineering in 1869 with a thesis on 'The fundamental principles of equilibrium in solid bodies', which inspired a number of his later ideas on economics and sociology. He was appointed a director of the Florence branch of the Rome Railway Company in 1870 and held this post until 1874, when he became managing director of the Società Ferriere d'Italia.

During these years he increasingly took part in political debates as an ardent supporter of universal suffrage, republicanism, free trade and disarmament. Borkenau and H. Stuart Hughes regard his later debunking of humanitarian and democratic ideas as a reaction to his father's Mazzinian beliefs. Yet, as Finer has pointed out, there is no evidence for this interpretation.[4] On the contrary, he was plainly attracted by these ideas, regretting the 'inauspicious circumstances' that led to his being born in France rather than Italy, and regarding someone opposed to the goals of the Risorgimento as a 'bad citizen' and 'a disgraceful being who lacks one of the prime qualities of man: patriotism and the love of liberty.[5] Far from rejecting his paternal heritage, Pareto's writings, in both economics and sociology, have their roots in his attempt to analyse the conditions governing the development of democracy in post-unification Italy, and to struggle for its realization in an uncorrupted form.

The difficulties confronting such schemes can be imagined by anyone with a cursory knowledge of Italian history. The moderate conservatives, the 'Historical Right', who ruled Italy from 1861 to 1876, were obsessed with reducing the debts incurred by the Risorgimento, the Italians becoming the most heavily taxed populace in Europe as a result. This was combined with a centralized and heavily bureaucratic administration, distant and remote from the people, only 2 per cent of whom had the franchise in any case. As attention was focused increasingly on internal problems, the right's inability to stimulate the economy or ameliorate the social conditions of the masses drew increased criticism. Popular unrest manifested itself in violent mass movements – Bakunin's anarchism enjoying a spectacular new lease of life – and culminating in an attempted insurrectional *putsch* in 1874. Unfortunately the parliamentary opposition did little to solve these problems either. The 'Young Left' dropped the Mazzinian programme for the privileged of office, seeking little more than a reduction of taxation and a small increase of the electorate (to 7 per cent of the population) to ensure their continued stay in office. Under their leader Depretis, Italian politics became a matter of bargaining and the exploitation of government patronage to obtain the necessary balance between northern and southern interests by the various party or faction leaders to maintain their administration power. This policy of *trasformismo* character-ized public life for the next fifty years, and effectively blocked any radical change in government.

Pareto's first political writings were primarily directed against the abuses of the Italian parliamentary system and the ruling classes' lack of concern for the plight of the people. An admirer of Mill and Spencer and the British political system generally, he argued from the principle of individual liberty for a policy of universal suffrage and free trade. Pareto contended that the opposition of the bourgeoisie to both of these policies was motivated by the desire to protect their privileges, rather than a principled defence of freedom, as they maintained. They argued that the franchise must remain limited, because only those who paid taxes had a stake in the nation, adding that the illiterate masses were unable to make a reasoned decision in any case. Pareto retorted that responsible government would only result when all, through elections, were involved in it. The vote was not, he wrote, a right, but 'the exercise of a necessary function for the good working of civil society.' The voter required, as 'a first and indispensable quality', the possession of 'the culture and the necessary knowledge to fulfil adequately his task.' Compulsory education was therefore a prerequisite in a country where 78 per cent of the people were illiterate, if universal suffrage was to become not just 'an empty word, but a beneficial reality.'

Following Mill, he defined liberty as 'the faculty of doing everything which in a direct and immediate way does not harm others.' Like Mill, however, some of the conclusions he drew from this principle which have more in common with T. H. Green's 'new liberalism' than 'classical liberalism'. For example, he argued that compulsory education, far from conflicting with liberty, was essential for its exercise:

> Now it is manifestly clear that compulsory education should rather be called freedom of education, since the parent who does not educate his son harms him greatly and in a direct way . . . The new born son is a citizen to whom the law owes guardianship and protection, and in fact this principle prevails in the modern legislation of civilised peoples . . . even taking away the father's right to dispose of his entire estate in his will. In virtue of what principle, I ask, must this guardianship, which is exercised over material goods, be diminished when treating that other patrimony, education, which is indispensable to all but above all to those, and they are the majority, who have no other?[6]

Pareto defended the workers' right to combine and strike on analogous grounds. The innovative studies of Franchetti, Sonnino, Fortunato and Villari, from 1874 onwards, had already revealed the abject poverty oppressing the southern peasantry.[7] Pareto's own experience made him aware of the similar conditions prevailing amongst factory workers in the north.[8] Commenting on a proposal to set a minimum wage and a maximum margin of profit, he sarcastically speculated on where the 'lovers of liberty', who opposed it, had been hiding

> when the tide of government interference was growing, instituting monopolies of every sort. It must be because of my weak mental faculties that I can't understand such a subtle distinction, but I fail to understand . . . how the principles of economics are unhurt when one punishes a citizen who does not want, either in agreement with others or alone, to sell his labour for a supposedly fair price and are mortally wounded when one imposes this just wage not on the worker but on the person who exploits him. For my own part I believe that justice leaves open only two paths: either the state does not meddle either in this nor in many other even graver ways in the relations between capital and labour and only exercises the office of maintaining free competition, or if it intervenes, it does so impartially, in everyone's favour, and not constantly for one side and to the detriment of the other. Either the state protects nobody or it protects everybody; beyond this there are only arbitrary acts, injustice and damage to national prosperity.[9]

Pareto argued that if there were really uncorrupt elections and free competition then everyone's welfare would improve, because the opinions and talents of the best would prevail to the advantage of the whole community. In many respects this remained his conviction. Yet it was equally clear to him that, given the current state of affairs, the workers' use of extreme tactics to get their grievances heard was both justified and reasonable.

Increased familiarity with parliamentary politics did little to improve his poor view of it. He stood twice as a candidate, in 1880 and 1882, and declined a third opportunity in 1886 in no uncertain terms: 'I've already had too many opportunities for seeing at close quarters the bad faith and cowardice of certain people without seeking out other ones. I'm content with the satisfaction of despising them and of saying it loudly to everyone.'[10] He withdrew increasingly from active participation in politics and business, resigning as managing director of the Italian Iron and Steel Company in 1889 in order to devote himself to writing.

His career as an economist and political journalist took off in these years, and be began to develop many of the core ideas of his sociology. His liberal convictions and his growing cynicism were fuelled by a deterioration, even by Italian standards, of the political climate. Depretis died in 1887 and was succeeded as Prime Minister by Francesco Crispi. Originally a Mazzinian Republican and a follower of Garibaldi, in power he became an authoritarian demogogue. An admirer of Bismark, he mixed repressive domestic measures with abortive schemes for colonial expansion, whilst continuing to exploit the system of *trasformismo* to retain his parliamentary support. A disastrous economic and foreign policy, combined with government corruption, produced a number of financial scandals which supplied Pareto's caustic pen with plenty of material.

He had become friendly with the liberal economist Maffeo Pantaleoni, and began to gain a reputation as an economic theorist because of his development of the market theories of Walras and Edgeworth through the application of sophisticated mathematical techniques. He combined the two activities of polemicist and economist when, at Pantaleoni's invitation, he began to contribute numerous comments on contemporary politics (*'cronache'*) to the *Giornali degli Economisti* from 1891 to 1897. The themes noted in his earlier polemics continued to predominate. Pareto retained his commitment to individual liberty, and his conviction that militarism and protectionism originated from the selfish and ultimately short-sighted desire of the bourgeoisie to keep their dominant position. This led him to express sympathy for the socialist cause – a fact which may surprise those who only know him for the ridicule he poured on the 'socialist myth' in *Les Systèmes Socialistes* (1901). Pareto's early support was, however, not inconsistent with his later scorn for the doctrine, which he never accepted.

Pareto had already warned the middle classes that 'it is to count over much on human ignorance, to expect that one can persuade the workers of the inefficiency, or worse the damage, that would come from measures wholly analogous to those adopted by the wealthy for their own ends'.[11] The protectionist policies subsequent on Italy's joining the Triple Alliance, which led to a drop of 40 per cent in exports previously secured by a free trade agreement with France, seemed to confirm his worst fears. 'Popular socialism', he now argued, was but the natural response to 'bourgeois socialism', the only difference being that the latter pursued the less laudable aim of favouring the haves rather than the have-nots.[12] Pareto bemoaned the lack of scientific judgement amongst the populace which could allow two such erroneous doctrines to hold sway, because once in power the socialists acted no differently from the others.[13] Even 'if power should pass into the hands of the masses, they would make no better use of it, on the contrary, as they are still more ignorant and brutal than the *bourgeoisie*, their oppression would be worse.' The remedy was not in a change of masters, though that might be necessary by way of transition:

[A]s I look at it, the only way of diminishing the sum total of suffering in the country is to withdraw the individual as far as possible from the power of the government or of the commune, – that is, to follow a path opposite to that which has led us to the existing *bourgeois* socialism, and which will lead us, in the future, to popular socialism.[14]

The problem lay 'not with the men', or not only with them, but with the system of ideas they espoused.[15] He greatly admired individual socialists, such as Napoleone Colajanni, who risked prison by denouncing the wrongs of contemporary politics. Moreover, he appreciated that it was faith in a socialist future which gave them the strength to risk their personal liberty in so doing. This position is well expressed in the following passage from a letter to Colajanni:

I am not a socialist, and I'm saddened by that, because if I could have that faith I would see a better moral reward for the work of those who fight to better the lot of the people than can be expected from Political Economy. But it seems to me that socialists and economists should be able to travel some way along the same road, to oppose the evil ways of our rulers.[16]

Pareto remarked that he felt his position 'in comparison to the socialists and supporters of our governments is similar to that occupied by the positivists with respect to the various religious beliefs.' Indeed, anticipating his later theory of ideologies and his use of Sorel's theory of myths, he maintained that socialism and reactionary conservatism had exactly the same attraction as Christianity, from which they derived their form. However, whilst they undoubtedly appealed to genuine emotional needs, and had a practical value in inspiring people to act, their 'scientific' value was nullatory, 'unfortunately lacking the use of the experimental method to make them profitable, the sole secure guide to human reason'.[17]

Pareto contended that the attempt to define the best society for humankind was inherently authoritarian, since the possibilities for human expression and fulfillment defy classification. As a result freedom, even occasionally to make mistakes, must be conceded so that full scope could be given to human diversity. Mill and Spencer were still very much at the forefront of his thinking, and he demonstrated a faith in the progress of reason worthy of these heirs of the Enlightenment. He exhorted the liberals to employ rational argument, rather than force or deception, to make their case, 'thereby paving a way down which they cannot be followed or blocked by those who derive their power from lies and fraud.'[18]

Pareto succeeded Walras as professor of political economy at Lausanne in 1893. Here he took on the task of laying the foundations for a science of society, grounded on the 'sure basis' of the logico-empirical method of the natural sciences, in his lectures on economics. The *Cours d'Economie Politique* of 1896 are perfectly consonant with the liberal principles of the youthful social reformer. He aimed to expound the 'uniformities' underlying human behaviour, 'stripping man of a large number of accretions, ignoring his passions, whether good or bad, and reducing him eventually to a sort of molecule, susceptible solely to the influence of the forces of ophelimity [self-satisfaction].'[19] Drawing on Spencer, Pareto argued that society evolved through the progressive development of needs and desires as individuals sought ever more varied and higher forms of self-satisfaction. Societies consequently ceased to be simple homogeneous units and diversified into a heterogeneous organic community. He asserted that an ideal equilibrium between different individuals pursuing their divergent but ultimately compatible projects, could be discovered by a 'science of utility'. However, given the current state of our knowledge, he argued, the presumption must be in favour of individual liberty and the free market, and all attempts at intervention, be it from socialists or protectionists, strongly resisted.[20]

Discussion of the important innovations in econometrics made by Pareto in pursuit of this goal are beyond both the competence of the author and the present study. However, he saw fit to expound his theories in a sociological rather than a purely economic context in two chapters of the *Cours* – on 'social evolution' and 'social physiology' respectively. The argument of the first has already been outlined above; the second is more innovatory. Numerous scandals during Crispi's second administration, from 1893 to 1896, convinced him that the ruling classes were willing to use any expedient other than free and open government to preserve their interests. His friend Pantaleoni's resignation from his post at the Scuola Superiore di Commercio at Bari, due to government pressure after he had criticized their policy of a customs duty on wine, symbolized this further decay of public morality. Pareto felt particularly bitter since he had drawn attention to this paper in an article in the *Revue des deux mondes*.[21] The bank crises led to the further smothering of criticism by free-trade economists. More than ever before, Pareto shared common cause with the socialists, whose followers in the Sicilian *Fasci* were brutally suppressed and the party forcibly dissolved in 1894. This sympathy is reflected in the *Cours* in Pareto's first sketch of what later became his theory of the circulation of elites.

As Finer has pointed out, Pareto neither adopted nor rejected Marxism; he absorbed certain salient features into his own theory and thereby denatured it. Acknowledging a debt to Marx and the *soi disant* Italian Marxist Achille Loria, Pareto agreed that 'class struggle . . . is the great dominant fact in history', but argued that it took two forms. In the first, beneficial form, it was equivalent to economic competition and produced maximum ophelimity. Usually, though, it took the second, harmful form, 'whereby each class endeavours to get control of the government so as to make it an instrument for spoilation.'[22] Pareto argued that it mattered little what the declared principles of the government might be – democratic, socialist or liberal – the effect was the same: the exploitation of the poor for the benefit of whoever was in power. Class war in the healthy sense, he believed, originated from the natural differences and inequalities obtaining between individuals, and was therefore an ineradicable aspect of all societies, the Marxist dream of an egalitarian communist community being a dangerous utopia. However, the class war justifiably attacked by Marx arose not from differences of ability, which might ultimately serve the good of all, but as a result of differential access to the organs of power. In this latter instance, the governing class abused its position in order to serve its own narrow ends. The only solution was to reduce drastically the capacity for governments, of whatever political disposition, from intervening to curtail individual or economic freedom.

The *Cours* puts Pareto's subsequent desire to unmask the irrational and essentially self-interested origins of political behaviour into perspective. His later attacks on humanitarian and democratic arguments did not indicate an aristocratic lack of concern with the plight of the people. On the contrary, they were motivated by a profound sympathy with their condition. He directed his cynicism against those whom he regarded as hiding self-interest behind a veneer of false altruism, not those who had a genuine interest in helping their fellow citizens. However, this reveals a contradiction in Pareto's own analysis and remedy – namely between his belief that efficiency, in the sense of optimal individual utility, could be attained in a perfectly competitive market composed of egoistic individuals, and the need for an assumption of altruism if the necessary redistribution of rights and power which would allow the market to operate in the desired manner were to occur. As we shall see later, a number of problems related to Pareto's defence of individual liberty follow from this paradox.

Government oppression steadily increased in the last years of the 1890s, culminating in an attempted palace *coup d'état* in 1898 when reactionary liberals, led by Sidney Sonnino, attempted to invoke the royal power to exact legislation directly by statute, rather than through parliament. In a series of articles in the socialist journal *Critica Sociale*, Pareto urged genuine liberals to unite with the socialists in their fight against the growing authoritarianism of the state. He remained a fervent opponent of socialist theories, 'but the fact is, that throughout Europe the socialists are almost alone in effectively resisting government oppression and fighting superstitious patriotism, which should not be confused with a healthy love of one's country . . .'[23] This and similar statements, written as late as 1899, might well seem to render Pareto's massive attack on *Les Systèmes Socialistes*, only two years later, inexplicable. Indeed, a change of tone is present only months afterwards in a number of academic articles warning of 'the dangers of socialism', and elaborating his theory of ideology.[24]

This change can partly be accounted for by political developments. On 29 July 1900 Umberto I was assassinated by an anarchist. Instead of inaugurating an even darker period of reaction, this event lent authority to the warnings of the liberal parliamentary opposition, forming under Zanardelli and Giolitti, of the need to conciliate the new social forces or be destroyed by them, a point emphasized by a crippling general strike in Geona in December 1900. Giolitti heralded the new mood in a speech which was to bring the conservative rule of Crispi's successors, Pelloux and Saracco, to an end:

> For a long time attempts have been made to obstruct the organisation of workers. By this stage anyone who knows the conditions of our country . . . must be convinced that this is absolutely impossible . . . The rising movement of the ordinary people accelerates daily; it is an invincible movement common to all civilised countries, because it is based on the principle of equality between men . . . Friends of institutions have one duty above all: to persuade these classes, and persuade them with deeds, that they can hope for far more from existing institutions than from dreams of the future.[25]

This passage neatly sums up the policy followed during the next fifteen years of largely Giolitti-led administrations. He added a new element to the *trasformismo* of his predecessors – that of reformism. He aimed to woo the socialists gradually with piecemeal social legislation and bring them into the existing system, disarming their revolutionary potential by 'putting Marx in the attic.'

Pareto's attack on the socialists should be examined in this context. The period from 1900 to 1902, when *Les Systèmes* was composed, witnessed an unprecedented number of strikes – 1,034 in 1901, and 801 in 1902 respectively. To many commentators it appeared that the leniency of Giolitti was to blame. Pareto's analysis went deeper, fully according with the earlier castigation of the right-wing government and his sympathy for the left. Part of the answer lay in the fact that the strikes were an understandable backlash after years of repression and exploitation. To this extent he still supported the workers. What disturbed him was the manner in which they turned on their fellows who had declined from joining their action, accusing them of a lack of solidarity. This seemed to him to reflect the authoritarian measures of the right. Even worse, though, was Giolitti's connivance at this in order to retain the political support of the PSI (*Partito Socialista Italiano*) and organized labour. Clearly a new elite or aristocracy of power-brokers and 'spoilators' was forming, even more adept at manipulating the institutions of government than the reactionary bourgeoisie had been. Their influence was all the more persuasive, since socialism acted like a new religion and diverted the people's attention away from their true interests with the hope of a mystical and totally illusory future paradise.[26]

*Les Systèmes Socialistes* did not signify the historical break between the young liberal and the future fascist. It sprang from the same liberal belief in the rights of the individual against all forms of authority and the claims of reason against those of religion and tradition. However, Pareto was now convinced that pure economic analysis was incapable of explaining human behaviour. As he wrote in the introduction, it ascribed too much importance to human reason, forgetting that 'Man is not a being of pure reason, he is also a being of sentiment and faith.'[27] Pareto aimed to place the study of these latter elements on a scientific basis in order to build a complete picture of political economy. Yet instead of complementing each other, his sociology became the inverted image of his economics – describing the pursuit of self-interest by irrational rather than rational means.

To the extent that Marxism and socialism had a similar enlightenment heritage, Pareto continued to sympathize with them. He distinguished the 'learned interpretation' (*l'interpretation savante*) from the 'popular' view of Marx: 'The learned interpretation of the materialist conception of history is close to reality and has all the characteristics of a scientific theory'. However, in this form, Marxism was 'at bottom, no more favourable to socialism than to any other doctrine; it is even absolutely opposed to sentimental and ethical socialism . . .' Rather, class war, properly considered, was simply an aspect of the Darwinian struggle for the survival of the fittest.[28] Contemporary politics had quite convinced Pareto of the plausibility of Marx's thesis, but the fight was not just between capitalists and workers, nor could it ever be overcome in a communist society. It was inherent in the essential inequalities prevailing amongst human beings. He still retained his liberal belief that in a free market these differences were mutually enhancing. But in a society which enabled the ruling group to extend its privilege and power, it inevitably led to the exploitation of the weak. Pareto had yet to elaborate his notion of the circulation of elites into its developed form, largely attributing the rise and fall of 'aristocracies', as he here calls them, to natural selection.[29] His firm conviction of the rather brutal reality underlying social processes had nevertheless toned down his crusading liberal zeal, though it derived from similar premises concerning the nature of human action. This thesis, though, was only the background to the principal theme of the *Systèmes* – the demolition of the 'popular interpretation of socialism.'

Influenced by Sorel, whom he came to admire and correspond

with, Pareto developed his comparison between socialism and religion. He distinguished 'between the concrete *objective* phenomenon and the [*subjective*] form in which our mind perceives it. . . .' The first corresponded to our 'scientific' knowledge of an object or of society. The second, on the other hand, often gave quite a different picture and could be found in most of our theories and beliefs. Pareto wished to discover why the subjective viewpoint held such sway over men's minds. The main source of error, he contended, 'lies in the fact that a very large number of human actions are not the outcome of reasoning. They are purely instinctive actions, although the man performing them experiences a feeling of pleasure in giving them, quite arbitrarily, logical causes.' As a result, there were two aspects to any doctrine: 'the real facts" which gave rise to it, and 'the methods of reasoning employed in their justification.'[30] Pareto applied this dual perspective to socialism and argued that whilst the 'scientific' theory corresponded to the 'objective' reality of the struggle for survival, 'popular socialism' covered this up in a mass of high-sounding, humanitarian language.[31] The task of sociology was to classify the 'hard core of sentiments' from which the various and often seemingly contradictory beliefs and theories derived.[32]

This task was only sketched out in the *Systèmes* and formed the subject of the *Treatise of General Sociology* of 1916. His concern for the moment was to show that however well-intentioned 'popular socialists' might be, their ideas had but one consequence – the expropriation of one part of the nation by the other, ruling section. The motivation for his attack on communist ideals has often been misinterpreted as a desire to bolster the power of the bourgeoisie. This interpretation mistakes Pareto's purpose entirely. He did not attack those who genuinely felt for the poor and oppressed, and supported individual freedom, but maintained that those who argued for these causes on socialist grounds were either deluded or charletons. Politicians like Giolitti claimed to be working a peaceful social revolution, Pareto regarded this as simply a cover for their own ends. They hoped to retain political power by meeting the workers' demands, but he saw it as the last desperate effort of an exhausted class. 'Bourgeois socialism' was being replaced by the new leaders of 'popular socialism'. The bourgeoisie's new-found enthusiasm for liberty, democracy and equality was indicative of its inability to oppose the new social forces. When this became apparent he believed a direct clash would occur and the new elite of workers' leaders would take over.[33] This would not inaugurate the communist utopia, but another era of oppressors and oppressed. The struggle between different individuals he concluded could not be abolished.[34] Indeed, even in a free market system only the harmful consequences of this struggle were prevented, since it was instrumental to the progress of society.[35] Socialists who ignored this reality would become its victims. As his favourite Genoese saying expressed it: 'Play the sheep and you will meet the butcher.'[36]

*Les Systèmes Socialistes* was the work of an entrenched economic liberal, not a die-hard reactionary. Pareto was not alone in his disillusionment with Giolitti's regime. Young intellectuals of both left and right castigated his system of compromise as corrupt. Radical socialists believed Giolitti had undermined the revolutionary potential of the proletariat, buying them off with transient material benefits; and nationalists bemoaned his abandoning the creation of an Italian Empire.[37] As we shall see, a similar anger towards this belittling of their hopes for a revived new Italy expressed itself in all the major theorists of this period.

Compared with many of the accusations and fantastic projects of his contemporaries, Pareto's work seems both restrained and reasonable. A well-known review of *Les Systèmes Socialistes*, by the intellectual entrepreneur Giuseppe Prezzolini, illustrates this contrast. Like most of his generation, Prezzolini was somewhat maverick in his political allegiances, regarding himself as part of an intellectual elite which praised creativity and individuality, and damned conformity and the second-rate. He regarded Pareto's book as a warning to the bourgeoisie not to become the dupes of the socialists, whose leaders sought to replace their benign rule and set up as an 'aristocracy of brigands.'[38] Pareto responded that he had not taken sides on the issue, showing if anything more sympathy for the socialists' energy than for the pathetic acquiescence of the middle classes.[39] As he had made plain in the *Cours*, he viewed Prezzolini's elitist nationalism with a distaste matching his aversion to socialism, regarding it as 'equally exaggerated, only in the opposite direction'. The 'neo-aristocrats' had simply reversed the socialist 'gospel of complete equality . . . According to them, the whole human race existed merely in order to produce a few superior men; it was only compost for some flowers'.[40] Prezzolini captured the difference of their approaches in his reply: 'In a word, you see in the theory of aristocracies a scientific theory; I see it instead as a scientific justification of my present political needs.[41]

If Pareto desired to write 'scientifically' on the subject, this did not entail an absence of political passion. In fact, this ambition was the expression of his point of view. He had long divorced himself from the existing parties and decided to limit his own political activity to his study.[43] His bitterness at the political scene was no more a sign of support for the bourgeoisie than it had previously been for the socialists. He opposed oppression from either side, but the hope that the socialists would be more tolerant than their adversaries seemed to have become a chimera. He succinctly expressed his position in the following passage from an article of 1905:

> Before, the restrictive legislation was all to the advantage of the bourgeoisie, and against the people; whoever fought it, therefore, could honestly believe he was working to create a just regime, which would not favour either side with privileges. I do not see how you can demonstrate such a conception to be erroneous *a priori*, and it seems to me that only subsequent events have the power to give such a demonstration, as they have done. They have shown that we have not stopped even for a moment at a mid-point, where there are no privileges; instead the bourgeois privileges have been abolished only to make way for the popular privileges, so that he who fought all privilege, in reality and contrary to his intention has succeeded only in substituting one kind for another.[43]

The *Trattato* originated as an indictment of human cupidity and foolishness, rather than a Machivellian handbook on how to use irrationality and force to undermine the aspiration to set up a humanitarian and democratic society. On the contrary, Pareto shared this goal, but despaired of its ever being realized. His ideal liberal polity assumed that individuals acted as rational calculators, able to work out where their self-interest lay. Unfortunately, as he had written to Pantaleoni, the study of society had convinced him that 'reason is of little worth in giving form to social phenomena. Quite different forces are at work. This is what I want to demonstrate in my sociology . . .' He thus ignored the exhortations of his friend, and gave up what he now viewed as the utopian study of economics for the real world of society.[44] However, by turning the political practices of contemporary Italy into universal laws of human behaviour, he had the effect of legitimizing the very attitudes which he had previously sought to condemn. In the next two sections I shall show, first, how Pareto transformed his bitter characterization of Italian politics into a general sociology; and, second, demonstrate that this led to an endorsement of fascism.

## PARETO'S SOCIOLOGY OF POLITICS

Although not published until 1916, the *Trattato* was the product of 'twenty years of study'.[45] Vast and 'monstrous' as it is,[46] a guiding thread can nevertheless be discerned. Pareto desired to unmask ideologies of all kinds, and reveal the true structure of society. He aimed at separating factual analysis from evaluation. He achieved this by denying the validity of discussing the ultimate value of any political system. Politics consisted of necessarily subjective emotional responses, conditioned by our nature and social experience.[47] All science could do, he argued, was describe those psychological states which correspond to particular values, and show how people attained their goals. But the worthiness of aspirations and ends could not be judged. He consequently made an important distinction, implicit in his earlier work, between the claims people make for their acts and the real motivations behind their behaviour, and he attempted to show that there was no necessary connection between the two.

Pareto divided actions into 'logical' and 'non-logical'. The former adhered to the criterion of scientific rationality he had outlined in *Les Systèmes*. He defined them as actions 'logically linked to an end, not only in respect to the person performing them, but also for those who have a more extensive knowledge . . .' The latter consisted of all the remaining actions, which failed to adopt 'logico-experimental' modes of reasoning. These 'other actions' were 'non-logical; which does not mean illogical.' Pareto noted that the subject believed most of his deeds belonged to the first category – 'For Greek mariners, sacrifices to Poseidon and rowing with oars were equally logical means of navigation.'[48] However, he argued that because only the second belief was susceptible to empirical verification, it alone was 'logical'.[49] Regrettably most human behaviour therefore belonged to the 'non-logical' class.

This rather narrow definition of rationality led Pareto into a number of difficulties, since almost no normative proposition is of this nature. Yet axioms such as 'Do as you would be done by' form part of the moral fabric of any society. Pareto, by suggesting that only action towards a definite and attainable end was valuable and meaningful, risked undermining the complex web of tacit understandings that make up social life, and replacing it with a crude utilitarian rationalism. This danger was signalled by Croce who, in a review of the *Manuale*, argued that Pareto's instrumentalism turned men into machines.[50]

The justice of this criticism became clear in Pareto's analysis of 'non-logical' actions, which he held to govern the vast majority of human activity. Pareto maintained that most behaviour of this class emanated from certain 'non-rational' states of mind. The theories which apparently guided action were a 'logical veneer', subsequent to the original motivation to act. The operative forces in society were not ideas, therefore, but the psychic states and dispositions of which these ideas were manifestations. The social scientist's task consisted of elaborating the 'residues', the constant element, of which theories were the 'derivations',[51] Pareto discovered some fifty-two residues, which he broke down into six classes.

In spite of this diversity, he explained most political conduct in terms of the first two classes of residue. Class I he called the 'instinct of combinations'. The Italian word, *combinazione*, connotes a range of meanings suggesting shrewdness and wit, as well as the usual English sense of the term. According to Pareto, it functioned as an intellectual and imaginative attribute, employed equally by the scientist using the logico-experimental method, the poet in his creative fantasy, and the schemer playing on the sentiments of others.[52] Class II was the 'persistence of aggregates'. This was a conservative tendency, which held on to conventional ways of seeing the world and resisted the establishment of new combinations. Each category corresponded to a broad set of attitudes and behaviour on the part of all human beings.[53]

Pareto claimed that his framework provided a scientific, value-free description of social activity. Yet, though Pareto swamped his readers with a mass of anecdotes and recondite facts, he was not content to remain at the level of simply describing the external aspects of events. Appearances to the contrary, he goes beyond the random collection of facts. Instead of simply stating, for example, that Prussia defeated France in 1870, he provided an explanation of the course of events in terms of his theory of human motivation.[54] However, as Croce was to show, any attempt to go beyond crude empiricism introduces innumerable conflicts of interpretation over the choice of facts and the attribution of motives to the agents involved. I shall argue below, that far from providing a 'neutral' description of human behaviour, Pareto merely endowed his own ideological leanings with a spurious scientific status.

Pareto held that all societies were governed by an elite, the composition of which was constantly changing. The rise and fall of governing classes he put down to the alternation within them of the proportions of Class I and Class II residues.[55] Government, he maintained, required both qualities: the invention, cunning and persuasiveness of the 'foxes', in whom the combining instinct predominated; and the strength of purpose and willingness to use force of the 'lions', moved more by the 'persistence of aggregates'.[56] He classified different types of polity according to the proportions of the two different classes present in the governing elite.[57] Moreover, there was no perfect balance which would keep an elite in power for ever. History showed a constant circulation between these two types of ruling class. 'Foxes' gained power in civilized countries, manipulating the political machine to their advantage to obtain the consent of the populace. But ultimately they would give too much away to the opposition, in order to appease them, and were incapable of wielding force to protect their position. The 'lions', who replaced them, willingly employed coercion and even violence to obtain their ends, but their rule would become stultified and mechanical, and they in turn would fall to the 'foxes', who cleverly exploited them for their own ends.[58] Finally, the political cycle was paralleled by changes in the economy between two similarly-motivated economic groups – the speculators and the *rentiers* respectively.[59]

Although Pareto tended to draw on ancient history for his examples, his theory was clearly inspired by his interpretation of contemporary Italian politics, examined in the previous section. This need not invalidate his position; indeed if his view of events was correct it would tend to support it. However, not content with limiting his thesis to an explanation of the current political situation, he elevated it into a universal law of social behaviour, valid for all times and places. Pareto professed to have tested his system by an appeal to the 'facts of history'. He implied that he could provide empirical evidence of the presence of classes I and II and then show an event to be produced by them – a claim he illustrated with the equation

$$q \text{ (event)} = \frac{A \text{ (Class I)}}{B \text{ (Class II)}}.$$

However, he then admitted that such a procedure was next to impossible, and that we must infer the presence of $A$ and $B$ from variations in $q$. Thus, he first described historical events in terms of his theory of residues, e.g. Bismark's victory over the French in 1870 as the result of his combination of cunning and force. He then explained and purportedly verified his thesis by explaining Bismark's conduct by the existence of the appropriate balance of Class I and Class II residues! By this method Pareto could make any event fit his scheme.[60]

Pareto desired to render the study of human kind scientific in the manner of the natural sciences. The meaning agents ascribed to their acts was taken as a potentially verifiable fact about the presence of certain residues within them. This procedure was entirely arbitrary, since the very choice of which features to study was prejudiced by the interpretative framework Pareto employed in the first place. He ignored differences of scale, organization, economic structure and systems of belief between societies throughout history. However these might vary, he believed, the underlying political reality of the circulation of elites had always been the same.[61] The protagonists of the Franco-Prussian war of 1870 displayed identical characteristics to those of the Athenians and Spartans during the Pelopennesian war, whilst socialists and liberals in modern Italy relived the conflicts between rival factions in ancient Rome.[62]

Yet there are clearly important differences between classical and contemporary politics, for example in the social composition of their democracies, which Pareto dismissed because of his obsession with discovering elites. In particular, two quite different conceptual schemes governed political behaviour in the respective periods. The Greeks regarded the human world as displaying an inherently rational order, as the embodiment of an underlying meaningful scheme in nature. The modern view rejects this parallel between the natural macrocosom and the social microcosm. This produces two divergent notions of personal identity. The ancients regarded themselves as part of a larger order, to which they must become attuned; moderns see themselves as characterized by a private set of drives and goals. Clearly Pareto adopted the latter view, but he thereby missed the point that the political practices of ancient Greece were quite different from those of today. For example, he stated that 'the controversies that raged at Athens over the profanation of the Hermic pillars and the Eleusinian mysteries, and the quarrels that raged in France over the Dreyfus affair, were largely masks and pretexts to cover passions and interests'.[63] This conclusion only seemed plausible because, in his account of the two affairs, Pareto attributed modern drives to the ancient Greeks. Yet the self-interested desire for power and wealth, in many guises quite acceptable today (as in the successful entrepreneur), was universally condemned as a kind of madness by Greek moralists. He criticized the Athenians for recalling Alcibiades from command of the fleet because of 'superstitious' beliefs, at a time when his skills were required against the Spartans.[64] But to describe the act in these terms gives an inaccurate picture of what was involved, since in Greek eyes someone who defied the Gods was *ipso facto* a disastrous leader of men. By attributing the decision to a preponderence of conservative Class II residues over the more realistic Class I, Pareto superimposed a parochial view of the nature of politics, totally at odds with that available to the agents at the time. He treated their religious beliefs as if they could be adopted or dropped at will, as simply the private opinions of the individuals concerned. But this was a presupposition of his sociology, not of those who actually held them. For the Greeks, these ideas and norms were rooted in their social relations, they constituted the practices they adopted and provided guidance about the appropriate attitude to take in a given situation.[65]

Pareto believed he was providing a factual account of Greek and French politics respectively. In fact, he was redescribing them in a fashion which misconstrued the motives of the principle actors so that they conformed to his scheme. However, he went further than this, to impose an image of politics in which anyone who did not seek to serve his or her own narrowly-defined egotistical interests was either a fool or a charleton. Little surprise then, that Pareto should have fallen into the role of the advocate of the Machiavellian use of force and persuasion to maintain oneself in power.[66] Since no political goal could be regarded as more rational than any other, success became the only measure.

This conclusion has led many commentators to attribute a change of political allegiance to Pareto, from liberal to proto-fascist. However, the assumptions behind his sociology were clearly the same as those inspiring his earlier liberalism. He retained the atomistic model of society, as made up of independent individual units continuously seeking different states of equilibrium.[67] He was equally committed to the belief that the best balance of forces was that which yielded the greatest social utility, in terms of the maximum want-satisfaction of each individual, and that this would be achieved in a libertarian free-market society.[68] Pareto's hostility towards ideologies expressed his frustration at what he deemed the irrationality of humankind. But arguing for his own case involved him in a paradox. For all people to adopt the free market and accept the redistribution of rights necessary for the system to work optimally, there must be a prior commitment on their part to the type of society it entails. However, this conflicts with the advantage claimed for free markets over centralized allocation – that they function by leaving the actor as the ultimate judge of his or her own preferences and projects. In fact the necessary measures would have to be imposed, or a sudden single flash of altruism be presumed, if those currently benefiting from the injustices of society were to accept a more equitable division of power.[69] This provides a further explanation for Pareto's later endorsement of fascism. Authoritarian politics appeared to be the only way to free the market from the political spoilation of a democratic order. In this respect he remained perfectly consistent, carrying through to the 1920s his convictions about the proper relation between the market and the state developed in the 1890s. Had he lived long enough to see Mussolini's economic policy, he would undoubtedly have withdrawn his support.[70]

Pareto's programme had two serious and interrelated drawbacks.

i The attempt to construct a science of society based on certain constant phenomena is vitiated by the relation between thought and action. Changes in how we define ourselves produce changes in how we act. Since the conceptual scheme governing human behaviour has not been the same throughout history, no sociological system can fail to take philosophical and ideological mutations into account and accurately describe past acts.

ii Pareto's understanding of his own society was similarly affected. By reducing politics to the circulation of elites, Pareto effectively closed the door on other political options, such as democracy or socialism. Statecraft, according to his theory, consisted solely in the manipulation of sentiments and the presence of the requisite balance of residues amongst the ruling group. Instead of creating a new 'value free' science of society, Pareto constructed a justification of the corrupt practices he had previously criticized. As the next section shows, this conception of politics was easily amenable to fascism.

### THE TRANSFORMATION OF DEMOCRACY

Pareto's methodology hinged on establishing certain polarities between 'objective', 'scientific' thought and action, and 'subjective', 'non-logical' modes of conduct. This epistemological position had consequences in his social and political thought extending beyond the immediate domain of sociological method. According to his scheme, the moral and the rational were quite distinct, the former simply being certain ends particular to the individual who held them. The conflict between competing ethical systems could not be solved by the growth of rationality. For Pareto, reason corresponded to what Weber meant by *zweckrational* – that is, action to attain a given practical end by the most appropriate means.[71]

Since values were largely subjective illusions, politics was the art of the practicable rather than the desirable.[72] The struggle between different individuals could not be transcended, because the goals people pursued were irreducibly diverse. Conflict is therefore endemic to the human condition and the 'scientific' politician could appreciate this. Democracy, in Rousseau's sense of leading to a general will of the people, was impracticable, as no genuine intersubjective values were possible.[73] Instead politics consisted of battling interest groups. Thus 'humanitarianism' was not a true expression of concern for your fellow human beings, but a rationalization of self-interest. When expressed by socialists it was used to weaken the strength of the elite in power. Bourgeois politicians, on the other hand, used it in the hope that piecemeal reform would prevent their overthrow by a violent revolution.[74]

A rational consensus between rival groups being impossible, Pareto put forward two alternative strategies. The first was the use of manipulative technique, appealing to the irrational sentiments of some groups and to the self-seeking greed of others. This was the tactic of the 'foxes' and, he believed, of the Italian middle-class policy of *trasformismo*. However, this approach could only work whilst economic growth kept the populace largely aquiescent and allowed opponents to be bought off. The system broke down in a time of crisis, when the governing class had to use force to remain in power. In such a situation the 'lions' would have their day.

Examining post-war events in Italy, Pareto saw the government as a weak and outmoded party of 'foxes' attacked by socialist 'lions'. The *biennio rosso*, of 1919 to 1920, produced a fresh wave of strikes, far better organized than ever before. The government's attempts to appease the workers, rather than tackle them head on, convinced Pareto of their imminent demise.[75] These events provide the context in which Pareto's appraisal of fascism should be viewed. Mussolini was the man of the moment because, whilst not devoid of the cunning of a 'fox', he could apply force with the strength of a 'lion'. From a 'scientific' point of view, therefore, he was Pareto's consummate politician.[75] What purpose he put these skills to, though, is a matter of personal opinion.[77]

This quandary bedevils Pareto's last writings. Initially he claimed he had simply described the conditions which had given rise to fascism. However it is clear from his letters, and his remarks about the 'red tyranny' of 1919 to 1920, that he welcomed it. He saw it as ending the stranglehold of the two power-blocks of producers and organized labour, who he believed had despoiled Italy before and since the war. His motivation was thus that of the early agitator, appealing to the petit bourgeoisie, whom he regarded as having lost most from the situation.[78]

The only difficulties arose from fascism's lack of an alternative ideology to arouse the sentiments of the people sufficiently to make it a lasting political force. Pareto feared that Mussolini was simply doing Giolitti's dirty work for him, and that nothing would change as a result. His initial support, therefore, differed from that of Croce and other moderate conservatives, who hoped Mussolini would strengthen the liberal regime without destroying it.[79] If fascism failed to establish itself as a new elite, which required fox-like cunning as well as leonine strength, violent anarchy would result. As he warned Pantaleoni, an earlier enthusiast of Mussolini than himself, 'There are growing signs in Italy, very slight it is true, of a worse future than one ever could have imagined. The danger of using force is of slipping into abusing it.'[80] Unfortunately, Pareto had deprived himself of any grounds for isolating what was or was not an abuse.

Efficacy or social utility was the only standard by which he could judge a particular regime. Without further defining an objective standard of human happiness, a claim at variance with his liberalism, this depended solely on whether a group could persuade people that their rule was better than another. The veracity of the claim was immaterial.[81] Pareto could not appeal to our 'real' interests when evaluating the policies of different parties, because this would have infringed the liberal belief that people should be free to decide for themselves what their wants were. Thus once Mussolini had successfully seized power, after the march on Rome, Pareto's earlier doubts faded completely. He applauded the use of force and fascism's anti-democratic stance for only in this manner 'could a radical change in Italian politics take place.'[82] Whereas 'Italian bolshevism' had exhausted itself in sporadic violence, Mussolini had laid the foundations for a new regime via a fox-like appeal to conservative sentiments.[83] 'The victory of fascism', Pareto wrote to Lello Gangemi, 'confirms splendidly the previsions of my *Sociology* and many of my articles. I can therefore rejoice both personally and as a scientist.'[84] He now hailed Mussolini as 'a statesman of the first rank',[85] who would be a historical figure 'worthy of ancient Rome.'[86] He was his Machiavellian Prince – 'the man the *Sociology* can invoke', who would bring about 'the resurgence of Italy'.[87]

There is therefore a certain circularity in the reasoning behind Pareto's sociology. Disillusionment at the frustration of his liberal ideals led to a cynical view of politics as the preserve of various elites composed of 'foxes' and 'lions'. His sociology then elaborated upon this jaundiced interpretation. Finally, the application of these categories to the study of contemporary politics actually confirmed his thesis, though in a manner he would have repudiated. For his theory provided a re-conceptualization of politics which made fascist practice respectable. As Adrian Lyttleton has remarked, 'if Pareto's theory had not existed, fascism would have had to invent it.'[88]

# 3

# GAETANO MOSCA

Mosca is habitually obscured behind the shadow of Pareto. Both are lumped together as the founding fathers of elite theory, and Pareto praised for his more rigorous and 'scientific' approach.[1] This characterization misleads in several respects. Mosca developed his concept of the 'political class' from a quite different ideological standpoint to Pareto – that of the moderate conservative, rather than the classical liberal. As a result, in spite of a similar methodological commitment to create a science of society on the model of the natural sciences, his theory evolved in a manner divergent from his Swiss colleague's, and they reached opposing conclusions about the future of democracy and the nature of fascism. The contrast between the two provides a vivid illustration as to how personal political preferences can completely transform the character of a purportedly neutral social theory. Moreover, it renders senseless the largely sterile debate, carried on by Mosca, as to whether Pareto had or had not derived the notion of the elite from his earlier writings on the same subject.[2]

Unlike Pareto, Mosca did not construct a system of general sociology. His work is far more impressionistic and often contradictory. Although he too appealed to history for proof of the validity of his ideas, he openly addressed the problems of contemporary politics and subtly changed his thesis accordingly. Thus what he lost in logical rigour was amply compensated for by the flexibility and richness of his analysis of political life.

The changes in his thinking are easily traced. Mosca was something of a monomaniac, and essentially wrote three versions of the same book. He gave his first account in the youthful *On the Theory of Governments and Parliamentary Government: Historical and Social Studies* of 1884. Twelve years later he expanded and added to the argument in the first edition of his most famous work, the *Elements of Political Science*, which was later translated into English as *The Ruling Class*. Finally, in 1923, a second edition of this book appeared, with a new volume appended, and this version essentially constituted a third rendering of his famous theory. Formally Mosca only admitted to amendments and additional refinements; taken as a whole, however, they provided a transformation of the original theory. In this Chapter I shall give an account of each successive version, and show that the constant factor behind each extension of his thesis was the changing social and economic situation of the upper middle class in Italian society, whose political role he sought to define and defend.

THE POLITICAL CLASS I

Mosca was born in Palermo, Sicily, in 1858, and his political vision exemplified the southerner's distinctive perspective on Italian politics. As I have already observed, the southern question came to epitomize all that was wrong with the new state. The *Teorica* was conceived at a crucial time, when the upper middle-class elite who had ruled Italy since the Risorgimento – the Historical Right – had lost their parliamentary majority. Mosca's work shares the general condemnation felt by intellectuals for the corrupt practices of the so-called Left. However, he linked his criticism with a direct appeal for a return to government by the ousted political class of 'disinterested' men of the middling rank.

Mosca's diagnosis of the situation follows on from a particular line of thought prominent at the time amongst fellow *meridionalisti*.[3] They laid the decline in the standards of public life at the door of parlimanetary democracy. The enlargement of the electorate to include members of the largely unlettered masses had, they claimed, simply increased the powers of landowners and other influential groups to manipulate the government. Whilst the landlords economic hold over the peasants remained complete, the notion of free elections was a farce. Worse, it provided a spurious legitimacy for their political ascendency. The only solution was the creation of a middling class of independent proprietors, who were free from the influence of quasi-feudal landlords.

The following two examples of Sicilian electoral practice amply demonstrate the accuracy of this analysis:

> In 1881 communal elections were held at Villalba . . . and the Marchese of Villalba, supported by the Mafia, took his precautions ten days in advance. The 214 citizens possessing the qualifications

entitling them to vote were locked up in a granary from which they
were released, eight at a time, and escorted by the Marchese's armed
guards to the polls. The Marchese was elected'.

By 1900 new methods of democratic persuasion had been perfected
to cope with the enlarged electorate. One observer, Alongi,
provided a vivid description of the new voting arrangements:

> Some short distance from the polling station the road was barred by a
> group of sinister figures. Here each voter as he approached was
> seized, thoroughly bastinadoed and forced to drink a huge glass of
> wine. There followed a thorough search of his person, after which the
> government candidate's voting slip was put into his hand and he was
> led or dragged to the ballot box, where the president took the slip
> from him and put it in.[4]

Cynicism about the virtues of democracy is hardly surprising, given
the novel application of its procedures prevalent in the Italian south.
The studies of Sonnino, Villari and Fortunato were largely empirical.
Mosca provided a theoretical dimension to their work, although still
in the positivist mode. However, he also sought to undermine their
contention that democracy was in principle workable once the
sources of economic and physical coercion available to certain
minority interests had been abolished. In this respect he aligned
himself with the conservative wing of southern analysts, like
Pasquale Turiello, who maintained that only rule by a restricted
group of public-spirited citizens could prevent 'a violent return to
barbarism.'[5]

Mosca' intentions were plain in the very organization of the
*Teorica*, which had three main sections. First, a criticism of the
Aristotelian division of polities into tyrannies, aristocracies and
democracies, and the assertion that all political systems are products
of elite rule. Second, a historical survey of past states in order to
prove this thesis. Third, the application of his theory to the
conditions of parliamentary democracy, a discussion which significantly concluded with an analysis of the 'social question', more or
less identified with the problems of the south. The main thrust of his
argument is plain – the democratic aspiration of government by the
people for the people was an illusion, since all rule was by a minority
over a majority. However, the details of his discussion led to a
slightly different conclusion, namely the justification of the rule of a
particular type of minority political class.

Like Pareto, Mosca aspired to ground the study of politics in
certain constant laws of human psychology. As many commentators

have remarked, the methodology adopted to arrive at this result was underdeveloped and inadequate.[6] The main difference between the natural and the human sciences, he believed, was that the latter required an infinitely greater wealth of detailed data to arrive at its laws. However, once historians and anthropologists had gathered together a vast store of solid facts 'it is a case of saying to ourselves: who has eyes to see, sees'.[7] Fortunately for Mosca's subsequent reputation, nothing like this crude empiricism guided his studies. Whilst he was intent on showing that all societies had and would be ruled by a minority, he did not, in Paretian fashion, assume a set of uniform human traits which could explain all the resultant social patterns. Indeed, he damned as a prioristic the racial, evolutionary and materialist schemes put forward by Gumplowicz, Spencer and Comte respectively – thinkers whom he largely admired.[8] Mosca's implicit awareness of historical change, both material and cultural, may have been at odds with his methodological premises, but it gave his thought an extra dimension. In particular, he acquired the ability to appreciate the new conditions of modern society and adapt his ideas to meet them, a virtue noticeably lacking in the system of his rival in Lausanne.

Mosca attributed elite rule to the 'indisputable properties of the social nature of man':

[i] that a superiority of moral character usually prevails in the long run over a superiority of numbers and brute force . . .

[ii] more important and less observed . . . that an organized minority, which acts in a co-ordinated manner, always triumphs over a disorganized majority, which has neither will, nor impulse, nor action in common.[9]

This passage suggests that Mosca thought the political class was necessarily composed of 'inherently superior persons',[10] and that they shared a common purpose and acted in unison. However, it soon emerged that he appreciated that this was not always the case, and that it merely represented his ideal.

He claimed that we do not generally know how political classes come into being. However, he did admit that the two features he had isolated varied over time. In particular, he noted that in modern industrial societies there is a far greater accumulation of power in the hands of government than ever before. The revenue generated through taxes, the presence of a standing army and a bureaucracy that entered into every aspect of public life, gave the contemporary political class an unprecedented accumulation of economic and political power, rendering their organized action irresistible.[11] The qualities of the ruling elite were correspondingly different too. In the middle ages military prowess led to wealth and political success. However this was rarely required, apart from exceptional periods of social unrest when force again became important, and the strong leadership associated with 'Caesarism' was called for.[12] 'Very civilised societies', however, 'which have arrived at a notable degree of maturity', laid the greatest stress on 'personal merit'. This arose not only because such societies valued equality and social justice more, but

> principally because the technical and scientific element is more developed in them, and, as in other departments of a civilised society, finds its applications in public life. Where a special culture, for those who are called upon to rule the destiny of the country, has been formed, and it necessarily is formed in any cultured and civilised nation, it becomes an indispensable quality which every member of the political class must possess to a greater or lesser degree.[13]

Mosca maintained that the requisite degree of culture was most likely to obtain when accompanied by a moderate degree of wealth. Great riches reduced the will to work, whilst poverty did not provide the necessary leisure time for study. Men of moderate means were less effected by private interest and were both more able and more prepared to devote a large part of their time to the common weal.[14] This was Mosca's model public servant – a modern equivalent of the Aristotelian 'great-souled man'. A man of slightly higher rank than the independent peasant proprietor advocated by his fellow meridionalisti, yet below the status of the aristocratic landowner – in sum, a member of the professional middle classes like himself. The class which in his opinion came closest to this ideal was that of the English country gentlemen, who performed the duties of J. P. and Alderman, not as elected representatives or career bureaucrats, but because 'they are called to exercise certain offices by virtue of the social position they occupy. It would appear', he went on, 'that with this system one has functionaries who are the most independent influences.'[15]

The argument outlined so far constituted Mosca's core thesis. Different renderings of it appeared in all three versions of his theory. However, it was all too evident to him that the natural ascendency of the upper middle class no longer pertained. The bourgeoisie had had their brief moment of glory during the Risorgimento, and declined thereafter. Mosca appreciated that quite a different kind of elite now ruled. He therefore turned to an examination of how democracy encouraged corruption and a decline in public standards, as a preliminary to suggesting reforms which would bring about a political revival of the middle classes. A Paretian aspiration to produce a universal law which merely described practices operating in all social systems was therefore superceded by an overtly prescriptive argument for a particular type of rule. Instead of asserting that the rulers were always composed of the best, he was forced to argue that rule should be by those who possessed 'personal merit'.

Mosca began his explanation of the rise and acceptance of democratic practices by offering an account of why political classes, and the moral justification they offered for their rule, changed. As Meisel and others have noted, his thesis was remarkably Marxian for a committed critic of socialism:

> [T]he political elements in a society, he wrote, are never very stable; they continually change with changes in the level of culture and of the general social and economic conditions of a people. As a result there are always new elements in a position of entering into the political class, and usually entering it under the aegis of a new formula, which replaces the old.

Each new class justified its position according to certain 'abstract principles' or 'political formula'. This did not necessarily correspond to the real reasons for a class's success – indeed it rarely did so. However, it had to be attuned to the dominant mores of the age. Thus 'from changes in the formula we can easily infer the changes which occur in the political class, and from the examination of the abstract principles, which inform the first, we can divine the real elements which enter into the composition of the second.'[16] Mosca contended that a political class which did not alter with the times could not maintain its rule indefinitely. Another elite would form amongst the ruled, which in the fullness of time would replace them, if necessary by force.[17] Nor did he believe that a given social and economic situation required a certain ideology – rather the political class chose the 'formula which best suits them' from a number of possibilities.

He did not claim he had discovered an inevitable process of 'elite circulation'. He had merely provided an understanding of the factors militating in favour of alterations in the ruling strata of society. Despite superficial similarities with Marxism, he did not argue that changes in the composition of the rulers indicated the substitution of a whole social class by another; in his view only the men in power varied. This enabled him to explain the apparent paradox of elite manipulation of democracy. Industrialisation had produced new social conditions and increased social mobility so that new political

elements had to be satisfied: namely, the masses. This meant that
the legal and political superstructures of power had to be altered.
Moreover new, largely intellectual, qualities were demanded of
rulers. But the true nature of government remained the same – only
the appearance, the type of justification, the 'formula' and procedures needed to maintain it, were different. The reality was still
rule by an elite. Mosca proceeded to push home his views via an
analysis of the practices of modern Western democracies; con-
centrating his study on Italy. He aimed to show that first, although
the French and industrial revolutions had necessitated a new
'political formula', democracy had no substantive basis as majority
rule[18] and second, that democracy actually corrupted the elite.[19]

He argued that 'whoever has assisted at an election knows
perfectly well that *the electors do not elect the Deputy, but usually the
Deputy has himself elected by the electors*', or more accurately, 'his
friends have him elected'.[20] The electoral system favoured the prime
factor leading to elite rule: the advantage of an organized minority
over a mass of isolated individuals. Voters could not pick at will
candidates from amongst themselves, but were presented with a very
limited number of parties to choose from. Given the 'artificial'
environment created by representative democracy, victory went to
those elements best able to impose themselves, and the notion that
elections reflected the decision of the popular masses '*is a lie*'.[21]

The choice of candidates, he continued, was really made by one of
three different sources of power. Prefects, 'grand electors', and
'political and workers' societies in all their infinite subdivisions and
variety'. The influence of the first, Mosca warned, had progressively
increased with the growth and acceptance of state interference in
local affairs. Once deputies were elected and formed part of the
government, ministers could use their control of the bureaucracy to
manipulate elections. This power largely derived from the vast
sources of patronage available to them from the dispensing of state
jobs, finance and contracts. By this method the strength of the
'political class' could in theory grow indefinitely.[22] The 'grand
electors' were those individuals whose personal social position and
wealth allowed them to impose their will on voters dependent upon
them for their livelihood. Mosca had southern landowners chiefly in
mind, but factory owners in particular circumstances would fit just as
well. As in the first example of malpractice in Sicily cited above, the
system added to the 'grand elector's' already considerable local
power political influence at a national level to protect his interests.
*Trasformismo* consolidated their power, Salvemini pointedly
remarking that the 200 deputies elected by the south from 1880 to

1900 had been 'eternally ministerial'.[23] As long as they could reliably get their candidates chosen, governments which sought to cultivate their votes were unlikely to pass measures which might ameliorate the condition of the oppressed. Democracy had thus considerably worsened the peasant's lot.[24] Finally, the influence of political and workers' associations was predominately an urban phenomenon. Mosca seemed to be primarily concerned with the trade unions and employers' associations, which collectively acted – through their links with political parties – in much the same fashion as the 'grand electors'.[25]

The upshot of these different methods for buying the electorate had been a general decline in the standards of both political practices and of deputies. The independent men of the Right no longer had the stomach for politics, for 'one can no longer use only honest and legal means, one must act like a gangster (*camorrista*) if one does not want to be a victim of a gangsterly attack (*atto di camorra*)'.[26] The system was prone to an infinite degeneration, as everyone, 'from the Minister to the voter, finds their private interest in betraying the public interest which is entrusted to them'. The 'precious qualities' of 'independence of character, boldness and impartiality . . . which constitute the true moral force of . . . political organisms, are increasingly sacrificed', excluding from office the men who possessed them. In parliamentary democracies '. . . moral cowardice, lack of a sense of justice, cunning, intrigue, which are precisely the qualities which bring peoples and states to ruin, are best suited, [and] lead to the advancement of their practitioners, and therefore develop and become increasingly evident'.[27] Mosca argued that democracy was inherently bad, and that the desire to rectify these problems via reforms aimed at instituting 'true democracy' were totally misconceived. They would only make matters worse.[28] He similarly rejected the notion that a genuine two-party system would produce beneficial effects by preventing any one group obtaining a monopoly of power. No genuine competition would take place, he argued, because the parties would always collude together to keep important issues off the electoral agenda, thus protecting their common interests as rival members of the same political class.[28] Anticipating one of his later arguments, he identified the problem in the already quasi-universal authority of the elected chamber. Although constitutionally both King and Senate acted as countervailing forces, they could not realistically perform this function. They lacked an alternative 'political base', representative of 'political elements different and independent from those which create and compose the Chamber of Deputies.' This was the role Mosca carved out within the democratic system for the middle classes. The ministers, the top echelons of the civil service, and the Senate should be royal appointees, and not those designated by the majority party in the lower house. Independent of both popular elections and government patronage, these positions would be formed from 'the most cultured and independent elements of the nation; to which class would be confided the whole provincial administration, and a wide participation in the work of the provincial bureaucracy'. If these reforms were effected '[t]hen King and Senate would indeed have both great prestige and great power, and the Chamber of Deputies would be not only counter balanced, but also effectively braked . . .'.[30]

Mosca readily admitted that such measures would only seem desirable, let alone practicable, if one had 'entirely left the orbit of ideas and the spirit which inform the parliamentary system'.[31] However, he was adamant that this was the only path to take. He likened his project to the 'admirable [English] system of self-government; by which almost all the administrative duties and a good part of the judicial ones, are performed by gentlemen, who serve the country gratis, who are neither dependent on Ministers nor the electorate, and do not have to conform to any other regulations than those proscribed by the common law.'[32] Ideally, he believed, this role could have been performed in Italy by a new aristocracy of merit, a utopian goal whilst differences in economic wealth and power brought such great political advantages. In the present situation of near anarchy, a simple return to respect for law and order took precedence over idealistic schemes from whatever quarter.[33] Reform must therefore occur within the paradigm set by the current political formula.[34]

This last pronouncement appears to contradict the whole gist of Mosca's earlier contention that democracy could never be reformed from within. However, he was clearly moving towards his later position where he re-conceptualized democratic theory away from the notion of popular majority rule and towards modern-day doctrines of pluralism. This revision did not entail dropping the 'political formula' of democracy, although it departed dramatically from the ideals of classical theorists such as Mill or Rousseau. I will give fuller consideration of this development when examining the later versions of his theory, since Mosca expounded it at greater length in the two volumes of the *Elementi*.[35]

The concluding section of the *Teorica* addresses the crucial problem of the social question, presenting a synthesis and application of the analytical instruments developed in the body of the book. This is hardly surprising, given that it had provided the original impetus behind the entire project. The nub of the problem, according to Mosca, were the great inequalities of political leverage arising from disparities in wealth. He rejected both the liberal contention that they were the natural result of free competition, and the socialist belief that they could be abolished in an egalitarian communist future.[36] Government intervention was needed to redistribute the grosser discrepancies between rich and poor. The chief drawback in this scheme arose from the domination of government by the wealthy, who 'to better the condition of the poor will never damage their own interests'.[37]

The solution lay, therefore, in the introduction of non-economic elements into the political class. Whilst riches were an important requisite for membership, other criteria should count as well, particularly 'technical expertise and a high level of cultural attainment', qualities which 'daily acquire ever greater importance' in modern society, 'such that someone who is totally ignorant cannot perform the tasks of high office for long'[38], or as Mosca somewhat naively stated:

> It does not seem possible to us, that a political class, in which a superior culture was obligaotry . . . and to which the children of all social classes can come to be admitted, could then have such base, egoistic and mean aims to subordinate every government action to the interests of gross capital and the big landowners . . . Thus that government is in the hands of the most educated class, and that it takes resolutely the initiative for the betterment of the lower classes, such according to us is the sole means which can lead to a peaceful solution to the so called social question.[39]

Mosca provided two applications of his theory. Elite rule as a description of contemporary politics revealed the manipulation of democratic procedures by economic interests – a view similar to Pareto's. To remedy this, Mosca invoked the prescriptive side of his theory – rule by a disinterested educated elite, serving the common good. Without their countervailing influence, Mosca intimated in the conclusion, a 'new barbarism' would arise in Europe, in which the 'feudal barons' of capitalism and landed property would hold unlimited sway.[40] Maintaining this double perspective involved Mosca in a number of potential contradictions. After all, if the masses were as base as he believed, and greed a universal human characteristic, why should the persons of merit who rose from the ranks of the people devote their superior talents to the common interest, rather than their own?[41] When writing this first version of *The Ruling Class*, Mosca could still hark back to the ideals of the

Historical Right. However, without debating the validity of his (inordinately) high estimate of their merits, it was increasingly evident that as an economic and social group their days were numbered. The new elite would have to be drawn from the masses. This led Mosca to see democracy in a new perspective and try to unite the formation of an educated political class with the procedures and even ethic of democratic government. As the two subsequent sections will show, his continued attachment to the rule of the nineteenth century gentleman class doomed this scheme to failure.

### THE POLITICAL CLASS II

The first edition of the *Elementi* appeared in 1895. In the intervening twelve years since publishing the *Teorica*, Mosca had had ample opportunities to observe the parliamentary system at work as Revisore[42], from 1886, at the Chamber of Deputies. He had obtained this post through the patronage of his friend and protector, the Sicilian politician Antonio Di Rudini. Along with Sonnino, Di Rudini led the right wing of the liberal party and was Prime Minister in 1891 and 1896. His stance sheds light on Mosca's political allegiances during this period. An opponent of Crispi, whose Abyssinian adventures and financial scandals he criticized, Di Rudini also oppressed the socialists and the Catholics – a policy which did not endear him to anybody. However, in his last administration he attempted a moderate conservative parliamentary reform, which sought to counterbalance the power of universal suffrage at the centre by a considerable degree of administrative decentralization, precisely what Mosca had proposed earlier.[43] The additions to Mosca's theory clearly reflected the political concerns of the times. As in his first book, the presentation of principles is followed by their explicit application to contemporary parliamentary politics.

The first two chapters read like a succinct restatement of the methodological criteria and the theory of the political class elaborated in the opening chapter of the *Teorica*. The 'constant element' in all political organisms was still the presence of 'two classes of persons: the one that governs and the other that is ruled', the former consisting of an organized minority which imposed its will by 'manipulation and violence', even, indeed especially, in a democracy.[44]

Mosca both clarified and extended other aspects of his earlier work. In particular, he elaborated upon his explanation of elite circulation. All ruling groups had, he maintained, to become hereditary.[45] Yet when 'there is a shift in the balance of political forces' and new talents are called for, then the ruling class must adapt or (more likely) topple:

> If a new source of wealth forms in a society, if the practical importance of knowledge grows, if the old religion declines or a new one is born, if a new current of ideas spreads, then, simultaneously, powerful dislocations occur within the ruling class. One might say, indeed, that the whole history of civilised humanity can be summed up in the conflict between the tendency of dominant elements to monopolise political power and transmit possession of it by inheritance, and the tendency . . . towards a dislocation of old forces and an insurgence of new forces, which produces an unending ferment of endosmosis and exosmosis between the upper classes and certain portions of the lower.[46]

He reasserted the link between changing social forces as society became more civilized, and the rise of a new political class from amongst the governed. He also noted, in a later passage, that the split could even occur within the ruling class itself, and that the different sections of the minority would appeal to the masses for support.[47] As in the *Teorica*, he is vague about the relations between the 'political formula' adopted and the prevailing social and economic conditions, suggesting it was to some extent autonomous. Like Pareto, he was clearly impressed by the effect ideas could have no political processes, and was deeply troubled by the increasingly ideologized nature of contemporary politics.[48] However, he was less cynical than his rival. Whilst opposed to religion, he recognized it as a legitimate need of human nature, impossible to replace with secular 'rational' modes of thought.[49] He did hope, though, that a liberal moral ethic would emerge, adapted to the needs of the modern age.

Unlike the cynic of the Villa Angora, Mosca only flirted briefly with the discovery of a 'universal psychological law' to link the role of ideas with the circulation of elites.[50] If he elaborated his thesis less rigorously, however, it was largely to his advantage in this instance. Mosca made two general observations about the influence of ideas. First, he distinguished 'social' and 'national' types. The former, as in the great religions, could command universal allegiances which cut across or even opposed duties to the state deriving from the latter. A political class would therefore be ill advised to deny the religious aspirations of a people, but should seek to increase the ties to the state as much as possible.[51] Such Machiavellian advice, rare in Mosca's writings, clearly emanated from his traditional anti-clericalism, fuelled at the time by Di Rudini's recent struggle with the

Catholics, who still denied the authority of the newly-formed state over former Papal territory. Second, he argued that whilst 'feudal' governments could impose a 'universalistic' political formula, 'bureaucratic' organizations are necessarily pluralistic.[52]

At this point, Mosca's supposedly 'neutral' categories clearly emerged as aspects of a normative theory. Whilst bureaucratic government increased the scope for central control of social life, its functions were dispersed amongst a plurality of officers. The feudal lord may have ruled over few people and had less power over their lives, but he filled all the functions of judge, general and tax man. He had a direct and personal relationship with his subjects, and could impose a unified moral code upon them. Contemporary life, in contrast, was much more atomistic due to the division of labour and the concomitant specialization of work and leisure. Mosca, as we shall see, was well aware of certain drawbacks arising from this situation. However, he saw a possible solution in 'bureaucratic' organization. Certain norms of behaviour and attitude emerged from the procedures of administration itself, both products of a progressive rationalization of social life. Unlike Weber he did not fear humanity risked entrapment in an 'iron cage' of bureaucratic uniformity, since he maintained somewhat illogically that it could never be extended to the whole of society, denying even its applicability to the production and distribution of wealth.[53]

The reasoning behind Mosca's additional thoughts on the links between the political class, social change and systems of belief became clearer in the fifth chapter, entitled 'juridical defence'. His remarks here provided preliminary clarifications for a major development of his theory. By broadening the political class to include both 'in' and 'out' groups, which needed to woo different sections of the lower classes, and who had to appeal to a variety of ideological viewpoints to do so, Mosca had laid the groundwork for a theory of elite rule adapted to the conditions of modern society. The increased organization of society, by joining people together in greater mutual dependence rendered

> moral discipline indisputably greater, and the overly egoistical acts, which by the control and reciprocal restraint of the individuals, who make up society, are prohibited or prevented, are more numerous and more clearly defined. . . . The social mechanisms which regulate this disciplining of the moral sense form what we call the 'juridical defence.'[54]

Mosca noted that his scheme did not have recourse to any altruistic or virtuous instincts – 'we believe instead, that as social organisation has the consequence of the reciprocal restraint of human individuals, it makes them better, not by destroying their wicked instincts, but by accustoming the individual to tame them.'[55] Quoting Guiccardini, he argued that a government of law and authority established political liberty by curtailing the selfish appetites of particular men.[56]

So far Mosca appeared to be tracing the development of a natural process within a civilized nation. However, as we have seen, he was all too aware that it did not reflect current Italian experience. Instead he was advocating a particular constitutional reform, similar to Di Rudini's, which he had been developing in a number of legal writings.[57] 'The degree of perfection that juridical defence can attain in a given people' was, he observed, denoted by the 'political arrangements, which establish the character of the relations between the governing class and governed, and between the various levels and the various sections of the ruling class.[58] Should a single political force ever manage to monopolize and exploit the advantages of power totally for its own benefit, then despotism would result.[59] This danger existed in representative democracies, where deputies could claim supreme power. The remedy, implicit in his very definition of a political organization, was to have competing groups within the political class, which would balance each other out. One might have expected him to develop this into a theory of indirect democracy, whereby competing elite groups would curry favour with the electorate. Although all the elements were there, he still cherished a place in the sun for his cultured class, so instead he made the following two proposals. First, drawing on Montesquieu, he advocated separating the functions of government. The church, army, judiciary and bureaucracy must all be autonomous, and not under the control of elected representatives.[60] Second, economic and political power must be kept apart – 'There is no use in cherishing illusions about the practical consequences of a regime, in which the management of economic production, and the distribution of political power, are linked and conferred upon the same persons.'[61] Like Pareto, Mosca applied this criticism even-handedly to corporate socialism and monopoly capitalism alike. The danger of the former though, was that democracy appeared to give these procedures some legitimacy – it provided for the complete hegemony of a single 'political formula' as a cover for particular interests. Its humanitarian pretensions were only a veneer, for

> when all the moral and material advantages depend upon those who hold power, there is no meanness that people will not do to please them; just as there is no act of violence or deception which will not be

resorted to to attain power, or rather to belong to the number of those who distribute the cake, rather than remaining amongst the many others who must be content with the portion given them.[62]

Socialism therefore constituted a double danger, combining a universalistic religious appeal with the concentration of absolute political and economic power in the hands of a party cadre. To criticize the particular measures of socialism did not suffice to undermine its impact – *'to a complete metaphysical system one must oppose a complete positivist system'*.[63]

Mosca clearly offered his own work as filling this role. But his neutral political science was obviously ideological too. Mosca followed Pareto in making two main objections to socialism. First, he contended that the abolition of private property would not solve the problem of inequality. Relations of subordination were based on a variety of factors in different societies, such as the ability to fight or intellectual skills in Military and Bureaucratic societies respectively. Second, he elevated present attitudes into a universal law of human nature, denying *a priori* the possibility for altruism to win over egoism.[64] However, unlike his rival, and in contradiction with his basic thesis, he saw one class whose position fitted them for public duty and were able to transcend self-interest. By now we are no longer surprised to learn that society can be saved by an economically independent group

> Who are sufficiently comfortable, to be able to dedicate a part of their time to perfecting their culture and acquiring that interest in the public good – that quasi-aristocratic spirit – which alone can induce men to serve their country with no other satisfactions than those stemming from self-respect [*amor proprio*].[65]

The gentry ideal surfaces again, and with it the renewed hope of replenishing their ranks to form a meritocracy from a new educated elite: the professional men – lawyers, scientists and technicians – required to service the needs of modern industrial society. A note to the third edition of 1939 reveals the dream to have been no more substantial than that. He claimed:

> This passage corresponded in great part to the truth of the epoch in which it was written, that is 1895: after the war the middle classes of almost all nations were, if not destroyed, more or less declimated . . . This decline of the middle classes has been one of the principal causes of the major difficulties affecting the functioning of the representative system in most of Europe and America.[66]

Preparing a third version of his thesis after the First World War required substantial revisions to cope with this harsh reality.

## THE POLITICAL CLASS III

Twenty-seven years separated the first and second editions of the *Elementi*. In the Preface he said it had been conceived over the past two or three years to take into account both new facts, occasioned by the changed times, and the effect recent events had had on his way of seeing things. He chose not to update the first edition, but to add instead a second volume written from his new perspective.[67]

The critical approval of parliamentary democracy is the most striking aspect of this version. Two factors no doubt contributed to this. First, although he secured an academic post in 1896 at Turin University, and from 1902 taught constitutional law and the history of political thought at Bocconi University in Milan as well, he did not desert the active world of politics. After the death of Di Rudini in 1908 he became a deputy. He remained in the lower house until 1919, serving as under-secretary in the colonial office from 1914 to 1916, during Salandra's administration. In 1919 he became Senator. Although he continued to attack the actual working of democracy, by which 'any party label, conservative or clerical, radical or socialist, only serves to cover up purely personal ends',[68] he did come to believe in the spirit which animated them – namely the ideal of 'free discussion, and the limitation of the exercise of sovereign powers' by governments.[69] Democracy, he now argued, produced bad effects as an abstract ideal, but not if it corresponded to the 'real conditions' of a society – 'According to this criteria the best electoral system would succeed in drawing on all the political values that a nation contains and uniting within an assembly the representatives of all the sentiments, and the ideas and all the interests of a people.'[70] In other words, he saw the possibilities the system offered as an arena for different interests to meet and debate and mutually control each other.

The second factor working towards this appraisal of democracy, was his anxiety about the social divisiveness of the unions. As interest groups operating outside the parliamentary system, he believed they cut workers off from any sense of the general interest. The dependency of the modern economy on certain specialized groups gave miners or steel workers, for example, tremendous economic power, which did not necessarily operate within a legal constitutional framework. The unions acted like feudal barons, disputing the authority of government and the state.[71] He was

perceptive enough to appreciate that fascism offered no solution to
this problem. Its violent methods took it outside the legal matrix,
which he now regarded as vital to political liberty, whilst its
proposed system of corporate representation perpetuated people's
concern with the narrow economic interests of their group.[72]

Mosca's reconciliation with representative government was none-
theless far short of wholehearted acceptance. In two parliamentary
speeches on 7 and 14 May 1912 he opposed Giolitti's proposal for
universal male suffrage and the further extension of the vote to
women respectively. He remained firm in his belief that democracy
only worked if the precondition of an independent middle-class
electorate obtained. His attempt to incorporate this elitist element
into the democratic system was, I shall argue, fraught with
contradictions, which ultimately doomed the project to failure.
Unlike contemporary theorists of democratic elitism, Mosca had the
presence of mind to realize this.

Mosca's notion of 'juridical defence' offered a constitutionalist
solution to the conflict of interests, but was inadequately related to
their origins within society. The new edition of his work sought to
remedy this defect. The central chapter here is the fourth on 'the
principles and diverse tendencies which affect the formation and
organisation of the political class.' Mosca began by broadening this
class to include more than just those who wielded political or
economic power. 'Below the ruling class', he now noted, 'there is
another much more numerous, which comprises all the capacities for
government of the country', and without which the upper strata
could not manage. The stability of a political organism ultimately
depended on the level of morality, intelligence and activity attained
by this lower strata, and increased in proportion to 'the degree of
pressure that the sense of the collective interests of the nation or the
class, succeeds in exerting upon the selfishness of the individuals
who make it up.'[73] The qualities of this second stratum were crucial
therefore, and Mosca's attention turned to the principles and
tendencies regulating its recruitment.

The two tendencies were the aristocratic and the democratic, the
two principles the autocratic and the liberal. The tendencies referred
to the means by which the ruling class was replenished, either by
hereditary transmission or from the lower classes respectively. The
principles denoted the system of authority in vogue; autocratic rule
being of a single person or small group for their personal ends,
liberal governments sharing power with other citizens and expressing
the general will of the people. Although the aristocratic and the
autocratic, and the democratic and the liberal generally went

together, this need not occur. China, for example, mixed autocratic rule with the democratic tendency to recruit the mandarins from the best candidates amongst the masses. The Venetian republic, on the other hand, was governed by a liberal aristocracy.[74] The health of a society depended upon having the right balance appropriate to the prevailing social conditions. The ideal was a mixture of both tendencies and both principles, so that the political class did not atrophy, nor become unstable through a lack of continuity, and the efficacy of government was combined with a certain accountability to the interests of the people as a whole.[75]

Having provided a sociological account of how to ensure a healthy political class, Mosca integrated it into his constitutional scheme for a perfected 'juridical defence'. He achieved this by constructing a system of indirect democracy. Rival groups for office formed in the second stratum of the political class, and competed for the vote of both their peers and members of the lower classes. Mosca argued that if the second stratum was sufficiently large, so that not everybody could hope for office, this would prevent collusions between the different factions to manipulate the electorate for their collective interest. There would remain a large number of independent voters capable of enjoining responsible government.[76] However, a difficulty arose if universal suffrage was granted too soon, so that the ignorant masses could outvote this middle group. By appealing to the basest sentiments, the ruling groups could gain the support of the masses for their self-serving policies.[77] Thus, whilst the democratic tendency was beneficial in rejuvenating the political class, it was disastrous if adopted integrally and the aristocratic virtues dropped altogether. Similarly the liberal principle of free debate should always be tempered by a respect for authority, and vice versa.[78]

This conclusion placed Mosca in a quandary, since he freely admitted that the balance he desired had only obtained during the brief 'belle epoch' of the late nineteenth century. Mosca's reflections had come full circle, irrevocably wedded, throughout all their different versions, to a view of society which was anachronistic even in 1884, at the start of his career. Unlike recent advocates of democratic elitism, Mosca was aware of the interrelationship of political organization and social forces. In turn of the century Europe there was a large enfranchized middle class, whose ranks could be joined by upward social mobility from the working classes. Whether the system worked quite as well as Mosca's encomium made out may be doubted. Yet even he had to admit that 'the greatest and most magnificent of all the eras that humanity has traversed' came indisputably to an end with the First World War.[79]

Only the confrontation with the autocratic rule of fascism finally reconciled Mosca to the representative system. Democracy at least offered a modicum of control over the government, providing 'a regime of liberty' in the only manner possible at the time 'given the extent of modern states and the complexity of their structure'.[80] However, to be totally consistent, Mosca would have had to drop the exclusivity of the political class *vis à vis* the masses. He was unwilling to do so because he realized that only if education and increased prosperity had turned all the electorate into middle-class voters would democratic elitism be a plausible option.[81] Its champions of the 1950s, like Dahl and Lipset, clearly believed this had occurred. A presupposition of pluralist theories, evident in the companion thesis of 'the end of ideology', consisted in an assumed general and fundamental agreement on values in society. If there were no such agreement, then the clash between diverse interests would foreclose the possibilities for conciliation and accommodation between rival groups. Pluralists claimed that the diffusion of power creates the necessity to respect the needs and demands of others. However, unless the forces involved were really equal, a highly unlikely event, arbitration between the two would always reflect the prevailing balance of power. For impartial government to result, there must exist certain ground rules and principles of justice or equity commonly accepted by all parties.[82]

Mosca had realized early on that the capacity of a political class to govern depended upon the degree of acceptance of its political formula. His theory of 'juridical defence' was not a substitute for this notion, but built upon it. He assumed a 'collective moral sense' as the key to the successful operation of a political organism.[83] Adopting the elitist model of democracy posed a real difficulty. Classical theorists of participatory democracy argued that it was intrinsically good, and that involvement in decision making together with others transformed the individual into a citizen. Proponents of indirect democracy, in contrast, regarded the masses as self-interested and essentially inactive. Mosca appreciated that paradoxically this system of government would not work either, unless the electorate had attained the same degree of cultural and moral awareness that classical theorists regarded as the product of participation alone.[84] Mosca maintained that this posed an insuperable dilemma: liberalism and democracy presupposed a common cultural and moral base, yet, contrary to what Mill and Rousseau believed, they undermined the consensus necessary for them to function. Both doctrines were based on the belief that 'the good sense of the people suffices to distinguish truth from error and to bring to justice anti-social and harmful ideas.' Mosca contended that this notion was defeasible, and far from producing 'a better and more moral system of social and political organisation in the future, is certainly well suited to destroy that presently existing.[85] The problem was that the world which had produced a healthy balance between the two principles and the two tendencies no longer existed, for the First World War had destroyed the younger generation, which would have renewed the ranks of the middle classes, and created deep social and moral divisions. He despaired of a new class arising amongst the masses, as he lacked faith in the practicality of the ideals of liberty, equality and fraternity espoused by democrats.[86] As a result, his liberalism no longer had a foundation, and his stoic defence of it lacked conviction. Patriotism, which he feebly clutched at as the basis for a new secular religion, had already revealed its destructive side in the rampant nationalism of the First World War.[87] Instead he feared a return to a new barbarism, 'which this time will be without God, and hence without the observation of oaths, and will have at its disposition in exchange the aeroplane, asphyxiating gasses and dynamite.'[88] The basis of the modern state would be force alone.

The attempt to rebuild a community, based on a common faith, from the ruins of the war, was one of the prime considerations of the idealist school, and in particular the two thinkers Mosca most influenced – Croce and Gramsci. Similarly preoccupied by the existence of two classes within the new nation, they rejected positivism as inadequate for the necessary task of creating a moral framework for political action. The first steps towards their alternative treatment of the problem were prepared by Antonio Labriola, to whom we must now turn.

# 4

# ANTONIO LABRIOLA

Labriola has suffered the curious fate of being much praised and little written about.[1] First-hand knowledge of his writings is relatively rare even in Italy, yet he was tremendously important for the development of the main currents of Italian political thought in the twentieth century.[2] A pupil of the prominent Hegelian Bertrando Spaventa, he rescued Marx from the positivist and Darwinian interpretations of Achille Loria and Enrico Ferri respectively. His influence on Croce, and to a lesser extent Gentile, gave the second generation of Italian Hegelians a pronounced Marxian colouring and ultimately favoured the Hegelian Marxism of Gramsci.[3] More generally Labriola's work and career exemplify the richness and the vicissitudes of Marxism during the Second International.

## EARLY WRITINGS

Antonio Labriola (1843–1904) was born in southern Italy at Sangermano (Cassino). When he was eighteen he moved to Naples in order to finish his studies at the University and came under the philosophical and political influence of Bertrando and Silvio Spaventa. Croce was to see Labriola's conversion to socialism around 1886 as an almost inexplicable 'leap' from the 'moderate and conservative Spaventa circle', even if 'there was much intellectual radicalism in that conservatism and therefore the possibility for the transition'.[4] There was, however, greater continuity between Labriola's early writings and his later Marxism than Croce allows. This is true both of his philosophical and his political thought. As he later wrote to Engels

> When I came to Rome as a professor (1873) I was a socialist without knowing it and a declared adversary of individualism for abstract

reasons alone. I then studied public law, administrative law and political economy and, between 1880 and 1897, I had already almost completely converted myself to socialism, but more from a general conception of history than because of the internal impulse of an active conviction. A slow and continuous approach to the real problems of life, disgust for political corruption and contact with the workers gradually transformed the scientific socialist *in abstracto* into a true social democrat.[5]

The three key features of Labriola's 'abstract' socialism – his opposition to individualism, his disgust at the present social order and his interest in the philosophy of history – all derived from his contact with the Spaventa brothers and via them with an Italian reading of German philosophy.

Bertrando Spaventa, unlike his colleague Augusto Vera, was not an orthodox or dogmatic Hegelian. He attacked the dominant positivist school, but in the name of an 'idealist realism' which owed as much to Bruno, Campanella and Vico as it did to Hegel. Spaventa sought to reform the Hegelian dialectic by avoiding its 'mystical' tendencies, the origin of this error, he believed, was Hegel's famous transition from the *Logic* to his *Philosophy of Nature*. Having integrated being into thought, Spaventa argued, Hegel could not separate it out again as a new world for thought to conquer without falling into 'panlogism' – i.e. the reduction of empirical reality to a preconceived logical schema. Spaventa felt this confusion derived from a conflict in Hegel between two forms of thought – that of Spirit, the essence of God which informs everything, and that of humanity, the thinking subject. If Spirit, he wrote, was not to be banished to an 'empty and ideal sphere', it was necessary to concentrate on its concrete manifestation in the present, in our actual experience, which was all we can legitimately claim to have knowledge of. Spaventa avoided a subjectivist epistemology by uniting historical or universal consciousness of the whole process of becoming, with our immediate consciousness of one of its moments. Our thought in the present was both the product and the continuation of the history of thought.[6] The inspiration for Spaventa's reading of Hegel derived from Vico's view of the historical world as issuing from the human mind.[7] However he rejected the Vichian distinction between a natural world made by God and a social world made by humankind, since the latter was the product of the transformation of the former by human thought and labour. Spaventa therefore used Vico to transfer the attributes originally ascribed by Hegel to Spirit to the human species.[8] History became the progressive unfolding of human consciousness towards the attainment of moral autonomy in the ethical state, a process brought about via philosophical reflection. To sum up in his own words

> If experience is certainty of oneself, to be limited to experience is to never *leave* oneself, not to have any other foundation than oneself, both in thought and in will; thought is *truth*, will is *duty*. To give any other foundation, the transcendent or bare external existence, to thought or to will, is to deny truth and morality. So that, precisely because he is limited to experience, man makes of himself what he is: his world, his knowledge and his happiness, all that which he is as a man, is his own work. This is in general the grand concept and meaning of *labour* and of *work* which at bottom are the same thing.[9]

The idealist aspect of Spaventa's philosophy was to be developed by Gentile and to a lesser extent by Croce. However, these themes were equally important for Labriola's interpretation of historical materialism. Indeed Spaventa has been called, with some justification, the Italian Feuerbach.[10]

Labriola's earliest writings, a critique of Zeller and the neo-Kantians (1862) and a study of Spinoza's theory of affections (1867), were clearly inspired by Spaventa's denial of a metaphysical foundation for knowledge or morals. At the same time, Labriola began to elaborate on Spaventa's view of Hegel with ideas drawn from the psychology of the contemporary German neo-Kantian J. F. Herbart. Herbart believed Hegel had over-emphasized the unity of the manifold of experience. This unity, he argued, was only a secondary product of the more fundamental plurality of groups of simpler elements which made up human experience. Ideas and beliefs were therefore essentially instruments for the interpretation of the given historical conditions, not the subjective embodiment of universal categories of thought, valid for all time. Labriola applied these insights to the interpretation of Socrates in a study of 1869. He did not aim, he wrote, 'to collect the authentic pronouncements of Socrates, in order to then place them according to the scheme of this or that philosophy', but to show 'that the doctrine of Socrates sprang naturally from the personal conditions of the author and remained so closely linked to them that they entirely coincided with the practical requirements which had produced them'.[11] This objective is clearly related to Labriola's later Marxian belief, that philosophy reflected the practical needs of the age. However, this is quite different from the view that philosophy is simply the product of the age. In his next book, *On Moral Liberty* (1873), he stuck firmly to the Kantian notion that '[l]iberty consists of the possibility of willing according to motives: and not only according to accidental impulses which are occasioned by the natural course of things.'[12] History was seen in the Spaventian perspective of a progressive development of the conditions necessary for humans to act autonomously, a theme he stressed in another book of the same year, *On Morality and Religion*. Historical progress was neither continuous nor inevitable. Like Spaventa, he had to face up to the awkward period of Italian 'decadence' following the Renaissance and the dashed hopes for a national revival after the Risorgimento.

Thus a number of aspects of Labriola's later Marxism stand out in these early works – namely an aversion both to materialist or evolutionary determinism and abstract *a priori* metaphysical speculation, resulting in a concomitant rejection of any theory of uninterrupted historical progress in favour of a view of history as the product of consciously directed human labour. These themes were all systematically developed in his last non-Marxian work, *Problems of the Philosophy of History* (1887). If history, he wrote, was to be more than mere dry erudition, it had to be organized around 'an epigenetic theory of civilisation'. However this must not lead to the loss of 'the critical sense in the use of the regulative concepts of research' common to 'the idea of a transcedent God . . . or to the fantasy of a germinal predetermination . . . which they now call according to the fashionable jargon *evolutionism* . . .' Labriola remained 'always firm in the Herbartian directive to consider metaphysics not as a conception of the whole world, but as the critique and correction of the concepts which are necessary to think experience'. The course of history was not a single undisturbed development, but an arduous making in which accident and illusion were as important as purposeful action. These complementary perspectives on the past of Herbart and Vico respectively were essentially retained in Labriola's interpretation of Marx.[13]

Whilst the above explains why Labriola should have had, like Croce, a 'scientific' interest in Marxism as a method for understanding the past, it does not reveal the reasons for his becoming a politically committed socialist. A number of historical and biographical details will help us to account for this. When he moved to Rome in 1873, to take up the chair of philosophy, he entered the circle of Silvio Spaventa, a chief spokesman of the Historical Right, or conservative liberals, who had governed Italy since unification. As we observed in the introduction, Spaventa drew on Hegel to describe the state as fulfilling an ethical mission, inherent in the national consciousness. The governing class had a directive role in educating the people towards the realization of their destiny. He contrasted this conception of the state, as a 'natural organism', with the liberal view that it served simply as a legal and institional framework for the pursuit of individual interest. Without a sense of national purpose, he believed the art of government would degenerate into the use of manipulation and demogogary for private gain. The fall of the Right from power in 1876, and the development of the policy of *trasformismo* by Depretis and the Left to maintain themselves in office, seemed to confirm his worst fears. For the rest of his life he belonged to a small opposition group who refused to accept government favours, and sponsored numerous parliamentary inquiries into the corruption of the new administration.

Labriola had long shared the moral vision of the Neapolitan neo-Hegelians and the Right, collaborating on various of their journals like the *Monitore di Bologna* at this time, and ultimately standing as a parlimanetary candidate in 1886. However, if he agreed with the moral tone of Spaventa's party, his reasons for holding these views increasingly differed. Indeed he wrote to Bertrando Spaventa in 1876, that in some circles he already passed for a socialist. For whilst the Spaventas held to the Hegelian doctrine that the contrasts of reality could be assimilated by thought but not structurally altered, Labriola came to agree with the Marxian contention that only by uniting theory and practice to change the world could alienation be overcome and a moral community arise.[14] As Croce recalled in his 1904 obituary of Labriola 'Once he told me of having come to socialism through the critique of the idea of the State. When the ethical State cherished by German publicists, revealed itself to be a utopia, and the antagonistic interests of the various classes appeared the sole harsh reality, he found himself in the arms of Marxism'.[15]

Labriola's socialism therefore resulted from his political as well as intellectual appreciation of the relevance of Marx's criticisms of Hegel. He devoted himself thereafter to the study of modern history and of Marx. Unfortunately he never completed his project of interpreting the former in the light of the latter, though he lectured on this topic until his death. His reputation rests on his theoretical contribution to Marxism therefore, but his concern to make it a practical tool of historical analysis and political action remained the focus of his interpretation.

### HISTORICAL MATERIALISM

Labriola's three main works on historical materialism appeared in rapid succession between 1895 and 1898. The first two, *In Memory of the Communist Manifesto* (1895) and *Of History Materialism* (1896), were published together in French by Sorel (1896) and in

Italian (1902) by Croce as *Essays on the Materialist Conception of History*. They became classics of Marxist literature, earning the praise of Engels, Lenin and Plekhanov – unlikely bedfellows, which casts doubt on how well they understood Labriola's ideas.[16] The third book, *Talking about Socialism and Philosophy* (1898), was a series of letters to Sorel disputing a number of points raised by him in his preface to the French edition of Labriola's *Essays*. None of these works was a systematic treatise on Marxist doctrine, such a project being alien to Labriola's cast of mind.[17] As the subtitle of his second book put it, they were 'preliminary clarifications' of Marx's theory of history. He concentrated on the use of Marxism as a method for understanding historical reality, rather than as a self-sufficient philosophy of history.[18]

Labriola's principal concern was to attack the excessively determinist interpretations of Achille Loria and Enrico Ferri.[19] In fact Loria's ideas were developed within the Spencerian positivist tradition of Ardigò, and bear little relation to Marxism at all – a point Labriola never tired of making. Indeed Labriola had already criticized Loria's doctrine on these grounds in *Problems of the Philosophy of History*. Loria argued that the economic factor determined the cultural and institutional superstructure, identifying the economy with the different forms of land appropriation. These changed and 'evolved' through the struggle for existence as increases in the population and humanity's egoistic search after self-satisfaction required a more efficient exploitation of natural resources. Capitalism was an intermediate stage between a society of self-sufficient individual proprietors, and a future community of voluntarily co-operating freeholders. He regarded this as the final economic stage towards which society was 'unconsciously tending'. Capitalism required the 'connective institutions' of 'morality, law and politics' to maintain the exploitative class of capitalists/landowners in power. These would disappear in the 'final form of society', in which land and produce would be shared equally, and it would be in everyone's interest not to exploit others and thus diminish the productivity of the whole community. Relations between people would be governed by a self-regulating 'enlightened egoism'. Loria's future society was thus very different from that envisaged by Marx, being entirely consumption-orientated – a primitive agrarian communism like that of Henry George, in which humanity's natural inclinations could be fully satisfied. Loria never attributed his ideas to Marx, and the evolutionary Marxist, Enrico Ferri, regarded them as an important corrective to Marxism, rendering it more 'scientific'. Whilst Loria was a somewhat embarrassing sympathiser, Ferri was within the socialist camp. A famous criminologist, he linked Spencer, Darwin and Marx as the trinity of nineteenth-century thought, ascribing to economic factors directly, or indirectly through heredity, a decisive role in the genesis of crime. His views were highly influential owing to his position as leader of the 'left' anti-Turati group in the Italian Socialist Party.

At this time views akin to Loria's and Ferri's, for example those of Lafargue, were popularly identified with historical materialism, largely as a result of the use of evolutionary theories by Engels. As Labriola ruefully remarked, it was not Loria's fault if the main socialist journal, *Critica Sociale*, mistook him for the Italian Marx. There is thus some irony in the fact that Labriola's criticisms were to lead to Engels' denunciation of Loria in the preface to the third volume of *Capital*. Labriola regarded Loria's theory as totally incompatible not only with Marxist theory but also with the socialist movement. Loria's naturalist determinism worked against the development of a revolutionary consciousness, whilst his concentration on land and his crude psychology were totally inadequate for the analysis of modern industrial society. Labriola saw the correction of these errors as having a direct practical import. As he commented *à propos* of the unrest of the unemployed in 1891

> There is a missing link in Italy between these spontaneous phenomena and the consciousness developed by the revolutionary proletariat, it is socialist culture. Our workers will certainly not be the heirs of *classical German philosophy*, precisely because that philosophy barely enters with difficulty the solitary brain of the odd Italian professor. The new generation only know the positivists, which for me are representatives of a cretinous deterioration of the bourgeois kind.[20]

His essays were therefore conceived as his contribution to the practical struggle for an Italian socialist movement.

Labriola distinguished between historical materialism and 'naturalist materialism', and he was particularly scathing of the Darwinian cult of 'Madonna evolution'. As he put it in *On Historical Materialism*

> Reasonable and well founded is the tendency of those who aim to subordinate the sum total of human events considered in their course, to the rigorous conception of *determinism*. There is, on the contrary, no reason for confusing this derived reflex, and complex determinism, with the determinism of the immediate struggle for existence which is produced and developed on a field not modified by the continued action of labour. Legitimate and well founded in an absolute fashion,

is the historical explanation which proceeds in its course from the volitions which have voluntarily regulated the different phases of life, to the motives and objective causes of every choice, discovered in the conditions of environment, territory, accessible means of existence and conditions of experience. But there is, on the contrary, no foundation for that opinion which tends to the negation of every volition in consequence of a theoretical view which would substitute *automatism* for *voluntarism*.[21]

Labriola continually repeated Engels' caveat that the economic base was all-determining 'only in the last analysis'. 'Only an idiot', he wrote, 'could believe that the individual morality of every one is proportionate to his individual economic situation.'[22] The links between the two were 'very complicated, often subtle, tortuous and not always legible.'[23] He was perfectly orthodox in regarding the motor of history as human beings' progressive transformation of nature to serve their needs, which themselves developed as they were satisfied. The economic base was composed of the productive forces – the technology and expertise which determined the relations of production, and these in turn were the foundation of social life. Historical research therefore had to be directed towards showing that, at every stage of history, needs conditioned social relations and consciousness. Human needs did not develop according to universal laws of natural evolution, but were the result of the conscious shaping of nature by human labour.[24] There was no inherent necessity about this process, so that humankind would inexorably be led from primitive agrarianism, through feudalism and capitalism, to communism. According to Labriola, historical materialism provided a broad interpretation of human history so far, but could not be used to explain every individual event. 'Accidents', 'the element of chance' and the contingent conditions of a given time and place meant that history was a series of zig-zags and reversals, rather than a straight line. Similarly, Marxism was not a prophecy of an inevitable socialist future, except in the most general sense. As far as Italy went, Labriola believed this might well take centuries.[25]

Historical materialism was above all a philosophy of praxis. Technical progress did not occur through some internal dynamic of its own. The improvement of the forces of production was the result of mental labour. Marxism's strength resided in not seeking to provide a universal interpretation of reality. It was bound up with the historical process as an explanation of a given set of circumstances. The *Communist Manifesto* itself was inexplicable unless seen as a response to a particular stage of history. As we saw, this was very much the view of philosophy Labriola had taken over from Herbart.

It was absurd, he argued, to subordinate consciousness to the relations of production, since the former created the latter. Both, however, were related to the requirements of society, which was itself a product of human mental and manual labour. History was thus a cumulatative and self-developing 'rhythmic process' between thought and labour, which 'facilitates the production of new thought by new forces'. Marxism was above all a practical philosophy:

> Historical materialism, then, or the *philosophy of praxis*, in so far as it sees man in his entirety as a historical and social being, just as it puts an end to all forms of idealism, which regard empirically existing things as the reflexion, reproduction imitation, example, consequence or whatever of *a priori* thought of some kind, so it also marks the end of naturalistic materialism using this term in the sense which was traditional up to a few years ago. The intellectual revolution, which has led to the consideration of the processes of history as absolutely objective, is coeval with and responsive to that other intellectual revolution, which has succeeded in *historicising* physical nature. This is no longer, for any thinking man, a *fact*, which was never in the making, an *event* which had never *become*, an eternal *entity* which does not *change*, and much less the result of a *single act of creation*, which is not a *continuous process of creation*.[26]

*Praxis* was both a tool for changing the course of history and a criterion for historical evaluation:

> The first corresponds to the practical requirements of the socialist parties, demands the aquisition of an adequate knowledge of the specific conditions of the proletariat in each country and adapts socialist activity to the causes, prospects, and dangers of the complications of politics. The second can lead, and will certainly do so, to a revision of the methods of writing history, for it tends to establish this art on the field of class struggles and the social relations, which result from them, in the basis of the corresponding economic structure, which every historian must henceforth know and understand.[27]

The two strands are intimately related. Revolution was not, as the later writings of Engels and evolutionary Marxists supposed, the necessary result of an internal collapse of capitalism. For Labriola it was only a historical possibility. To become real, the proletariat would have to become conscious of its position with regard to the specific historical conditions governing it. This consciousness, which could only come from a historical awareness, created needs which required a revolution in order to be satisfied. Only if the proletariat were aware of their historical situation would they grasp that it could be changed. This clearly went against the orthodox view that revolutionary consciousness was simply an awareness of the 'objective' forces of history, since intellectual labour was one of those forces. For Labriola the doctrine of *praxis* was 'the kernal of historical materialism'. It was the meeting point of the various influences – Hegel, Vico, Spinoza, Herbart and Marx – upon his thought. It marked the end of 'the vulgar opposition between theory and practice' in favour of the continuous process of historical change which humankind brought about when 'scientific' knowledge of the given historical conditions led to the political modification of those conditions.[28]

Labriola's doctrine was clearly a very sophisticated version of Marxism. Given his ignorance of Marx's early Hegelian works, the predominance of Darwinian and positivist interpretations of Marxism under the influence of Engels's later writings and the generally positivist intellectual climate of the day, it was a truly remarkable achievement. It did not receive much recognition at the time, however. Undoubtedly this partly derived from the ambivalence of Labriola's message. He inveighed against crude determinist theories, but still claimed that Marxism was 'scientific' and praised Engels' *Anti Dühring* as 'the greatest book of general science to come from the pen of a socialist, and in addition the book of greatest objective value that there now is of philosophy generally.'[29] In effect Labriola had brought out a number of the ambiguities inherent in Marxism *tout court*. For example, he clearly maintained that 'relations of production' could not be separated out as the determining factor of the 'legal and political superstructure' which defined how people regarded those relations and could in turn profoundly affect production. To admit this, however, was to undermine the base superstructure model which gave Marxism its distinctively 'scientific' character. Labriola appeared to avoid this dilemma by way of Engels' qualification 'in the last analysis', but if he had jettisoned absolute determinism it was meaningless to say that it nevertheless occured 'in the last analysis'.[30]

Labriola was equally adamant that history could not be seen as a uniform and unilinear process – it followed many different and independent paths in different countries:

How many times have we read – first comes associationism, then cooperationism . . . and finally collectivism: and having put the isms in line, the rest unfolds of its own accord. Wasn't the French working out of the sacred schema: slave economy, service economy, salaried

economy, extended to the whole human race? Whoever uses that
formula won't understand a single thing of, say, fourteenth-century
England; – and what about the good Norwegians who were never serfs
or servants? and what does one make of the institution of serfdom in
Germany beyond the Elbe, which arose and developed after the
Reformation?[31]

But to introduce this limitation, to argue, as he did, that Marxism
was a method rather than an all-embracing theory,[32] was to dilute it
so much that it became no more than a vague injunction to pay
attention to human beings' material as well as their spiritual life and
to be aware of the connections between them. For it would not, on
Labriola's own admission, lead to a set of universal laws which
would allow the predicition of a given result if the same conditions
were to arise on different occasions.

This has important consequences for Marxism as a political
doctrine. For to doubt its validity as a means of interpreting the past,
is to weaken its claim concerning the communist future. Labriola
was correspondingly ambiguous about this as well. He saw the state
in Marxist fashion as an instrument of class power, its existence
being a reflection of pre-existing class divisions. The state, which was
not just a collection of political institutions, but the conceptions of
morality and justice which invested them with legitimacy as well, was
thus a transient feature of bourgeois capitalist society which would
disappear with the eradication of class divisions. This would come
about when capitalist society had been developed to a point at which
the inevitable polarization of capital and labour became transparent,
and a revolutionary consciousness developed amongst the proletariat, bringing about the crucial transition to a classless community.[33] Whilst for most Marxists the revolution is a special case of
conscious goal-orientated action, for Labriola it was only a continuation of the unity of theory and action throughout history by which
human beings 'create an artificial environment'.

Labriola was at pains to reject any notion that Marx's theory was
utopian or a prophecy:

> . . . it is the endeavour to bring practical plans to a realisation by the
> help of a clear understanding of all the complicated and intricate
> interrelations which hold together the world in which we are living. If
> it were not so, with what right and by what claim could we speak of a
> vaunted Marxism? If historical materialism does not hold good, it
> means that the prospects for the coming of socialism are doubtful, and
> that our thought of a future society is a creation of the utopians![34]

Yet Labriola had himself cast doubt on the 'scientific' basis of the socialist future. If historical materialism was too vague to be able to relate everything to 'class-interest', then both the association of the whole intellectual and legal superstructure to class, and the future of a classless society brought about by changes in the economic base, were called into question. If the belief that there was a distinctive 'proletarian' interest, which could be satisfied by any compromise or amelioration of bourgeois society, could no longer be rigorously maintained, then socialism necessarily lost its revolutionary character. Labriola was perfectly orthodox in his view of the socialist future and its consequences for socialist practice in the present, but he was to find that his ideas reflected a 'crisis within Marxism' which called for quite different attitudes towards both of them.

### REFORMIST SOCIALISM AND THE 'CRISIS WITHIN MARXISM'

Labriola's Marxism was both complex and restrained. It was 'a method of research and of conception', calling for the careful analysis of society. The socialist condemnation of capitalism and the projection of a communist society were the product of slow and laborious 'scientific' enquiry into history, requiring and creating 'a certain queer humility' in those who espoused it.[35] A successful revolution could not be carried out on the basis of an unfounded desire for a future utopia or supposed knowledge of the laws of history. Utopian and evolutionary socialists alike 'seem to forget that this future society must be produced by human beings themselves in response to the demands of the conditions in which they now live and by the development of their own aptitudes'.[36]

The union of theory and practice was achieved in the complementary tasks of intellectuals and workers in the socialist movement. This consisted of the former providing a concrete analysis of the historical conditions shaping the proletariat, and bringing them to their consciousness. This would lead to an organized proletarian party capable of transforming capitalism to bring about the transition to communism. As Labriola wrote to Sorel

. . . the practical science of socialism consists in the clear observation of all the complicated processes of the economic world, and in a simultaneous study of the conditions in which the proletariat lives, becomes capable of concentration in a class party, and carries into this successive concentration the spirit which is proper to it, given the economic struggle in which that politics is rooted, which it is its job to do. Upon these present facts we can base sufficiently clear calculations of our forecast and make connection with that point where the proletariat becomes dominant and shapes the political parties of the state. And from this point, which must coincide with the one where capitalism becomes unfit to rule, from this point I say, which no one can very well imagine to be a noisy disaster [*patatrac*], will come the beginning of that which many, who knows why, persistently call the social revolution *par excellence*, as if the whole of history wasn't a series of social revolutions. To go beyond that point, with reasonings, would be to mistake it for a fabric of our imagination.[37]

Labriola's doctrine was thus opposed both to evolutionary socialism and anarchism. Yet during this period Italian socialism was dominated by just these two currents of thought. The first, owing to the influence of Loria and Ferri, was particularly strong in the PSI.[38] Turati, its leader, whilst sympathetic to Labriola, was very much a product of this positivist culture. There were a number of apparent similarities between their positions. Both believed that capitalism, especially in the south, had yet to develop in Italy to a sufficiently mature stage for the revolution to take place. This conviction even led to Labriola's support of Italy's abortive colonial adventures in north Africa.[39] There was, however, a world of difference between Turati's 'reformism' and Labriola's 'gradualism'. Turati believed there were two Italies – the mature, bourgeois, capitalist society of the north, and the semi-feudal south. As long as the backwardness of the south provided support for the forces of reaction there could be no nationwide socialist movement in Italy. The best strategy was therefore to co-operate with the progressives in the north in order to extend the liberal, democratic regime to the south. The justification for this strategy was that there were certain stages of economic and hence social development through which it was necessary to pass. As Turati put it

> . . . *For us the revolution comes from the nature of things.* We await it, and we live in the middle of it. Every school which is opened, every mind which is unclouded, every backbone that straightens itself, every gangrenous abuse which is uprooted, every rise in the tenor of life of the poor, every work protection law, if all that is coordinated towards a clear and conscious goal of social transformation, is an atom of revolution which is added to the mass.[40]

Turati believed that socialism could in this manner be brought about within the capitalist order. For Labriola such a strategy was completely mistaken in its analysis of the nature of historical change. It assumed underlying laws of historical development, whereas he believed history was what men made it. To co-operate with capitalism was not to foster its downfall due to its inherent contradictions, but to maintain its existence. This did not mean he belonged to 'the worse the better' school of Marxism, for this similarly presupposed that the socialist future was latent in the nature of things. On the other hand, he offered little in the way of a political programme for socialists, or any analysis of why or for what they were struggling. Labriola not only rejected the notion of immanent laws of historical development, he denied the existence of absolute principles of morality and justice as well. He limited himself to suggesting that society somehow required technical progress, and that in fashioning the tools of economic development, humankind was taking a step towards a new type of society. But to sustain this theory, Labriola would have to rely on an unproven metaphysical doctrine of historical necessity similar to those he had rejected. Otherwise why should capitalism not continue indefinitely and simply absorb technical change? As Labriola had pointed out, this was perfectly possible as long as the proletariat were kept in ignorance of their situation by a positivist culture portraying the capitalist ethos as implicit in the very nature of things. He had given up the traditional philosopher's task of relating a theory of the order of reality to how we ought to act as a hopeless endeavour. It could only issue in an 'ideology', a metaphysical blanket to cover up the exploitation of one class by another. Yet such beliefs were required to justify and provide the motivation for the criticism of the present. Without such an alternative, passive acquiescence or collaboration with the better elements of what existed were the most likely and rational strategies to adopt.

It was this second line of argument which did most to undermine Labriola's work and influence, and fuelled the strong anarchist current in Italian socialist thought. It was perhaps to be expected that his writings would be too academic and against the current to be well received by socialist politicians. Far more damaging, however, were the criticisms of his supposed collaborators, Sorel and Croce. Both had been instrumental in the writing and publishing of his works, forming in Labriola's imagination a 'holy trinity' for the defence of Marxist doctrine.[41] But they had expressed doubts about Labriola's interpretation from the beginning. Sorel summed up their worries when, in his preface to the *Essays*, he argued that Labriola had left socialism 'suspended in the air . . . so long as it does not find the means to develop its own philosophy . . . inherent and immanent in fundamental facts and premises.'[42] This led Croce to the conclusion that 'Historical materialism is not, and could not be, a new philosophy of history, nor a new method but is, and must be, simply this: a collection of new facts, of new experiences, which enter into the consciousness of the historian'.[43]

Croce perceived that Labriola's criticism of idealist, Darwinian and positivist interpretations of Marxism had rendered it no more than an exhortation to be aware of the interdependence of technology, property relations and civilization, offering no hard and fast rules as to how these relations were to be interpreted. Marxism, Croce continued, could not provide any criteria for the construction of a historical narrative 'as if the facts spoke for themselves and the historian was there to listen and record their voices'. Meaning could only be found within ourselves, based on 'individual persuasions and convictions about the ends of history and the course of progress'.[44] Marx's writings in 1848 had shown precisely these qualities: 'few works, he wrote, like these of Marx are able to give us the notion and the impression of what history should be: the study of a complex of facts, to which we are drawn not by idle curiosity but from the need to shed light on the problems of our spirit.'[45] He agreed with Labriola that such beliefs could not be given any objective or philosophical foundation, but that did not necessarily entail a denial of their reality or necessity. The materialist doctrines of Marx and Engels were, he argued, belied by their own actions:

> . . . the idealism or absoluteness of morality, in the philosophical sense of those words, are a necessary presupposition of socialism . . . And, without that moral presupposition, how would one explain, not just the political activity of Marx, but the tone of violent indignation and bitter satire which one notices on every page of *Capital*?[46]

Croce distinguished two aspects of human practical activity – the economic and the moral. To act morally was necessarily to act economically as well, but not *vice versa*. If that were the case, morality would degenerate into pure hedonism.[47] This had been the substance of his critique of Loria, written at Labriola's behest.[48] He now made the same criticism of Marxism, which without any notion of morality 'cannot give any succour to socialism nor to any other practical endeavour'.[49] This was the vacuum which he believed Sorel's theory of 'myths' had filled. For Sorel a myth was not a didactic allegory but a call to battle. It had no scientific value beyond inspiring the action of those who adopt it. It was a negation of the existing order, but not the promise of a future earthly paradise, which would rule out further similar actions. The myth of the proletariat was the general strike, which 'concentrated the whole of socialism', without 'the reconciliation of contraries in the gibberish of official intellectuals'.[50] It was this passional element, ignored by Labriola and positivist Marxists alike, which Croce praised Sorel for developing. It had liberated 'the healthy and realistic kernel of Marx's thought from the metaphysical and literary scribblings of their author and the worthless exegesis and deductions of the school.'[51]

Sorel's contribution, he was to later write, lay in his championing of 'a combative morality, capable of keeping alive the forces which move history and preventing them from stagnating and becoming corrupted.'[52] He shared Labriola's view that the proletarian consciousness had been weakened by Turatian reformism. The bourgeois liberal ideal of economic and intellectual equality was but an excuse for moral and spiritual sloth, and belief in the inevitable progress of mankind '. . . a recipe for assuaging the spiritual and moral forces of man'.[53] If socialism merely aped bourgeois decadence, then its force as a revolutionary movement would be lost. The proletariat should rather follow Sorel's lead and create a new moral viewpoint in opposition to that currently prevailing.

Labriola admonished Croce for being 'an intellectual epicurean' whose 'scholastic' separation of the economic and the moral marked him out as an outdated academic 'Platonist'.[54] But this was quite wrong – Labriola was by comparison much more of a *professorissimo*.[55] Croce denied the theoretical validity of Marxism, but not its practical efficacy; on the contrary, he dubbed Marx 'the Machiavelli of the proletariat'.[56] Much more disturbing, and essentially anti-philosophical, was Croce's espousal of Sorel's voluntarism. He regarded Sorel's myths as products of the 'moral conscience'. Yet they were immune to rational criticism – the product of instinct rather than reflection. Such a doctrine was more likely to breed immorality. As it was syndicalist ideas, disseminated by Labriola's namesake Arturo Labriola, had a far greater influence on Italian politics – ultimately inspiring Mussolini's fascism – than historical materialism. Meanwhile Labriola had returned to being a solitary figure, bitter at his continued association with two thinkers who had deserted the cause of 'critical communism' and worried that he had somehow contributed to the 'crisis of Marxism'.[57]

There is some justification in Labriola's fear that he had helped precipitate this situation. By submitting Marxism to a sustained analysis, he had uncovered a number of important gaps in Marxist theory. In particular he had shown that to relate, in an uncomplicated fashion, consciousness to the economic base, and to regard the latter as self-developing, was too crude to be acceptable. However, his attack on rigid determinism had equally undermined the

'scientific' claim of Marxism to offer clear answers about the future.
Socialism could only be justified, on his reading of historical
materialism, in terms appropriate to the current struggle within
capitalism. Such a strategy, however, seemed to accord well with the
reformism of Bernstein and Turati. If talk of the socialist future was
empty utopianism, then Bernstein's formula, that 'the socialist goal
is nothing and the movement everything', had some justification.[58]
A possible alternative would have been the route taken by
contemporary ethical socialists. They pointed out that the inevita-
bility of socialism did not prove that it was necessarily a goal worth
striving for, unless one believed historical progress to be inherently
necessary and good. Labriola was as scathing as they were of such a
naive progressivism, but he was equally opposed to any doctrine of
an absolute morality, valid for all times and places. He was perfectly
orthodox in regarding morality as nothing more than a function of
the class interests of a given mode of production, destined to
disappear under communism.[59] However, if this is the case, then he
had no grounds for objecting to Sorel's use of 'myths' for the limited
strategic purposes of providing a motive for action in the present.
For the pursuit of an unconditional good, which on Labriola's
reading is beyond definition, could provide no basis for action
guiding principles in the present. The dilemma of reformism or
utopianism could not be avoided by falling back upon the requirements of society, as Labriola tried to do, for this would be to commit
the very error of hypostatizing society which it had been Labriola's
main task to attack. He gave a clear summary of the problems facing
Marxists in his review of Masaryk's thesis, popular at the time, of a
crisis within Marxism:

> Since politics cannot be anything else but a practical and working
> interpretation of a certain historical moment, socialism is today
> confronted – generally speaking, and without taking into account local
> differences of the various countries – by the following difficult and
> intricate problem: It must beware of losing itself in vain attempts at a
> romantic reproduction of traditional revolutionism . . . and yet it
> must take care at the same time not to fall into an acquiescent and
> willing attitude which would cause its disappearance in the elastic
> mechanism of the bourgeois world by means of compromise.[60]

Unfortunately for Labriola, he had failed to show that Marxism held
any alternative to these two strategies; on the contrary, he had
convinced Sorel and Croce that it did not. Moreover, as we shall see
in examining Gramsci's writings and recent debates within the PCI
(*Partito Communista Italiano*), the problem continued to bedevil

subsequent Italian Marxists. Nevertheless he had posed the central issue, and largely framed the terms in which it was discussed, which was to occupy the three main Italian thinkers of the next generation – Croce, Gentile and Gramsci. Namely, was it possible to have a theory of reality which would not only provide objective knowledge of the human situation, but would equally give grounds for acting so as to change and improve the human condition? The validity not just of their answers, but of how they framed the question, will be the focus of the rest of this book.

# 5

# BENEDETTO CROCE

Born at Pescasseroli in Aquila in 1866, Benedetto Croce dominated Italian culture until his death in 1952. His copious writings on aesthetics, ethics and politics, and history constitute a comprehensive humanist philosophy, which Croce developed with the aim of constructing a secular religion able to direct all human activity. It is difficult to exaggerate the success of his project in Italy. The main intellectuals of both right and left were profoundly influenced by his thought, so that even under fascism and after the Second World War, when his teaching was viewed with official disfavour and popular disregard respectively, his ideas continued to be of crucial importance. However, his philosophy has aroused far less interest outside Italy. This has been particularly true of Anglo-American philosophers, who have generally been unconcerned with aesthetics or history – Croce's main areas of research. When they have plundered his works for illumination about these subjects it has been with scant respect for, or even knowledge of, his wider metaphysical and political ambitions. The frequent complaint of analytical philosophers about 'the obscurity of his exposition'[1] is symptomatic of this failure to appreciate the wider context of Croce's thought.

This chapter will be primarily concerned with Croce's historical theory and its relation to his theory of human action, which was the heart of his whole philosophical and cultural project. His ideas about history cannot therefore be relegated to the status of methodological precepts for professional historians. They constitute a more global theory about human thinking and action generally. It is possible to distinguish three periods in the development of Croce's philosophy, which are intimately related to his broader political concerns.[2] During the first period, from 1890 to 1906, Croce was the *enfant terrible* of Italian philosophy, in revolt against positivism and praising humanity's infinite creative powers. This was succeeded by the containment of his earlier ideas within a system – the conservative historicism of Senator Croce from 1906 to 1924 can be seen as an attempt to quell the expectations he had aroused with his *Aesthetic* of 1902 and his anti-establishment polemics. The final period, from 1924 to 1952, is the most crucial. For in opposing fascism he was forced to reconsider the practical implications of his own philosophy and review them in the light of their history. The constant revisions which were a feature of Croce's work derived not just from internal difficulties within his thought, but are related to the important cultural role he sought for his ideas as well. It will therefore be necessary to advert to both in tracing these three main phases of Croce's philosophy below.

## HISTORY SUBSUMED UNDER THE GENERAL CONCEPT OF ART

Croce followed Spaventa and De Sanctis in advocating an 'idealist realism' in opposition to both positivism and 'abstract' idealism, both of which, he maintained, deprived human thought and action of freedom and meaning. The chief problem relating to positivism was held to be its reduction of questions of value to questions of fact, thereby denying the human capacity to appraise and revise beliefs and desires, and act in a free and responsible, as opposed to a determined and mechanical, manner. 'Abstract' idealism was equally at odds with human autonomy, because it assumed a 'transcendent' morality separable from human activity and to which we should conform. Instead Croce concentrated on the ways in which people develop and use value judgements in everyday life. The emphasis was away from the notion of reality as a given – either abstractly or positively conceived – to reality as it was thought, acted upon and created by humanity. Left at a merely descriptive level, this provided no guidance about how to choose between different and conflicting values and judgements. The most common way of out this *impasse*, adopted by contemporary philosophers, was to attempt to group and classify these experiences. Croce, however, rejected both the 'under-labourer' conception of philosophy and the sociological approach for historicism. For Croce philosophy was not just a method, but identical with the spiritual development of both humanity and truth. The conception of human beings as either vainly seeking the approval of a transcendent deity or determined by natural laws was replaced by that of the individual creating reality by his or her thought and action. Philosophy operated as a faith, reintegrating humankind's practical activity into their search and need for a framework of meaning, value and certainty. In this

respect Croce's idealism shared many features with the general
current of thought associated with James, Bergson and more
particularly the development of German historicism by Dilthey,
Simmel, Rickert, Windelband and Weber, from which his principal
ideas derived.[3]

Although initiated into classical German philosophy through his
exposure to the Neapolitan Hegelians, particularly his uncles
Bertrando and Silvio Spaventa, and the literary critic Francesco De
Sanctis, he was introduced to contemporary German thought by
Antonio Labriola, who in the 1880s and 1890s was, as we have seen,
a follower of the psychology of Herbart.[4] Herbart regarded
philosophy as the elaboration of the concepts of experience rather
than universal statements about an 'objective' reality, and Croce's
early writings are consistent with this approach. His first philosophical work, *History Subsumed under the General Concept of Art*
(1893), was sparked off by an article by the Italian positivist
Pasquale Villari entitled 'Is History a Science?' (1891). It belonged
however, to the famous German debate between Dilthey and
Windelband about the nature of the human sciences.[5] Dilthey
maintained that history was special in studying the products of
human action, which could be understood through an empathetic
reconstruction of human 'life expressions'. Windelband, on the
other hand, argued that it was not the object of study which
distinguished human from natural science but the concepts used in
studying it. Whilst history was 'idiographic' or 'picture-making',
science was 'nomothetic' or 'law-making'. Croce's own solution
combined elements from both. He agreed with Windelband's
distinction and argued that history was the representation of
particular past events, rather than the elaboration of general laws of
human behaviour, and was hence 'subsumed under the general
concept of art'. However, history was different from art in depicting
'what actually occurred' rather than 'the possible'.[6] A novel about
Dante was different from an accurate biography. Yet there was a
further link between history and art which Croce owed to Dilthey.
Both were concerned with human 'life-expressions', the product of
mind, will and the emotions. The same skills of intuition and an
ability to empathise with our fellow human beings were required to
appreciate a work of art or a past political act.[7] Since history was the
result of human action, he rejected all speculative philosophies of
history which regarded it as the product of providence, reason or
natural evolution – 'We make history ourselves, taking into account,
to be sure, the objective conditions in which we find ourselves, but
with our ideals, our struggles, our sufferings, without it being

allowed us to unload this burden onto the back of God or the Idea.'[8]

Thus far Croce was in substantial agreement with the views of Labriola, examined earlier, for whom history and philosophy could only be understood as relating to the struggles of particular individuals in given circumstances to understand and transform their historical situation. Croce's writings on Marx reveal no substantial change in his position. He regarded Marxism as having simply added social and economic factors to the number of 'experiences' the historian must 'find within himself' and relive in his imagination in order to give an accurate historical account. But he regarded a Marxist philosophy of history as a descent into naturalism, and rejected it accordingly.[9] Nor did he attempt, like Dilthey, to provide a detailed historical methodology based upon the elaboration of types or classes of human activity. He held such a task to be impossible, given humanity's infinite potential to create new forms of life. He nevertheless believed that there was a structure to human activity, and here he was once more close to Windelband and the neo-Kantians. Croce argued that the form and the content of our knowledge were intimately related, so that the categories of thought reflected the nature of reality. This had been the basis of his distinction between science and art. In his writings on Marxism he introduced two further distinctions – between theoretical and practical activity, and economic and ethical willing. This schema produced a number of antinomies in Croce's philosophy – between thought and action, spirit and nature, ethics and politics, intuition and logic – which were at odds with his idealism and never fully resolved. The difficulties involved can be seen by examining Croce's first attempt to provide a systematic exposition of his *Philosophy of Spirit* in the *Aesthetic* of 1902.

The *Philosophy of Spirit* was intended to encompass human activity in all its aspects. Croce divided spirit into its theoretical and practical dimensions. The former was further subdivided into intuition and logic, the latter into economic willing and ethical willing, the two dimensions being so related that the second and fourth subdivisions implied the first and third respectively, but not *vice versa*. These four subdivisions corresponded to the four aspects of spirit – the Beautiful, the True, the Useful and the Good. All human activity could be understood within this schema, but this does not mean that Croce believed in certain eternal ideals of the Good, the Beautiful, etc. These 'pure concepts' were indeterminate – their content derived from human activity itself. Thus human beings performed particular acts which seemed appropriate to the circumstances as they understood them, and on certain occassions these would appear to be not only Useful but Good as well. Similarly, all human thought was necessarily intuitive, concerned with particulars, and representative, using language to express itself. However only certain types of thinking were logical, devoted to the elaboration of concepts and the relations between things. What counted as the Beautiful and the True was conditioned by the particular activities of individuals at a given time and place.[10] Croce elaborated his system over the course of the next ten years in the volumes of the *Aesthetic* of 1902 (the Beautiful), the *Logic* of 1905 and 1909 (the True), the *Philosophy of Practice* of 1909 (the Useful and the Good) and the *Theory and History of Historiography of 1912* to *1915*, which outlined his overarching historicist conception of philosophy.

Croce's first systematic work revealed problems in his radical idealism, which the historicism of the later volumes sought to correct. In the *Aesthetic*, Croce aimed to steer a careful path between positivism and *a priori* metaphysical speculation. He was particularly anxious to avoid any suggestion that human activity was predetermined by either natural or metaphysical causes. However, this led to his apparent praising of the self-sufficiency of human reason and the limitless powers and autonomy of human creativity. Although he claimed that his doctrine was 'a realistic idealism', it is hard to see at what point the constraints of the world entered the picture. By making philosophy dependent upon intuition and morality upon the practical will, Croce appeared to be arguing in favour of a kind of subjectivist relativism. Neither an appeal to reason nor the world could arbitrate between different viewpoints; they could only be distinguished in terms of the ways of living and feeling involved. It could not be said that one was truer or more faithful to reality than another. History remained 'subsumed under the general concept of art' as the accurate representation of past creative acts. Such was Croce's fear of 'abstract' philosophy, that he made no connection between the effects of past acts and thoughts on those of the present. The slate always remained clean for each artist or historical actor to start afresh.[11] The accompanying history of aesthetic doctrines was thus a study of how different thinkers had looked at the eternal but indeterminate problem of aesthetics, rather than a developmental history of how earlier studies had influenced the work of later thinkers – a feature of his subsequent histories of philosophy.

Croce's ideas were eagerly seized upon by contemporaries such as Papini and Prezzolini, already inspired by James and Bergson in their revolt against the official positivist culture. Prezzolini, in an article entitled 'The God-Man', praised Croce's *Aesthetic* for its affirmation of art 'as a personal vision', with 'the autonomy of the imagination as its foundation'.[12] Croce initially welcomed their support and looked favourably upon their magazine *Leonardo*. However, it soon became clear that their pseudo-Neitzschian posturing and elitist exaltation of limitless human creativity went much further than he was prepared to go, even though he had fuelled the emotivist ethic of the *Leonardiani* both in his *Aesthetic* and his praise of Sorel's syndacalism.[13] He retorted that the task of philosophy was 'to *understand* life, not to fashion a life different from reality . . .'.[14] But Papini merely replied that in that case he had fallen back into the very naturalism he had so effectively criticized.[15] Croce's historicism was an attempt to overcome this dichotomy between naturalism and rationalism within his philosophy. In formulating this doctrine Croce was indebted to his collaborator Gentile.[16] Their discussion of this problem was significantly occasioned by Croce's book on Hegel (1906) and Gentile's critical review of a recent work by Windelband. But it was also prompted by the need to answer the criticisms of Papini and to counter certain interpretations of his *Aesthetic* which seemed to Croce to have extreme consequences.[17]

## HEGEL, GENTILE AND THE IDENTIFICATION OF PHILOSOPHY AND HISTORY

Croce's interpretation of Hegel was always as ambivalent as the title of his famous study, *What is Living and What is Dead in the Philosophy of Hegel*, suggests. Indeed, although related to two of the major nineteenth-century exponents of Italian Hegelianism – Bertrando and Silvio Spaventa – his first encounter with Hegel had been one of almost total rejection. As he wrote to Gentile's mentor, the philosopher Donato Jaja, in 1892, 'I believe that the fundamental principles, and especially the method, of that system are entirely erroneous; and the damaging consequences of this error will become plain when applied to particular disciplines'.[18] Croce, as the title of his magazine *La Critica* reveals, shared the neo-Kantians' concern with the critical study of the categories of knowledge and their rejection of Hegel's assimilation of nature into mind. This was the substance of Croce's criticism of Hegel – he accused him of 'panlogism' and the consequent subordination of empirical reality to a pre-conceived metaphysical design. This lead to Hegel's second error, the failure to maintain the distinctions between the different aspects of human knowledge – between the moments of the Beautiful, the True etc. which he regarded as intrinsic to reality and hence to mind. However, if these criticisms made up the bulk of the

book, the first three chapters were a defence of Hegel. For Croce the
'life' of the Hegelian system resided in Hegel's dialectial conception
of reality – that is, the identity of infinite and finite expressed in the
formula 'what is rational, is real; and what is real, is rational'. It was
the 'exaltation of history . . . in which the infinite and the finite are
fused together, and good and bad constitute a single process, history
is the very reality of the idea: spirit is nothing, outside of its historical
development.'[19] This view of history, as the immanent development
of Spirit, was the essence of Croce's historicism. Gentile, however,
was quick to point out that Croce's criticisms of Hegel did not fully
accord with what he had chosen to praise.

Gentile and Croce had been in continuous correspondence with
each other since 1896. Although Gentile was the junior partner in
their collaboration on *La Critica* (from 1903), their epistolary
discussions reveal that he had had an important influence on Croce's
view of the nature and role of philosophy. Gentile's Hegelianism had
already led to a divergence of opinion over the interpretation of
Marx, but the debate came to a head when in 1906 Gentile sought to
publish his ideas on the relationship between history and philosophy
in a review of a book edited by Windelband. Gentile pointed to a
contradiction between Windelband's conception of philosophy and
his view of the role of the history of philosophy. Windelband noted a
certain circularity between writing a history of philosophy and doing
philosophy – without a conception of what philosophy was, it would
be impossible to write a history of philosophy, but philosophy was
itself a product of its history, so that to know what philosophy was
presupposed a knowledge of that past. Windelband's solution to this
predicament was to claim, in Kantian manner, that the subject
matter of philosophy was the same throughout history. There were
permanent forms of cognition by which reality was understood,
although the problems facing these varied according to time and
place. Gentile believed Windelband's solution still left the relationship of philosophy to its past unresolved. For if philosophy was
conditioned by the different problems which arose throughout
history, there was no reason to suppose that contemporary philosophical concerns would shed any light upon those of the past. To
escape this dilemma the circularity of philosophy and history must be
accepted. Thus, he argued, to understand Dante it was necessary to
know about the culture, the politics and opinions which coloured his
thinking. But it would be impossible to know what these were simply
by making an inventory of books Dante might have read, or events
he might have witnessed. It would be equally necessary to think
these writings and occurences as Dante thought them, as it was only

through his philosophy that they assumed the importance they did for him. Philosophy, the need to understand the world about us, was a permanent requirement of humanity. But that did not mean there were permanent problems of philosophy, for 'the eternal is in time; indeed it is of time'. We can think new thoughts in the present and add a new page to the history of philosophy, or we can be moved by a present need 'to go to school' with the philosophers of the past. In either case it would be impossible to separate philosophy and history, since philosophy was 'empty' once divorced from its history, and history 'blind' without philosophy to illuminate it. Philosophy was therefore always the product and the creator of its past.[20]

Croce was quick to point out that he shared Windelband's position.[21] As he had written in 1903, it was necessary first to 'philosophise' in order 'to discern, in the as yet indistinct mass of facts, the "philosophical" facts and write their "history" '.[22] He now reaffirmed this conviction that '[historical] reconstruction is only made possibly by the [logical] precedence of a strictly theoretical-philosophical moment'. As a result, whilst 'bad' or 'little' philosophy meant 'bad' or 'little' history, the converse was not true. '. . . [G]ood philosophy can be accompanied with little and bad history: precisely because the philosophical moment precedes that of historical reconstruction'. On the other hand, he admitted that he accepted '[t]he thesis that philosophy and history of philosophy are the same thing . . . in the Hegelian sense that ideal and real, idea and history, are the same'.[23] This concession led Gentile to reply that Croce must also concede that 'historical reconstruction' and 'philosophical appraisal' of a past thinker were identical. If this was true, 'the philosopher does not really possess his philosophy, of which he ignores the history, since in itself, apart from the subjective conditions of whoever actually thinks it, it has its own historical reality, from which it is indivisible'.[24] There was no objective reality of external facts apart from the thought which created them. Our conception of reality was therefore a product of the history of thought. The only way to be critical of the concepts we use to think about reality was to retrace their history and discover their immanent logic, as Hegel had done in the *Phenomenology*. Croce feared that Gentile was making the same mistake he had found in Hegel, of subordinating empirical history to a preconceived meta-physical design. Ideal and real must therefore be retained as 'distinct moments' of Spirit.[25] However, Gentile's arguments revealed that his own view ran this risk, leading him to revise substantially the earlier version of his *Logic* (1905). Yet whilst Gentile's actualism ultimately found the real within the ideal, history within philosophy,

Croce resolved the ideal into the real, philosophy into history – a dramatic turnaround from his earlier position.[26]

With the above discussion in mind, it will not be possible to examine Croce's two most famous pronouncements on the nature of history – the definition of history as 'individual judgement', made in the *Logic* (1909), and the characterization of all history as 'contemporary history', in his *Theory and History of Historiography* (1915). 'Individual judgement' was the unity of history and philosophy. To say 'Peter is a man', Croce argued, was not only to define a characteristic of Peter with a pre-formed concept of what a man is, but to reaffirm and change the concept of man in relation to Peter. Our notions of maleness were historical products of past meetings with other Peters and Pauls, and modifiable by similar future encounters. However, if what we meant by a man was in part constituted by Peter's existence, Peter's conception of himself was equally defined by a given notion of man. There was a unity between the language and the concepts used and the practices engaged in which developed and changed throughout the course of history. However this did not mean that past societies might be incomprehensible to us, because applying the concepts of the present to understand the past would be inevitably anachronistic. For although philosophy was the 'answer' to the 'problems' of a given historical moment, it conditioned the problems and solutions which followed on from it. To think philosophically was to include all the problems and solutions which history had thrown up and 'to translate them . . . into our language'.[27] This conception of history was further developed in Croce's analysis of why we study history – 'All history is contemporary history' because 'it meets a present need'. The collection of facts about the past, of documents ranging from accounts of battles to works of philosophy, whilst producing the best possible position from which to write history, was not yet history but, in Croce's terminology, 'chronicle'. It was a 'dead' past because it merely transcribed the past in its 'own terms', with no concern for how we in the present were to understand it, so that it remained as impenetrable to us as the affairs of an alien world. 'Chronical' only became 'history', a 'live' past, when 'translated' into the language of the present. Croce believed that this was both necessary and possible because we are what our past has made us. Our knowledge of the world and of ourselves derived from experience, which was historically conditioned. Our present state of mind was consequently to be understood in terms of past states. Our thoughts and actions belonged to the stream of history, but 'overcome' it by 'representing' the past in a new form which 'expresses' the new content (thought or action). It was therefore a new world of experience, which incorporated the past at the same time as it transformed it.[28]

Croce wished to avoid Gentile's 'actualist' belief that the thought of today recreated and superseded that of the past without it being necessary to resort to doing history. This desire led him to reverse his earlier position, which had made human creativity the subject and creator of history, to argue that 'history . . . is the work of that truly real individual, which is Spirit eternally individualising itself'. History was the concrete unity of universal and particular, idea and individual, so that 'It does not involve abolishing Pericles in favour of Politics, Plato in favour of Philosophy, or Sophocles in favour of Tragedy, but to represent Politics, Philosophy and Tragedy as Pericles, Plato and Sophocles, and the latter as each of the former in one of their particular moments.'[29] The emphasis, however, was away from the notion that humanity autonomously advanced its conceptions of what Philosophy, Politics etc. were, and towards the idea of them as emanations of Spirit: 'Not even the work of speculation and the work of poetry is attributable to the individual; even these works belong to the course of things and to the universal spirit'.[30] Action in the present, as Croce spelled out in *The Philosophy of Practice*, was only of value from 'the cosmic point of view', as part of

> . . . the plot of History, to which all individuals collaborate, but which is not the work, nor can be in the intentions, of any one of them in particular, because each one is intent exclusively upon particular work and only in *rem suam agere* does the business of the World. History is what has happened, which . . . one does not judge practically, because it always transcends particular points of view, which alone make possible the application of practical judgement. The judgement of History is the very fact of its existence: its rationality is its reality . . . [It is not] the work of a transcendent Intelligence or Providence. . . . If History is rationality, a Providence certainly governs it, but in a manner which becomes actual within individuals and works not above or outside of them, but with them. And this affirmation of Providence is itself neither conjecture nor faith, but evidence of reason. Without this intimate persuasion, who would find within themselves the strength to live? . . . That which the religious man says to himself with the words: 'let us leave it up to God' is said equally by the man of reason with the words: 'Courage and onwards'.[31]

The religious context of Croce's historicism now becomes clear. All history was, in Hegelian and (on Croce's interpretation) Vichian manner, sacred history – the work of providence.[32] What constituted providence was beyond definition. It rendered the past intelligible, but was of no relevance to the present. Such was Croce's fear of falling into 'speculative history' that he denied any special validity to the everyday need for practical judgements. They relied on 'pseudo-concepts', rules of thumb largely conditioned by circumstances. But ultimately all acts were worthwhile because nothing fell outside the bound's of history. To act 'effectively' the individual needed to 'search within himself' and 'establish what attitudes the course of reality has laid down within him . . . not to throw them off but to adopt them'.[33] There was an implied teleology underlying Croce's historicism, which at times amounted to little more than a historicist version of social Darwinism. Spirit, he wrote, brought 'order out of chaos' and via 'continual struggles' had 'effected the passage from animal life to human life . . . and creates ever higher ways of life'.[34] This interpretation of human history reached its extreme in his interpretation of the First World War as the 'life struggle, for the survival and prosperity of the best type [of social group] . . .'.[35] However the outcome of this struggle could never be pronounced upon, so that Croce's philosophy seemed to amount to little more than the justification of history *per se*.

Croce had accused Hegel of a mystification of the real, making it the tool of a transcendent rather than an immanent Idea. However Hegel, unlike Croce, did not identify the real with the sum total of empirical reality. It was the constrast between the Idea and nature, between an ideal order of reality and a disordered empirical reality, which acted as the spur to philosophical reflection. Croce, for all his polemic with positivism, appeared to naturalize this process. As history was infinite, its meaning was unknowable. Instead we had to see history as everything which had occured or would occur, and assume that it had been created by an Idea (the Crocean Spirit), immanent to natural and human wants alike. Philosophically this is totally barren, since no value can be attributed to the unfolding of an Idea unless it is concluded, at least in imaginative anticipation. As the empirical stream of history continues, the meaning of history can only be construed as a transcendental rather than an empirical drama. Croce's historicism not only prevents value judgements in the present, but about the past as well – 'History is the world's court of judgement' in a sense very different from that intended by Hegel, when he quoted Schiller. According to Croce, whatever had happened must have been meant to happen. All the historian could do was recount the past as accurately as possible. For if we did not know how history would eventually turn out, we could not presume to judge the past any more than the present. This seems to contradict

Croce's earlier definition of history as 'contemporary history'. Surely to foist our present concerns upon the past is to be not just anachronistic, but to assume superior knowledge about the essence of history. Croce avoided this dilemma by regarding history as a continuous and progressive process. As servants of Spirit we carried within us the whole of its past development, which conferred upon us who and what we were. The past could therefore be justifiably assessed by the lights of the present. But he offered no reason for this belief beyond the human need for assurance that our acts are ultimately worthwhile. It is hard to suppress the feeling that much of this circular argument is more rhetorical than philosophical.[36]

Croce's philosophy of history is clearly some distance from the concerns of contemporary analytical philosophers. His ideas cannot be adequately assessed simply as methodological recommendations to practising historians. His views are commonly assimilated to Collingwood's belief that to explain an action was 'to discern the thought' of the agent, and that the historian who 'emulates the scientist in searching for the causes or laws of events' was simply 'ceasing to be an historian'. Croce, however, did not make Collingwood's distinction between human events which could be known from the 'inside', and natural events which had only an 'outside' of external effects. Since Croce's Spirit was everything, it produced both the human and the natural world, hence Croce's injunction, criticized by Collingwood, that the natural historian 'become a blade of grass'.[37] This did not entail the view that human and natural history could be conceived as a single causal process, governed by certain general laws of historical development. Croce rejected this thesis in the course of an attack on the dictum of the French positivist Taine – 'Après la collection des faits, la recherche des causes'. Croce's objections were twofold:

i The 'vulgar positivist' (e.g. Taine, Buckle or Loria) conceit, that history was a continuous chain of events, ultimately collapsed into the error of speculative philosophies of history, of substituting a preconcieved skeleton plot, e.g. the development of civilization, for history and hence pronouncing on the ultimate meaning of history or Spirit.
ii There were no 'brute or disconnected' facts outside of the explanation which brought them into being. Human action could not be explained naturalistically, but only relative to the interpretation of events made by the agents at the time, which the historian had to 're-live'. Of course norms and conventions could be regarded as causal conditions of actions, but because

humans were self-interpreting animals, these were also subject
to change, and could not therefore be construed as fixed
determinants of human acts.

Analytical philosophers often regard this view as admitting an
undue degree of subjectivity and unassessable intuition into the
study of human events. Moreover, it also raises the spectre of
relativism, of societies and acts governed by conceptual schemata
incommensurable with our own and hence unknowable. These were
not difficulties for Croce, however, since human thought and action
did not properly belong to the individual, but to Spirit. There were
no false explanations of the past, but only those required of us in the
present.[38] This led Collingwood to criticize Croce's theory as
insufficiently idealist. In a review of Croce's *Theory and History of
Historiography* in 1921 he argued that 'there are two Croces, the
realist, dualist, empiricist, or naturalist . . . and the idealist, whose
life is a warfare upon transcendence and naturalism in all their forms
. . .'. He regarded Croce's historicism as the triumph of the latter,
noting that he claimed to have given up philosophy to write history –
a distinction which for an idealist did not really exist.[39] Collingwood's
review echoes Gentile's criticisms in his last, and this time published,
debate with Croce on the nature of philosophy. Gentile pointed out
that Croce never discussed, except in the most general terms, the
role thought played in judgement. He made great play of the
distinction between art and logic, theory and practice, but the life of
Spirit dissolved everything into its historical development. By
reducing all judgement to history, Croce had denied man the ability
to think or act on any basis other than faith. There was no guidance
to the historian beyond the injunction to trust in the intuitions which
Spirit had placed in him. If Collingwood and Gentile regarded 'all
history [as] the history of thought', for Croce 'all history is the history
of Spirit'. Croce had substituted a mystical belief in History for the
subjectivist idealism of Gentile's 'pure act of thought'.[40]

This difficulty is further compounded by his undisclosed conviction, noted above, that the present is somehow superior. Croce's
history of historiography, which accompanied his own theory just as
a history of aesthetics, logic and ethics had accompanied the three
earlier volumes of the *Philosophy of Spirit*, was written so as to
suggest that his own philosophy was the culmination of a historical
process called 'the development of historiographical thought'.[41] This
presumed that the history of philosophy was only 'contemporary' if it
reflected our own assumptions and ideas of the nature of philosophy.
To take the thought of the past seriously, Croce would have had to

entertain the possibility that it was superior to the thought of the present. This he was not willing to do in the decisive respect of its un-historicist nature, for he rejected any validity of thought beyond that conferred upon it by the historical process, a belief ignored or denied by most earlier thinkers. Yet this committed him to doing what he formally rejected – pronouncing on the meaning of history. There was no other way to justify the Hegelian view that the thought of the present transcended that of the past, except through the rational comprehension of the whole historical process – an attempt Croce repeatedly made in his histories of philosophy, but which he claimed to have rejected on the (correct) grounds that it was an impossible exercise.

This raises two crucial difficulties within Croce's philosophy. The first arises from the ambiguity of Croce's criteria of truth. He was adamant in his opposition to positivist empiricism or 'abstract' speculative theories, but did not define his own views. For example, he argued that the 'ideas' of the past 'were not truly ideas or intellectual formations, but . . . practical acts, sentiments, dispositions, customs, institutions . . .'.[42] This argument followed from his belief that there were no eternal ideas and that all thought reflected its context. Yet he was equally scathing about any notion of truth as correspondence to fact, since it was only in the positivist conceit that 'the facts speak for themselves'. He argued that we must enter into the thoughts of the participants, but this alone would not help us decide on the rationality or veracity of their beliefs. Croce sometimes wrote as if each age had its own criteria of truth, but to translate the past into the present some common assumptions must exist. Yet beyond the formal categories of the Beautiful, the True etc., Croce never tells us what these are.

This relates to the second area of difficulty, concerning the status of his highly selective version of the history of philosophy. Croce argued that the ideas of the past, as defined above, formed a 'patrimony of judgement' which was 'the capital with which and upon which our daily thought works'. We thought about our heritage when, as a result of 'new needs', these 'sentiments and institutions enter into crisis . . . [and] we attempt to understand their true "nature", that is their historical genesis'.[43] Whilst it was true that history took on philosophical importance when significant values were called into question, it was especially vital when present customs and beliefs had obscured important alternative ways of seeing things. Croce argued that the past was only relevant when the present sought to correct it, by developing all previous thinking on the subject. Yet this ignored an important alternative, namely that

the relevance of the past might well be in forcing us to become aware
of what our current beliefs implicitly ignore, and to reconsider them
in the light of this; possibly even to adopt an earlier set of ideas
rejected by our present norms. History has this ability to promote
criticism and hence philosophy by breaking the interpretative circle
of a society's self-interpretation of itself to itself. This capacity is
really essential for people living in an age of intellectual decline,
because it is the only practicable way in which they can recover a
proper understanding of fundamental problems. Croce's historicism
negated this point, because it was opposed to the conception of
philosophy behind it. Historicism sanctioned the loss of any criteria
of truth or rationality by denying the permanence of fundamental
problems, the existence of which made possible 'objectivity' and in
particular 'historical objectivity'. Had Croce taken history seriously,
he would have had to substantiate his assertion that philosophical
doctrines were only at home in specific types of historical and social
setting, an element which is conspicuously absent from his histories.
An enquiry of this nature would have forced Croce to investigate the
rationality and truth of past beliefs in order to understand both what
the thinker thought he or she was explaining and the related
question of whether he or she was correct in this belief or not.[44]

The conceit that such questions did not have to be asked, that
history in its unfathomable way would decide, was not a posture
Croce could responsibly maintain for long. Croce claimed that
historicism had 'served to liberate me once and for all from any
scepticism towards myself and towards the human ability to reach
truth' – that is, against the ultimate vanity of all human thought and
action.[45] The dialectic of the 'living' and the 'dead' reappears
throughout all his writing; an image powerfully evoked by his own
entombment in an earthquake as a child, from which he was the only
survivor. Historicism answered the basic religious need for '. . . an
assurance against the harms of this world taken on the capital of
another'.[46] All human thoughts and acts, no matter how trivial or
worthless they might appear at the time, belonged to the development of history and added to and were preserved in the construction
of the future. Yet, if philosophy was only the expression of the
Zeitgeist, which itself perishes in time, it could have no authority
outside of its particularity. Croce sought to rectify this paradox by
asserting that philosophy belonged to a continuing historical tradition
or 'series of systems'. But this tradition could not be validated by
reason since it was the basis of all reasoning. This was the central
difficulty of Croce's faith – that it was underpinned by a historical
tradition, the basis of which was insusceptible to critical examination

and hence open to arbitrary adulteration. His fight 'against all definitive systems' led to voluntarism on the one hand or resignation on the other. The former, in the hands of right wing nationalists like Papini, seemed highly irrational; yet so did resignation to history, urged with increasing shrillness by Croce throughout the First World War. The rise of fascism seemed to offer the worst of both alternatives. The product of a seizure of power, it became an ever more oppressive and apparently permanent historical reality. Following the war Croce became part of the liberal establishment, serving as Minister of Education under Giolitti from 1920 to 1921. He initially gave a cautious welcome to fascism, hoping it would create the well-ordered and regular form of government necessary for a free-market liberal economy to work effectively. However, by 1924 fascism was developing into a totalitarian regime and claiming a monopoly of knowledge and power over all aspects of life.[47] In order to oppose fascism Croce was forced to amend his view of history as inherently benign and hence redefine the relationship between historical consciousness and human action.

### HISTORY AS THEORY AND AS ACTION

Croce regarded the success of fascism as indicative of a weakness of the moral conscience amongst the Italian people. Yet his own philosophy appeared to justify passive acquiescence to the will of the strongest. His writings after 1924 therefore witnessed a return to the emphasis on human autonomy in the creation of history. However, his philosophical commitment to autonomy now had to be linked to both a defence of liberal politics and his absolute historicism.

As long as Croce was confident in his blind faith in providence, the two had supported each other in an unproblematic manner. Croce could pass over the possibility that the inner convictions of different individuals might ultimately be in conflict with each other, by positing a law of the heterogeneity of ends in classical liberal fashion. Even in the face of the palpable conflict of individual interests in the First World War, he urged his readers to resign themselves to the 'perpetual struggle' by which 'Reality makes itself.'[48] He was unwilling, however, to see fascism as the product of an idealist version of the doctrine of natural selection. Croce's new 'ethico-political' interpretation of history no longer stressed the need of individuals to adjust themselves to history, and examined instead how human ideals made history.[49] This had to be reconciled with Croce's historicist thesis that the real entities in history were not ideas but acts, produced by 'that truly real individual . . . Spirit eternally individualising itself'. The solution lay in the two possible interpretations of Hegel's phrase 'What is real, is rational, and what is rational, is real', which was the foundation of Croce's historicism. The German term rendered here as real is *wirklich*, and derives from the verb to act, *wirken*. By playing on the double sense of *wirklich*, either as a given reality or as what has been made actual by action, Croce could argue both that history *per se* was rational, and that it became rational through its actualization. In Hegelian terms the Idea and human will were the 'warp and weft in the fabric of world history'.[50]

There are correspondingly two aspects to Croce's liberalism. In common with other thinkers in the liberal tradition, he regarded the social and political structures as the product of free, undetermined individual choice – an ideal embodied in the concept of contract. On the other hand, he was less sanguine than many liberals that this was the natural state of humanity, grounded in certain innate human rights. Liberalism was only at home, and its theoretical pre-suppositions intelligible against, a more general historical back-ground – namely the history of Western Europe from the Renaissance to the Risorgimento. To be a liberal was thus not simply to espouse individualism, but also to locate it within the customs and beliefs of a particular historical heritage.[51] Croce argued that if this historical culture could be shown to belong to liberalism, then the legitimacy of the fascist regime in speaking for the Italian nation would have been undermined. Since the Italian people were no more than what history had made them, the acts which expressed their true nature derived from their historical past.[52] This did not mean, as fascist critics argued, that people were eternally trapped in the past, but that the concepts they used to guide their action in the present were historical creations. Moral judgement was *ep ipso* historical judgement. History was therefore the necessary preparation for action. As Croce expressed it in a famous passage:

> We are products of the past and we live immersed within the past which presses upon us from all sides. How then can we move to a new life, how can we create our new action, without putting ourselves above the past if we are within it, and it is us? There is only one way out, that of thought, which does not break the relationship with the past but ideally soars above it and converts it into knowledge.[53]

Croce's distinctions between theory and practice, thought and action, history and the present were thus as important as their ultimate unity. They enabled him to see the individual both as the servant of Spirit and as an autonomous actor. Both Gramsci and

Gentile argued that this distinction prevented Croce from developing a theory of praxis. Revolutionary change, a radical break with the past, was necessarily un-historical and hence outside Croce's doctrine. Historicist politics were restricted to piecemeal reformism.[54] There is some truth in this criticism – it was certainly the political stance Croce chose to adopt. Yet he could reply that even the thought of the revolutionary operated within a given historical framework, and that there were certain limits to human action which history could help people discover by making them recognize who and what they were. To presume there were no limits to people's ability to transform themselves was an error, which when lived out became a criminal illusion. Croce's distinction between theory and action had the salutory effect of forcing him to justify his doctrine by the actual writing of history. This is turn promoted a more thoroughgoing criticism of his historicism. It is only when theory and practice are kept distinct that the relationship of morals to action can be problematical. For unless the morality of politics is to be abandoned to the historical stream, or individual whim, some framework must be elaborated in which talk of the rightness or wrongness of actions makes sense.

## HISTORY AS THE STORY OF LIBERTY

Between 1924 and 1932 Croce wrote his four main historical works. Although related to his earlier writings, they were undoubtedly prompted by the new orientation of his philosophy which followed the advent of fascism. The first two, the *History of the Kingdom of Naples* and the *History of the Baroque Era in Italy*, were written between 1922 and 1926. Both defended the general thesis that the 'religion of liberty' developed from the Renaissance onwards, and was uninhibited by either the economic and social backwardness of southern Italy, or the 'moral decadence' of the Counter-Reformation respectively. They were not only considerable contributions to historical research, but a defence of the 'ethico-political' approach to history against the Marxist and the fascist schools. According to Croce, both doctrines mistook empirical categories for ideal ones – thus Marxist historians of the south related a reactionary social and political superstructure to the backward economic base. Instead, Croce focused on the liberal tradition, which he associated with the intellectual opposition to the authorities of thinkers such as Campanella, Giannone, Vico, Pagano and Cuoco, to name the most famous. This political tradition was a 'moral phenomenon', not a 'natural phenomenon'. The economic base did not determine their actions, but was the matter upon which they exercised their spiritual activity.[55] The political and cultural institutions of the Counter-Reformation were, in contrast, purely at the service of economic interests. Croce clearly intended his portrayal of the seventeenth century to be understood as a characterization of fascism as well. Yet even during this period of decline, the origins of liberalism could be seen in the growth of rational scientific enquiry and the claims of the protestant conscience against church and state.[56] Croce's argument was that if we looked for what was 'contemporary' in these two periods we would rediscover the ideals of the liberal tradition and identify the fascist regime for the reactionary baroque masquerade it was. In contrast, liberal ideals would not be seen as products of a determinate social-economic class, but of a culture which transcended material conditions.

These two histories provided the dynamic element of Croce's 'ethico-political' interpretation of history, whereby society advanced via the struggle of intellectuals to realize certain 'moral ideals' of mankind. Ethico-political history had as its subject

> not only the state, the government of the state and the expansion of the state, but also that which is outside the state, whether it co-operates with it or tries to modify it, overthrow it and replace it: namely the formation of moral institutions, in the broadest sense of the word, including religious institutions and revolutionary sects, sentiments, customs, fancies and myths that are practical in tendency and content'.[57]

These institutions were the creations of 'political geniuses and the aristocrats or political classes which give them life and in turn are created and supported by them'. Croce developed Mosca's notion of the 'political class', elaborating his ideas in a review of the second edition, which served as a preface to subsequent reprintings of the work.[58] Its members did not, he argued, serve their particular class interest, but aimed at serving the ideal interests of humanity as a whole. As a result, they rarely came from amongst the ruling group, but were drawn, as Mosca claimed, from the middle rank of any given society, which were always in a relatively independent position. Croce held that members of the 'political class' promoted the development of history by virtue of serving Spirit via the ideal moments of the Beautiful, the True, etc. Their membership changed with the circulation of ideals rather than of interests. He hoped that by removing Mosca's theory from its positivist framework, he could prevent the identification of the political class with the bourgeoisie of the nineteenth century, thereby avoiding the anachronism which bedevilled any practical application of his compatriot's ideas. Like Mosca, he turned to the history and analysis of contemporary political institutions to prove his case – that the liberal ideal had primacy over the democratic. Only by infusing the masses with the spirit of the former, he contended, could the two be reconciled.

Croce's next pair of histories were therefore much harder to execute, for they portrayed the liberal era itself and called for some explanation of the links between liberal theory and practice. His *History of Italy from 1871 to 1915* (1925) and the *History of Europe in the Nineteenth Century* (1932) were attacked by Gramsci as uncritical panegyrics which failed to address either the formation of liberal regimes and ideas in the French revolution and after, or their collapse following the First World War.[59] Had Croce wished to maintain that the liberal era was either inevitable or eternal, as Gramsci suggested, these would be crucial omissions, but he did not support either of these theses. His intention was to examine the nature of liberalism by returning to the period which had produced the most complete realization of liberal practice. It was only thus that the politics implied by liberal ideology could be brought to light. To this extent his account did not neglect the various elements in play during the formative period, since the opening chapters of both histories listed the diversity of social groups and expectations generated by the French and industrial revolutions; they marked the culmination of the development of modern rationality outlined in the two earlier histories. The industrial revolution was the product of man's progressive control of nature, and the French revolution brought the individual's emancipation from the authority of traditional customs and beliefs which had not been freely assented to. He maintained that the legacy of these movements had not been the simple hegemony of a particular class and set of ideas over all others.[60] The liberal belief in the neutrality of facts and the subjective nature of values was a response to this situation, for it operated as a defensive strategy against the attempts of some to act as moral legislators for others. Croce's histories aimed to shed light on why liberalism failed to produce a moral consensus opposed to fascism. His answer falls into two parts – the insufficiency of liberal politics, and the inability of liberalism to become a 'moral ideal' – and are treated in the *History of Italy* and the *History of Europe* respectively.

It would be a grave misunderstanding of the limited metaphysical pretensions of Croce's *History of Italy* to regard it as a vulgar-Hegelian deification of the liberal state. In fact it argued for a very narrow conception of liberalism. According to Croce, liberalism was more an attitude of mind, an openness to alternative points of view, than a set of political practices. For different policies would be appropriate at different times – it was the merit of liberalism that it appreciated this. The low-stock of liberalism derived from the 'lack of understanding of the ideal character of pure liberalism'.[61] Liberalism's ethical core, the defence or individual autonomy, had become unduly associated with the political and economic practices which had initially accompanied it – i.e. democracy and the expanding industrial free-market economy. To regard these as the only ways of realizing human freedom was to confuse the empirical with the ideal. Liberalism became a means rather than an end, so that the cultural achievements which gave human individuality meaning could be sacrificed to the material rewards of political power or an increase in gross national product. Liberalism became identified with the policies which had briefly accompanied its triumph in the nineteenth century – 'The fact is just this: that liberalism was then a practice and not yet a living and intimate faith . . . an object of solicitation and meditation, a sacred object to jealously defend at the first move which threatened it'.[62] This process culminated in the First World War – the result of the pursuit of material ends at the expense of ideal ones.[63]

Croce's liberalism was based on the relationship between the Good and the Useful elaborated in his *Philosophy of Practice*. The Useful logically preceded and was distinguished from the Good – morality thus subdued and refashioned economic activity. Fascists and democrats, socialists and laissez-faire liberals all made the same mistake of substituting an economic category for a moral one. No single political programme could be adopted to the exclusion of others, since that would be to impose an abstract ideal, be it a planned socialist economy or the laissez-faire policies of the free market, upon the unknowable design of Spirit. What was suitable, and hence moral, could only be shown *post factum*, as history. All the individual could do was to act as the situation, and hence Spirit, demanded, adopting socialist policies on some occasions, capitalist ones on others.[64] Croce's liberalism therefore provided no criteria for how to mediate between the conflicting projects of different groups or individuals, beyond a general injunction to act according to the liberal ideal of moderation and co-operation. Giolitti is singled out for having adopted this spirit of accommodation when ruling the country, and his hated policy of *trasformismo* praised accordingly – 'having freed the term from the pejorative meaning which was initially attached to it, and because every time that the antinomy between conservation and revolution is transcended and weakens and seems to vanish there follows a drawing together of extremes and a unifying transformation of their ideals'. He is favourably compared with Crispi, who sought to provide a social consensus through abortive schemes for imperial expansion, whilst repressing political expression by socialists and liberals at home. In contrast, Giolitti attempted to involve groups previously excluded from politics, and defuse both nationalism and Marxism. Unlike the Risorgimento liberals, who sought to hold on to their monopoly of power, he realized that the Italian political class was too narrow in numbers and risked exhausting itself, and that it was therefore appropriate to gradually call new stratas of society to public affairs.[65]

Croce's admiration for Giolitti would seem to commit him to the classic strategy of social democratic politics – the belief that the gradual extension of the franchise and the more equitable distribution of wealth would produce a fairer society and diffuse ideological divisions. However, he had long attacked what he stigmatized as 'the masonic mentality'. He argued that liberal individualism of itself could only produce an atomized society, lacking the shared commitments and values which endowed political practices with meaning. Liberal practices required an adherence to liberal ideals if the moderation and compromise involved were to be accepted as fair or rational. As Croce had written in an important article of 1911, 'Faith and Programmes',

> Programmes are not faith and cannot give rise to it; because faith is something secure and absolute, and programmes are contingent and changeable, faith must dominate every kind of event, and programmes must adapt themselves to events to the point of letting themselves be absorbed by them.
> The relationship between programmes and faith is, therefore, that the latter precedes the former and generates them; and, when it is lacking it is futile to replace it with grandiose programmes, just as a building without foundations is not strengthened by ornaments and decorations.[66]

Democracy, for example, understood simply as a mechanical political practice, undermined the claims of social norms upon the individual, by requiring the consent of the populace to render a given policy legitimate. If this consent was judged by purely numerical criteria, then any voter who disagreed could claim there was no real obligation upon him to obey unless there was a prior agreement that majoritarian decisions were in some manner inherently fair or just. This involved a common understanding of what these practices entailed, and not just the arbitrary adoption of a given mechanism. Democratic legitimacy implied a unity of will towards certain ends which linked all voters, a common sense of the meaning of voting, and not just an aggregate of votes. Democracy therefore assumed a degree of consensus amongst voters which its procedures alone could not provide. Unless a sense of responsibility and common political purpose existed, the extension of the right to vote would merely increase the divisions and disaffection within society and open up the possibilities for manipulation and demogogary to hold sway over the electorate. This had been amply demonstrated by the rise of fascism.[67] But if liberalism had failed to become a 'living ideal' under the 'Historical Right', it had certainly not succeeded under Giolitti. As his fellow liberal idealist, Guido De Ruggiero, pointed out, Croce had failed to develop his thesis fully enough and show how politics had been debased to 'administration' and liberal culture become 'the empty rhetoric of half-forgotten commonplaces'. The lesson of Croce's *History of Italy* was that liberal politics required the 'religion of liberty' to be a coherent doctrine.[68] Croce's aim in his *History of Europe* was to show that historically, and hence ideally, the former was implied by the latter. He ended up proving the opposite was the case.

The *History of Europe* is often criticized for being too philosophical, 'the most complete historiographical realisation of his providential view-point'.[69] This overlooks the role Croce's historicism plays in completing his defence of liberalism. For it is the belief in providence which moralises liberal practice, providing a secular language to express common needs, aspirations and fears which go beyond the immediacies of technique and social structure. Unfortunately for Croce's wider philosophical ambitions, he was too good a historian to actually think such a union of belief and practice had been anything more than a temporary historical conjunction. Even on the most optimistic reading, which he gave here, its hold was always tenuous and by 1915 gone altogether.[70] Croce's writing of history revealed the limitations of his philosophy, by showing its dependence upon the actual existence of a specific historical world. The politics of bargaining and accommodation of Giolittean *trasformismo* worked for as long as this ethos correctly reflected the self-understanding of all or most of the participants. As Croce well knew, the acquiescence of the liberal establishment (including Giolitti) in the fascist seizure of power had been largely because this situation no longer existed. Like Croce, they had welcomed fascism as the 'restoration of a stricter liberal regime, within the context of a stronger state'.[71] They had hoped fascism would enforce liberalism, since it no longer seemed to command the voluntary assent of the populace. However, by 1932 he appreciated that the lack of support for liberalism was indicative of a deeper dissatisfaction with the liberal ethic, of which liberal institutions had been only the temporary expression. This was not just the result of an instrumental failure of liberal policies to produce an efficient and expanding economy or maintain law and order, but a more general disillusionment with the norms of political behaviour and the goals which liberalism assumed in order to function. Moreover, the breakdown of the liberal consensus had been a product of liberal politics.

This paradox informed both Croce's histories, and reached it climax in the famous epilogue to his *History of Europe*. He did not want, he wrote, to predict the future but to provide

> indications of the paths the moral conscience and the observation of the present provide for those, who in their guiding concepts and interpretation of the events of the nineteenth century, agree with the narrative given of them in this history. Others, with different minds, different concepts, a different quality of culture and a different temperament will choose other paths, and if they do so in a pure spirit, obeying an interior command, they too will be preparing the future well.[72]

However, the 'moral conscience' had been debased by his liberalism to the status of a subjective ideal. This compromised any defence of liberalism as *the* moral ideal. He could not, he remarked, rule out the possibility of other moral standards which reflected different historical and cultural settings. The liberal could not even claim to be morally superior to the fascist, since fascism was a product of history like any other political regime or doctrine, presumably held honestly enough by many of its adherents. Both his liberalism and historicism failed to recognize that it was possible both rationally and genuinely to hold a false belief. For this presupposed an objective account of human rationality and interests distinct from the explicit statements and actions of individuals in history. The only consolation which Croce could offer the liberal was that he too had a historical role to play: 'Work according to the line which is here marked out for you, with your whole self, everyday, every hour in each of your acts, and leave the rest to divine providence, which knows more than we single individuals do and works with us, through us and above us.'[73]

Croce's liberalism and his historicism shared the same individualist and subjectivist assumptions, the latter providing metaphysical endorsement for the former. Thus the collapse of one brought the decline of the other. With the end of the liberal era, Crocean providence offered little comfort to the liberal beyond a grim

stoicism. Not surprisingly, few were attracted by it, even when Croce
later assured them, in the 1947 preface to his *History of Italy*, that
fascism had been 'a sad parenthesis' in Italian history. Croce found
himself in the same quandary as Mosca – unable to detach the liberal
ideal from the class and times to which it belonged, his hope for 'a
new aristocracy young and vigorous like that of other days',[74] mere
wishful thinking.

Croce's 'religion of liberty' was a civilization creed, and could
have no authority outside the particular society of which it was the
expression. To hold on to this creed when the historical world which
made it possible had passed away as simply anachronistic. He sought
to assimilate the Christian belief in providence to his 'religion of
liberty', but in reducing it to a cultural phenomenon he had denied
its spiritual force. Croce's predicament can be summed up in Eric
Heller's splendid phrase, 'the disinherited mind'. Croce's definitions
of liberalism and morality, by being linked to history, were
dependent upon the continued existence of the bourgeois Christian
world of nineteenth-century Europe. His liberalism was a product of
modern rationality, his moral conscience the Christian legacy.
During the nineteenth century the two had seemed compatible, but a
world of radical secularity, of human autonomy based on modern
technology, ultimately has no need for religious endorsement.
Croce's view of religion as a contribution to human culture was in
this respect revealed as a fatal compromise. In a final revision of his
historicism, Croce tried to incorporate a purely instrumental conception of rationality into his scheme of things, replacing the concept of the
Useful with that of *vitalità* – the raw material of history which has 'its
needs, its reasons, which moral reason does not know'.[75] However,
this was little more than a return to passive acquiescence to the given
– a resignation to the persistence of fascist rule. It was not a position
Croce found satisfactory for long.

Croce's analysis of liberalism can be usefully compared with
Weber's account of capitalism. Both studies are more than illus-
trations of a particular approach to the study of the past. Weber and
Croce's respective methodological principles are intimately related
to their chosen subject, and they aimed to provide historical
legitimation for both. Capitalism, liberalism and methodology are
products of a common theme in their work – namely the seculariz-
ation and rationalization of human culture. It is a topic about which
they were both highly ambivalent. On the one hand, it was the
triumph of individual autonomy, of our control over nature and
ourselves. But it equally marked the loss of a religious framework
capable of endowing human action with value and meaning, and the

substitution of merely instrumental forms of justification and endorsement. Their interpretations of modern culture were remarkably similar. For Weber, humanity had no choice but to act in a narrowly rationalistic manner. The evaluation of the ultimate worth of our acts was beyond human knowledge, so that they had no intrinsic value besides their effectiveness in satisfying certain short-term goals. However, he rejected the notion that human action was therefore purely self-interested and egoistic. The paradigm of the capitalist was the Puritan zealot, moved to carry out his or her duties by a sense of 'vocation' or 'calling'. The capitalist acts as if to be rewarded in the next world, but with no sense of his or her own merit in so doing; since all has been pre-ordained by God, and even this comfort is an act of faith or will. In the modern age there was no option but to adopt the Calvinist's rationalist creed; no longer a matter of choice or belief, it had become 'the iron cage' of modernity.[76] Croce similarly restricted human action to the sphere of the 'practical', its value being a matter on which only providence could decide. For both Croce and Weber, in the words of the latter's two famous essays, science and politics were a 'vocation' in a manner analogous to the faith of the Calvinist believer.[77] However Croce, less 'tough-minded' in William James's sense, attempted to retain the theological context of the rationalist ethic. But fascism had revealed that rationalization undermined religious and moral beliefs, leaving naked economic and political power whose might, as Gentile was infamously to argue, was right.

The writing of history ultimately undermined both Croce's liberalism and the historicist faith upon which it rested. History revealed not only the historical contingency of the union of liberalism and historicism, but also their incompatibility. For the liberal insistence on the self-sufficiency of individual reason mitigated against a common moral understanding. Croce recognized that a shared set of beliefs was indispensable to the life of a community; historicism was meant to substitute for religion in this respect. Far from making such commitments redundant, he realized liberalism only flourished during the brief period when liberal ideals were hegemonic. Yet liberal practice had ultimately dissolved this allegiance by simultaneously increasing individualist aspirations and demystifying social bonds. In this regard liberalism had prepared the way for fascism, for the re-creation of a moral community was liable to be forced and authoritarian in character when there was widespread disbelief in the possibility for any objective basis for such a regime. History could not provide a valid set of norms because liberalism lived in an eternal present, the individual's choices

supposedly unprejudiced by prior social or cultural attitudes. Yet
some such assumptions were required to reach to any agreement at
all and avoid complete anarchy. By the 1940s, with the political and
cultural world of nineteenth-century Europe irreparably torn apart,
Croce was led, yet again, to reconsider his historicism and the values
it represented.

## HISTORIOGRAPHY AND MORALITY

Croce's historicism had three main features:

  i The sublimation of the individual to being a concrete moment
  of the universal
  ii the identification of morality with the process of history
  iii the implicit progressivism of the belief in providence.

All three were intimately related and doubts about one aspect of
his doctrine inevitably called the other two into question. Croce had
attempted to reduce the individual to his or her acts, regarding them
as part of the historical drama of Spirit – the product of a special
'vocation' or calling. However, this provided no guidelines for how
to act in the present beyond the two unacceptable alternatives of
passive resignation or emotive whim, with Croce stressing one or the
other according to circumstances. This lead on to the second aspect –
Croce's definition of morality. The individual acts responsibly by
following the 'moral conscience', but to define this Croce was again
forced to adopt a circular argument. According to Croce, morality
was Spirit's dialectical manifestation in history, the product of
'grace' and 'providence'. Yet to act morally in the present, an
individual must act 'as if he was grace and providence for himself,
forcing the one and the other'. Taken literally this could only lead to
the will to power of Gentile's actualism, and so Croce added the
caveat 'or to adopt less paradoxical terms, to make himself worthy of
one and the other by his own acts and efforts'.[78] But the paradox
persists, for without knowledge of the meaning of history, one
cannot know what will make one worthy of it.

To avoid this dilemma Croce had to abandon historicism. This can
be seen in an essay of 1948, in which Croce reconsidered the
Hegelian motto concerning the rationality of the real, which was the
keystone of his philosophy. In a fictional discussion with Hegel he
reaffirmed the incontrovertible truth of the 'solemn aphorism', but
was moved to add that

  the unassailable truth of that aphorism sometimes appears to waiver
  in whoever feels the efficacious and terrifying presence of the evil

against which he fights, and therefore it is necessary to add that the dualism of rational and real, abolished by historical thought, is posited and always re-established by the conscience which is not theoretical truth but practical and moral action.[79]

To retain the 'moral conscience', Croce had to effectively drop the perspective of absolute historicism. For if morality and history coincided, which they had to do if the subject of history was Spirit, there could be no duality of the *sein* and *sollen*, 'is' and 'ought', within the moral conscience, for Spirit could not assume a duality in practice which was denied in theory.

In deepending his investigation of what constituted morality, Croce became aware that although the source of civilization, it could not be identified with it.[80] This was particularly evident in a review of the pioneering studies of witchcraft by the 'Crocean' anthropologist Enrico de Martino. Croce pointed out that history broke down present day preconceptions by revealing the varieties of moral experience. This did not mean the past should be accepted at its own evaluation any more than the present, nor that there could not be permanent objects of human enquiry outside a particular discourse which defined or omitted them. History rendered our contemporary philosophizing more self-critical by urging us to give an account of the human situation which was more adequate than those of its rivals. Magic could not be understood apart from the concepts and practices of the culture which supported it. But this did not entail acceptance of it as a rational belief, even if rationally held, nor a patronizing dismissal of it as a surpassed stage in human development. Rather, it invited enquiry into what needs and purposes such beliefs served – something which might transcend different societies and cultures.[81]

These were reflections which Croce, then at the end of a long life, could develop only in a sketchy form. They pointed to a dropping of historicism, but not of history, which was reaffirmed as vital for philosophy and particularly ethics, since it was the only way to become aware of all that humanity was and could be. It was also the best solvent of ideology, since it undermined the closed and self-defining nature of ideological systems which prevented criticism by denying alternative points of view. By confronting philosophy with its history, Croce was led away from historicism and ideology and back to philosophy. Unfortunately his example was not emulated by many of his contemporary followers and critics, frequently with disastrous political consequences.

# 6

# GIOVANNI GENTILE

Giovanni Gentile was born at Castelvetrano in Sicily on 30 May 1875, and assassinated by communist partisans on 15 April 1944. Best known as the philosopher of fascism, he was as important as Croce, with whom he collaborated until 1924, in reviving the idealist tradition in Italy. In some respects his influence was greater than Croce's, since his university position gave him more opportunities for building up an academic school. This was particularly true after the fascist seizure of power when, as Minister of Education in Mussolini's first government, he was able to apply his ideas in a comprehensive reform of the educational system, and ultimately became the official cultural spokesman of the regime. Above all, the principle doctrine of his social philosophy – the unity of thought and action – forced upon him the moral duty, as he saw it, of putting his ideas into practice. This chapter will therefore investigate the extent to which 'actual idealism' necessarily leads to fascism.

## THE REFORM OF THE HEGELIAN DIALECTIC

Gentile's philosophy was more firmly rooted in the native idealist culture than Croce's. His philosophical works are written at a high level of abstraction and assume a detailed knowledge of his sources. His thought is therefore best elucidated in the context of the tradition of post-Kantian idealism in Italy which he aimed to develop.

Actualism was a radical attempt to integrate our consciousness of experience with its creation, thereby abolishing the distinction between thought and practice. He claimed that his main thesis could already be found in his doctoral dissertation of 1897 on the Italian neo-Kantians, Rosmini and Gioberti, where 'to explain the value of Rosmini's philosophy and hence of Kant's [I maintain] that a profound difference exists between the category (which is the act of thought [*l'atto del pensiero*]), and the concept (which is the fact thought about [*il pensato*]). From then on I have considered thought as real only in its actuality, as *a priori*.[1] Kant rejected the empiricist epistemology which regarded human knowledge as the product of sense impressions of external objects. He replaced this model with the notion of an *a priori* synthesis, whereby the concepts by which we interpreted reality constituted the objects of experience. Thus the causal connection of events was not supplied by experience but by the Understanding, as a necessary condition of our awareness of causality. However Gentile, following Hegel, did not believe Kant was radical enough in his criticism of 'realism'. Having rejected the empiricist idea that objects were given in experience, Kant re-introduced it in the guise of a given in the Understanding – his fixed set of categories for interpreting the world. By positing a fixed noumenal world as the transcendental ground of phenomenal experience, Kant ended up denying the truly creative faculty of the Understanding.[2]

According to Gentile, Hegel was the first to appreciate the fully autonomous nature of thought, in virtue of which different 'forms of consciousness' produced different concepts and categories of Understanding. In the *Phenomenology*, Hegel attempted to show that these 'forms of consciousness' followed a logical sequence from 'sense certainty' to 'absolute knowing'. Empiricism and Kantian Understanding were therefore stages in the development of consciousness. However, Hegel did not wish to replace transcendental idealism with subjectivist idealism. The contribution of the thinking subject was vital, but this did not mean that all knowledge was relative to the knower. Hegel's epistemology was underwritten by an ontological argument, which regarded being and consciousness as logically related as part of the development of a metaphysical entity – Spirit or the Idea – immanent to them both. This was a historical process, which Hegel identified with the revelation of God to humankind within Christianity:

> The *world spirit* is the spirit of the world as it reveals itself through the human consciousness; the relationship of man to it is that of the single parts to the whole which is that substance. And this world spirit corresponds to the divine spirit which is the absolute spirit. Since God is omni present in everyone and appears in everyone's consciousness, and this is the world spirit.[3]

Spirit or mind was thus a self-constituting subject which culminated in philosophy, the 'inwardizing' of the successive phases of Spirit's unfolding. The ontological status of the content of human thought was thus solved by bringing humanity to recognize it as the working of *Geist*, of Spirit or reason, in humankind and the world. As we saw, this is the fundamental tenet of Croce's absolute historicism. Gentile, in contrast, was unsatisfied with Hegel's solution because, he argued, the Hegelian Spirit was as transcendent from the human viewpoint as the Kantian categories. This stemmed from the Hegelian distinction between the *Phenomenology*, or the development of individual consciousness, and the *Logic*, which regarded reality as the product of Spirit, thereby creating an apparent dualism between Spirit, as the essence of everything, and human thought.[4]

Gentile's argument was again occasioned by the study of an Italian thinker – the Neapolitan Hegelian Bertrando Spaventa, whose follower, Donato Jaja, was Gentile's mentor at the Scuola Normale in Pisa. Under Jaja's influence, Gentile came to regard Spaventa as the principal continuator of the idealist tradition, and republished his main writings. Spaventa's radical solution to the alleged Hegelian dualism, which Gentile made his own, was to identify the individual mind of the *Phenomenology* with the Spirit of the *Logic*. Transcendence was finally overcome in a philosophy of absolute immanence, in which the activity of the thinking subject was the sole basis for human knowledge, and hence of the objects which constituted experience.[5]

Gentile, via Hegel and Spaventa, concluded by transferring the faculties originally ascribed by Kant to the transcendental subject, and by Hegel to Spirit, to thought *tout court*:

> The method of immanence, therefore, consists in the concept of the absolute concreteness of the real in the act of thought, or in history [past thought]: an act that one transcends when one begins to posit something (God, nature, logical law, moral law, historical reality conceived as an assemblage of facts, spiritual or psychological categories beyond the actuality of consciousness) which is not the self-same Ego positing itself, or as Kant put it, the I think.[6]

Thought is a 'pure act' that is presuppositionless – the absolute foundation of the human world of experience. Gentile revised Vico's aphorism *verum et factum convertuntur* to mean that the criterion of truth was within the thought of the agent, through whose activity the world of fact was created. Vico's motto was hence rephrased *verum et fieri convertuntur*.[7] This was the unity of thought and will in the self-constitution [*autoctisi*] of reality – the true *synthesis a priori* of self and world which made objective knowledge possible.

Gentile provided two proofs of his 'theory of spirit as pure act'.

First, he aimed to show that it was the logical outcome of Western philosophical thought since Descartes and, borrowing from Hegel, the essence of Christianity. Second, it was equally the phenomenological development of human self-consciousness. Philosophy and history coincided, therefore. To illustrate his first proof, Gentile adopted Bertrando Spaventa's theory of the 'circulation of European thought' to show how the ideas of the German philosophers he admired were adopted, or independently conceived, by Italian thinkers as part of a single philosophical tradition reflecting the unity of Spirit.[8] The concept of *bildung* – of the development of self-consciousness through the education of experience – was central to the second aspect of Gentile's theory, and was elaborated in a number of his works devoted to pedagogy.[9] The history of culture and the theory of education were the twin poles of Gentile's demonstration of the truth of his ideas, and formed the bulk of his writings. They will only be examined here, however, to the extent that they affect his social and political thought.

## UNIFYING THEORY AND PRACTICE

Gentile's 'actual idealism' entailed the unity of theory and practice, since for Gentile to know the world was to make it. This doctrine was at the heart of Gentile's social philosophy, and was first formulated in his early writings on Marx. This was hardly coincidental, for as we saw, Labriola's Marxism had its origins in the Spaventian reform of Hegel which actualism develops. Gentile's interpretation of Marx was largely based on Labriola's commentary on the Preface to *A Contribution to the Critique of Political Economy*. He also attributed great importance to *The Theses on Feuerbach*, which he translated into Italian for the first time.

He assimilated the Marxist doctrine of praxis to the Vichian principle that history was a human product – '. . . thought is real, because it is to the extent it posits the object. Either thought is, and thinks, or it does not think and isn't thought. If it thinks it acts (*fa*). Therefore reality, the objectivity of thought, is a consequence of its own nature. This is one of the prime consequences of Marxist realism.'[10] The eleventh thesis on Feuerbach was read in a strongly idealist manner to mean that thought creates reality. This, he claimed, vitiated Marx's professed materialism, leading to (Gentile's habitual criticism of other philosophers) a 'more or less Platonic dualism' between mind and matter within Marxism. This could only be resolved within an idealism which regarded everything as the product of Spirit. Indeed 'the matter of historical materialism, far from being opposed to Hegel's Idea, is contained within it, is one with it.'[11] Marx's theory of *praxis* could therefore be assimilated to the reform of Hegel in the direction of a subjective idealism by which human beings' self-critical activity, rather than Spirit's, produced their environment.

Gentile regarded his actualism as the only philosophy compatible with human freedom and morality, in the Kantian sense of autonomy. Moral freedom was brought back to earth from the noumenal world where Kant placed it, to become part of our everyday experience for which we are totally responsible.[12] In many respects Gentile's theory seems to involve a subjectivism so radical in kind that it falls into complete solipsism. It is hard to see what political consequences are likely to follow from this theory beyond the anarchism of *bellum omnium contra omnes*. For there is no basis for presupposing that my conception of my interests should coincide with that of my fellows. We each have equally valid grounds for regarding our own will as an autonomous spiritual creation, and those opposed to it as objects to be absorbed and organized within it. The only solution to an otherwise eternal conflict would be via the domination of a particular will over all others. In many respects. Gentile's fascism can be traced to this *impasse* in his thought.

His *Foundations of a Philosophy of Right*, published contemporaneously with his *General Theory of Mind as Pure Act* in 1916, provided a vivid illustration of this problem. Gentile's book was clearly modelled on Hegel's *Philosophy of Right*; however, he accused Hegel of having an *a priori* and rationalistic view of law and morality.[13] Gentile, on the other hand, regarded society as the product of the dialectical development of conflicting interests towards a unity supplied by a universal consciousness common to all. Just as a plurality of particular objects was resolved within the single unifying consciousness which created connections between them, so the 'naturalistic' conception of particular individuals was overcome in a common conception of society:

> Robinson Crusoe on his island, before meeting Man Friday, can only realise his own will by going through the same process that is proper to the will of every individual living in society: that is by negating what is opposed to his own will within its universal value, which constitutes the particular or finite moment of the will in society. Hence [society], though empirically it is the accord of individuals, is speculatively definable as the reality of the will in process of development. The universal value is established through the immanent suppression of the particular element. [Society], therefore, is not *inter homines*, but *in interiore homine*, and it is *between* men only to the extent that all

men, with respect to their spiritual being, are one single man with a single interest that continually increases and develops: the patrimony of humanity.[14]

Gentile was only able to overcome the conflict of particular wills by presupposing a spiritual unity in the 'patrimony of humanity'. This solution, however, was in conflict with the fundamental tenet of actualism as a philosophy without presuppositions. Gentile explicitly rejected the Hegelian thesis that the social world was the manifest-ation of a metaphysical entity, *Geist*, within human affairs as *a priori* or 'transcendent'. He was equally opposed to the nationalist claim that membership of a given community automatically bound one to it, condemning it as 'naturalistic'. Gentile insists our obligation to the state was always 'internal', and that the social relations which unite us to others were a product of our will. He was therefore committed to showing how a community of will could emerge spontaneously amongst individuals interacting in society. This, as the above passage illustrates, he singularly failed to do. Instead each individual sought to negate the particular wills opposed to his or her, supposedly universal, will. The individual was only likely to recognize the universality of others if forced to do so.

This indeed is precisely what Gentile suggested when, in the next chapter, he identified force and law. 'Law is for the subject the very act of his self-realisation': force and law could only be abstractly distinguished therefore, 'because the law is neither a *prius* nor a *posterius* with respect to the power which posits it and freely obeys it.'[15] We were literally 'forced to be free' by virtue of recognizing the compulsion imposed by the will of the stronger. Nationality and culture, which in Hegel were the basis of communal life in the state, were interpreted by Gentile as a product of the state – that is, the effective will. The state was not the will of all the people to realize themselves, but the will which had successfully realized itself – be it that of the tyrant or the rebel. The result was that an individual's will was totally subordinate to that of the state, to the extent of being identical with it: 'I, then, as a citizen of my country, am bound by its law in such a manner that to will its transgression is to aim at the impossible. If I did so, I should be indulging in vain velleities, in which my personality, far from realising itself, would on the contrary be disintegrated and scattered. I then want what the law wants me to want'.[16]

Actualism would seem to have such radically subjectivist premises that as a social doctrine it could only lead to anarchy or dictatorship – a consequence foretold by Hegel in his criticism of the French Revolution as an attempt to remake society entirely according to the

prescriptions of human reason, what Hegel called 'absolute freedom'.[17] Croce had warned Gentile of this danger in his public
critique of 'actual idealism' of 1913. He argued that the insistence on
the simple unity of the 'pure act of thought' led either to mysticism,
the 'transcendental loneliness' of the individual subject, or megalo-
mania. The latter was, practically speaking, the most likely and the
most dangerous, because actualism abolished the distinction between
truth and falsehood, good and evil, since whatever the agent
believed or did at a given moment was *ipso facto* true or good. The
transcendental idealism of Hegel and Kant assumed an objective
foundation in Spirit or Reality which structured consciousness. By
abandoning any notion of reality beyond the 'pure act of thought',
Gentile undermined rationality as an independent standard as well.
Activity was praised regardless of its content, and the only standard
of worth was that of success.[18]

Regrettably, the First World War prevented their differences from
remaining purely theoretical. For Gentile regarded the war as
providing the moment of conflict necessary for the spontaneous
creation of a moral unity of consciousness and will amongst
individuals, by centring their thought and action on the defence and
extension of the state. That the vast majority of soldiers killed or
demoralized in the trenches were conscripts, rather than ardent
nationalists, does not seem to have bothered him. Unfortunately the
defeat at Caporetto was far from redeemed by the Vittoria Veneto;
and it required the authority of 'l'Uomo', in the shape of Mussolini,
to enforce the identity of individual and state that Gentile's social
theory required.

### THE PHILOSOPHER OF FASCISM

Gentile believed that the Italians' defeat at Caporetto in 1917 had
resulted from a lack of patriotism, of united moral purpose, which
was the real foundation of the state. However, the war provided the
opportunity to create this cohesion and to prove that the Risorgimento had been a genuine act of will, rather than a combination of
fortuitous circumstances and external aid.[19] He claimed the rout of
the Austrians at the Vittoria Veneto provided such a proof,[20] but the
peace soon showed this to have been an illusion and the years from
1919 to 1922 were probably, with the exception of 1943, the period
of greatest social and political agitation in modern Italian history.
Gentile placed the blame for this state of affairs on the 'realist'
attitude predominant in the schools and the political parties of the
time.

'Realism', in Gentile's terminology, was the antithesis of 'idealism'. Realism posited a reality apart from thought, which it should mirror. This led to individualism – the pursuit of purely material interests which could not be shared as a common spiritual interest – or passivity – acquiescence to the supposed natural order. Idealism, on the other hand, regarded the world as within consciousness. The individual was tied to his fellows via a common consciousness – national culture. Moreover, it was active, moulding nature rather than conforming to it.[21] The key problem, as we saw, was how this unity of purpose was to be achieved. In wartime it was provided by the need to defeat the enemy, but no similar common aim existed after 1918. Gentile believed that it could be created through education, and it was Mussolini who provided him with the opportunity to put his ideas into practice.[22]

As the same men who had ruled Italy since 1900 returned to office, Gentile became increasingly disillusioned with the liberal party. He regarded the fascist takeover as justifiably getting rid of the liberal old guard of Giolitti, and reaffirming the strength of the state. This favourable impression was confirmed when he was asked to become Minister of Education. Gentile had long argued for the reform of education in line with his idealist conception of mental development, and had helped prepare a comprehensive overhaul of the system for Croce, when he was the minister under Giolitti from 1920 to 1921. Mussolini now gave him to chance to complete this programme. Although the resulting *Riforma Gentile* was hailed by Mussolini as 'the most fascist of the reforms', it was not initially conceived as such. Gentile was not a party member when appointed, and his scheme was a continuation of his earlier ideas for a national revival produced by the return of idealist principles in the schools.

He aimed to increase elementary schooling and improve teachers' conditions, whilst making secondary and higher education more specialized and selective. His new curriculum centred on the Hegelian triad of art, religion, and philosophy as the ideal stages of human consciousness towards absolute knowledge. Thus Italian literature and the Catholic religion were the core subjects of the elementary schools, whilst classics and philosophy predominated in the *liceo* and university. Finally, a single state exam was to apply a universal standard throughout both public and private schools.[23] Gentile believed that the school completed the spiritual awakening of the child and prepared him for citizenship. The school therefore replaced civil society in Gentile's revision of the Hegelian triad – family, civil society, state – in the socialization of the individual.[24]

Education should have offered a solution to the problem, noted

earlier, of how to create a unity of will amongst conflicting wills which
was consistent with actualism's subjectivist principles. Gentile regarded this as 'the fundamental antinomy of education'. The pupil's
spiritual development should be ideally totally free and personal.
Education, however, usually required the imparting of knowledge to
the pupils by the teacher. This circumstance could potentially lead to a
conflict between the pupils' liberty to learn in their own way, and the
authority of the master to teach what he believed to be important.
However, Gentile simply resolved this problem in the familiar way
by arguing that the will of the master must become the universal will,
overcoming the particular wills of his pupils. This was achieved by
discipline, whereby the teacher's will became an active force uniting
the wills of his or her students.[25] His conclusion, that discipline
thereby achieved the moral freedom of the pupil, could only be
accepted if might was taken to be right, a view, as the last section
demonstrated, to which acutalism tends.

Gentile seems to have regarded his solution to the problem of
authority in the classroom to be extendable to the nation as a whole.
On 31 May 1923, with the *Riforma Gentile* coming to completion, he
applied to Mussolini to become a member of the Fascist Party. It
was, he wrote, 'a moral obligation' for him to join, since liberty only
existed 'within the law and therefore through a strong State, through
the State as ethical reality', an ideal represented in Italy 'not by the
liberals,' who are more or less openly your opponents, but on the
contrary by you yourself'.[26]

His view of authority in school and state was essentially the same –
it must be created by the teacher and by the politician respectively.
Yet at the same time he wished to maintain that the individual's
capacity to act was not thereby curtailed. This was achieved by
appealing to the doctrine of the state in *interiore homine*, referred to
earlier, and was central to Gentile's fascist philosophy. Gentile
argued that the state could not exist outside the consciousness of the
citizens who made it up. This would be plausible as a theoretical
proposition, an ideal to be attained, but Gentile asserted that it was
necessarily a reality as well, so that the actual state could claim to be
the conscience of the individual. As we saw, Gentile was only able to
achieve this unity by dint of force. He now justified the fascist
seizure of power in precisely the same terms used in his *Foundations
of a Philosophy of Right:*

> Liberty is certainly the supreme end and rule of every human life, but
> only so far as individual and social education make it a reality by
> embodying the common will, which takes the form of law and hence

of the State, in the particular individual . . . From this point of view State and individual are identical, and the art of government is the art of so reconciling and uniting the two terms so that a maximum of liberty harmonises with a maximum of public order not merely in the external sense, but also and above all, in the sovereignty ascribed to law and to its necessary organs. For always the maximum liberty coincides with the maximum force of the State.[27]

This argument follows the same stages noted in the passage from the *Foundations* quoted above. He asserted that particularity must be subsumed under the universal. This enabled the individual to realise his or her own moral autonomy, and was paralleled by society as a whole. Once this stage was accepted, then it followed that liberty and law were identical and that freedom was *ipso facto* power. Yet he had still to explain how the moment of particularity could be overcome. The answer was again the same – the universal was that which had the force to make itself such. It was impossible

to distinguish moral force from material force: the force of the law freely voted and accepted, from the force of violence which is rigidly opposed to the will of the citizen. But such distinctions are simple-minded when they are sincere! Every force is a moral force, for it is always an expression of will, and whatever method of argument it used – from sermon to blackjack – its efficacy cannot be other than that of entreating the inner man and persuading him to agree.[28]

Gentile sought to justify the fascist seizure of power further by claiming it to be the continuation of the Risorgimento. Mazzini, whose doctrine of 'thought and action' he interpreted in actualist terms, was turned into a proto-squadrista, whose revolution the fascists were completing.[29] He deployed this argument to deprive the liberal regime of any legitimacy. Like Croce, he maintained that the true Italy was within those who shared the spirit of its founders.[30] Gentile's reference to the history of Italy to bolster his political doctrine paralleled his use of the history of philosophy to support his actualism. Both could only claim universality if they could be shown to represent the working out of the immanent logic of human self-realization in thought and practice. Only then could he claim fascism to be 'God's will', and Mussolini to be a 'world historical individual'. However, unlike Croce, whose analysis of history produced import-ant revisions in his historicism, Gentile's actualism was self-confirming rather than self-critical, and his researches into the past increasingly propogandist and dogmatic.

The sophistry behind Gentile's identification of individual and state appears just as clearly in his constitutional programme creating the fascist system of corporate representation. The corporations were to organize the moral will of the people within the political force of the state. The unions or 'syndicates' constituted the corporate personality of the worker, which together with the employers' federations were to be brought within the framework of the national personality – the state. As a result, the individuals pursuing their private interest would come via the corporation to a consciousness of the general interest. Gentile's theory seemed to be little more than a mechanical exposition of the Hegelian state, in which people did not enter the political arena directly but via associations, guilds etc.[31] Hegel believed that the classes of society were so sharply differentiated from each other, that the notion of direct participation in politics was a non-starter, since self-interest could never generate a sense of the common good. It was necessary, therefore, to have a degree of corporate autonomy in public life, whereby groups could regulate their own affairs. He argued, however, that at a higher level the individual would become aware of the interrelatedness of the 'system of needs' – that all labour is social as well as individual – and that consciousness of this fact would promote the development of a community within civil society.[32] This was a perception open to the representatives and bureaucrats who formed a universal class through their direct allegiance to the state, rather than all members of society. Gentile, however, obviously trivialized the Hegelian analysis by simply creating the differentiation which existed in Hegel's day, and identifying the will of the individual somewhat arbitrarily with that of the fascist government. Under totalitarianism the citizen had no volition of his own at all. Gentile restricted the individuals to seeking their private interests in that of the group, since there was no incentive for them to transcend it. The general interest was the concern of the state authority. Thus the corporate state could in no sense be called a higher form of self-government, as individual interests were manipulated rather than allowed to develop freely.[33]

Far from providing an organic unity of state and individual, the corporations were simply the institutionalization of the liberal individualism Gentile claimed to have rejected. The individual was forced to identify with a particular set of narrowly-defined material interests, which were harmonized by being restricted to a particular sphere. This was the mechanical unity of the technical or bureaucratic state, not the organic unity of the state in *interiore homine*, which existed and developed in the thoughts and acts of autonomous individuals. The state was totalitarian only in the empirical sense that it included everything, not in the ideal sense desired by Gentile of organizing the whole of the nation's will, thought and feeling.[34] For Gentile's theory to escape this descent into coercive authoriarianism, he needed to provide some convincing account of the genesis of a will common to individuals and society alike, yet consistent with the radical subjectivism of the 'pure act of thought'. This he attempted to provide in his final work on the *Genesis and Structure of Society*.

### GENESIS AND STRUCTURE OF SOCIETY

Gentile's last book was written as a 'relief for the soul' following Mussolini's overthrow in 1943, and before the division of Italy into the allied occupied south and the German puppet Fascist Social Republic in the north.[35] Villified at the time by fascist and antifascist alike, because of his attempt to remain neutral between the two, the book made a serious attempt to consider what, other than force, united a society. It is certainly the most profound of Gentile's political works although, for reasons given below, ultimately mistaken in its central thesis.

In the preface Gentile directed the reader to the fourth chapter on the 'Transcendental society or society *in interiore homine*', as the most important and original in the book.[36] This doctrine had been the crux of his philosophical defence of the fascist state. Gentile now elaborated that thesis at some length in order to show why the subject of the self-creative activity, upon which actualism was premised, was not the individual but society, and ultimately humanity, as a whole. He began with the Aristotelian observation that 'man lives in society', but denied that this could be correctly understood as simply an empirical statement – one could not create a community from 'individual social atoms'.[37] Human self-expression was always social because, in attempting to be universal, it aimed at membership of an ideal society. Language was the most tangible example of the existence of this ideal community. Language was always expressive of the personality and the originality of the individuals – 'Yet no one talks so individualistically for his words not to echo all around as a human expression of something human, which all are disposed to welcome and recognise as real in the spiritual life which embraces all men of all places and of all ages.'[38]

Gentile then amended his account of the development of individual consciousness in order to show why this ideal community was not a personal vision, but necessarily one which included respect for others. The 'transcendental society' developed, ideally and

within the subject, via the self-distinction into subject and object –
'Because there is no Ego, in which the individual realises himself,
which does not have, not outside, but within himself, an *alter*, which
is his essential *socius*: that is an object, that is not simply an object
(thing) opposed to the subject, but is also a subject, like him'.[39]

The world and consciousness required each other to be, the latter
endowing the former with a spiritual life of its own so that it was not
just an object to be overcome, but an alter ego with which mind
could converse. This primitive spiritual unity occured in the childish
personification of the external world, and developed into an
'internal or transcendental dialogue', in which ego and alter-ego
could converse and collaborate in a common spiritual life. This
passage of the not-I from being an object of consciousness to
membership of an internal spiritual society was present in every
instant of human experience. In this manner the 'transcendental
loneliness' of the Ego was overcome.[40] This process occurred within
the individual subject alone, without the stimulus of other people –
'We speak to others because first of all we speak to ourselves'.[41]
Society, arose from this dialogue within the agent, in which the
object ceased to be a 'thing' and became a partner in the
transcendental society innate in the transcendental Ego. The
'moment of otherness' did not refer, then, to the empirical
separateness of different objects and persons, but was part of the
synthesis of I and not-I within the consciousness of the Ego. It was
analogous to the unity of love, which developed from the mutual,
but, he claimed, entirely separate development of sympathy within
the minds of two lovers.[42] Gentile, therefore, traced the origin of
society to the immanent dialectic of the 'act of pure thought',
unifying subject and object – 'All of society in its infinite forms is
here, in the dialectical union of *alter* with *ipse*.'[43]

This chapter must be considered his most successful attempt to
derive society from the self-constituting activity (*autoctisi*) of the
individual subject. Its claim to originality has been rightly criticized
as exaggerated, since this doctrine is fundamental to the political
thought of Plato and Hegel.[44] However, Gentile's search after an
ideal unity had the concomitant result of regarding all distinctions,
such as those urged by Croce, as empirical and insufferable in a
philosophy which 'overcomes' them. But human reason could never
fully absorb the real into the ideal. Hegel's moments of civil society
and the state, or Croce's distinction between the Useful and the
Good, recognized this basic aspect of human existence. The
individual remains a physical body, which is part of a physical world,
and the body within this self-conscious self is a partly but never

wholly transcended element. There can thus be no complete transcendence within the state of the practical individual. The ethical state as a practical reality will inevitably be totalitarian – the total subordination of the individual's practical and intellectual will to government. It was precisely this identification of real and ideal that Gentile sought to achieve via the unity of thought and practice. Philosophy was thereby always complete and self-sufficient – the contrasts of reality abolished forever, as Croce feared. Human experience, however, reveals an irresolvable asymmetry between real and ideal at all levels of human existence, so that no philosophy can be successfully constructed wholly *a priori*. This was the objection Aristotle made to Plato's *Republic* in the *Politics*, – that the heterogeneity of human goods could not be abolished by asserting a single moral and social order. The state was 'Man writ large' only by virtue of our continued participation at all levels of human existence, from the family through to the life of contemplation. If in pursuit of the ideal one forced development to the highest stage, then one destroyed human nature.[45]

This point was made by Professor Arangio-Ruiz, in an early ciritque of Gentile's doctrine of the state, when he argued that a distinction should be made between the state *in interiore homine* and that *inter homines*.[46] It was the complete resolution of the empirical distinction, implied by the latter, into the ideal of the former, which was Gentile's main error. As he replied to Arangio-Ruiz's article, the distinction was superfluous since he

> had clearly shown that the individual, who is in essence the State and from whom it eternally derives, is not the particular, naturally given, individual: but the individual who overcomes his own particularity in the universal will (which is neither more nor less than the universal will) . . . but then, if this is the case, to emphasise one term rather than the other is pointless, because they are not two terms, but one.[47]

Gentile simply avoided the whole problem of legitimating the relations between people by assuming away the particularity of the individual.

His whole fascist creed, assiduously elaborated in much of the rest of the book, flowed from this error. The humanization of culture was to be followed by the humanization of labour – the complete transendence of God and nature by man, for economic action was only moral action viewed externally.[48] All human activity was to be organized within the Fascist Corporate State which represented 'the fundamental unity of man, which is articulated in all its dimensions'.[49] This was the concrete human will, which was the essence of all history. Force remained indispensable to the life of the state, which was the true subject of history. But it was only by rewriting history that Gentile could prove fascism to be the ideal implied by all human activity, and hence justify coercion to realize it.[50] The belief that 'no love is a more secure and solid possession than that which is won via an apprenticeship of conquest and of brotherhood of the enemy with us'[51] had to be regarded as a pious hope that, which ever side lost, they would ultimately acquiesce and resign themselves to the rule of the other. Yet it proved no more realistic in 1943 than a similar sentiment, expressed in 1925, had been at the start of the fascist débâcle. Namely that 'A spirit of compromise will become more pronounced day by day, progressively as, when the second term is fulfilled, the first term of the great Roman admonition appears even more opportune and more just: *parcere subjectis et debellare superbos*.'[52]

Here lies the contradicition at the heart of Gentile's fascism – that the more authoritarian the state was, the freer the individual citizen would become. This paradox was necessitated by a philosophical theory which denied all opposition beyond the dialectic of a subject and an object, which is not the same thing as the contrast of real and ideal, or that between subjects explored above. It is noticeable that Gentile was much less tolerant in the ideal realm of ideas than he was in practical politics. As director of the Fascist Institute of Culture and editor of the *Enciclopedia Italiana* he attempted, against strong opposition from the authorities, to maintain a largely open policy towards opponents of the regime.[53] But he damned the belief that culture as contemplation was the highest truth as 'intellectualist'.[54] The only valid ideas remained those which were practically victorious over others – which succeeded as action and not as mere thought.[55] It is not surprising that Gentile should have ultimately sided with Mussolini's last-ditch stand against the allies, and his violent death by assasination was a sad but appropriate end to his career.

# 7

# ANTONIO GRAMSCI

Antonio Gramsci's life and thought have received greater attention in recent years than that of any other modern Italian thinker. His fame stems from his contribution to Marxist theory which, it is claimed, provides the basis for a more democratic version of communism than that practised in the Soviet Union. However, it is hopefully clear to readers of this book that the main elements of Gramsci's philosophy – the role of consciousness in determining human action and the consequent importance of ideological hegemony in maintaining social relations, and of intellectuals and the party in creating a revoluntionary alternative – are as much developments of the Italian political tradition as of Marxism. The *Prison Notebooks* are a creative reworking of the characteristic Italian theme of how to unite theory and practice and bring together the diverse classes and cultures which made up the Italian state. Despite the fragmentary nature of his writings, Gramsci provided the most comprehensive analysis of and solution to this problem. Yet I shall also argue that he revealed the limitations of Italian social theory when it turns from the criticism of present society to the construction of the community of the future.

## LIFE AND WORKS

Gramsci wrote his *Notebooks* during a period of enforced reflection on Italian society and on the strategy of the communist party in transforming it and advancing the interests of the working class. It is doubtful whether he would have had the desire or opportunity for such a task had the fascist authorities not wanted, in a phrase which was to prove ironic, to stop his 'mind working for twenty years'. In the tradition of Boethius and his hero Machiavelli, removal from politics led him to want to write about it 'from a disinterested point of view, *für ewig* [for eternity].'[1] For this reason it would be wrong to try to draw too close a connection between his role as a political activist prior to his imprisonment, effectively from 1926, and the notes written thereafter until his death in 1937. A brief sketch of this formative period is nevertheless a necessary preliminary before considering his major work.

Gramsci's life, according to his biographers, divides into the following five phases:

i his childhood and adolesence in Sardinia (1891–1911),
ii his studies at Turin University, and the start of his career as a political thinker as a commentator for *Il Grido del Popolo* (1911–18)
iii the experience of the 'red years' and the factory councils whilst editor of *L'Ordine Nuovo* (1918–20)
iv the resulting critique of the socialist party and the setting up of the Italian communist party (PCI) (1921–6)
v the Prison years (1926–37).[2]

At the risk of a certain over-schematization, it is possible to relate certain fundamental ideas of the *Notebooks* to each of the four earlier phases.

His childhood was marred by his physical deformity, he was hunchbacked, and his family's near destitution due to his father's imprisonment through involvement in local political intrigues. Gramsci found relief from both misfortunes in Croce's humanist philosophy and Sardinian nationalism respectively. Both coloured his later Marxism. Gramsci continued to see philosophy in Crocean terms as a surrogate religion, providing not only an orientation in this world but a confirmation of the value and meaning of our acts. Similarly, a concern with the problems of the peripheral areas, and of the influence of different social and cultural traditions, modified his later class-based analysis of Italian politics. The move to Turin initially led him to fuse and deepen the Crocean and regional aspects of his thought in the study of Sard dialectics under a pioneer of socio-linguistics, Professor Matteo Bartoli. Attracted by the militant Croceanism of Prezzolini's review *La Voce*, and in particular the group of southern activists gathered around Salvemini, Gramsci increasingly linked his scholarly concerns with those of politics. He was further encouraged in this direction by his new Turin friends Angelo Tasca, Umberto Terracini and Palmiro Togliatti (all later co-founders of the PCI), who urged him to join the socialist party.

Gramsci's early socialism reflected his idealist cultural background.

In a series of articles written for the socialist papers *Il Grido del Popolo* and *Avanti!* between 1915 and 1918, the most famous of which are 'Socialism and Culture'[3] and 'The Revolution against *Capital*,'[4] he rehearsed the arguments for a Marxist philosophy of culture which were later elaborated in the *Notebooks*. He rejected the 'positivist fatalism' of 'vulgar marxism', appealing instead to the spiritual and willed nature of social formations. '[M]echanical forces', he argued, 'never prevail in history: they are the men, the consciousness, it is the spirit which moulds the external appearances and always ends up by winning.'[5] Elements from Croce, Labriola, and to a lesser extent Gentile, were combined in a theory of social change which stressed the need for a period of cultural preparation prior to political action. An understanding of the present historical situation and the attainment of a certain moral stature and self-sufficiency were necessary to transcend the present and create new history:

> Marxism is based on philosophical idealism. Philosophical idealism is a doctrine of being and knowledge, according to which these two conceptions are identified and reality is that which one knows theoretically, our ego . . . History is a human product, of humanity divided into classes and cadres, of which from time to time one predominates and directs society towards its ends, fought by the other part which tends to affirm itself and *substitute* itself in the direction [of society]; not evolution therefore, but *substitution*, the necessary means to which is conscious and disciplined force.[6]

Lenin and the Bolsheviks had appreciated this 'living' aspect of Marxism, 'which is the continuation of German and Italian idealism, and which Marx has contaminated by positivist and naturalist incrustations.' He continued,

> . . . [T]his thought, always posits as the main factor in history not bare economic facts, but man, but the society of men, of men who are close to each other, who understand each other, who develop through these contacts (civilisation) a social, collective will and understand the economic facts, and judge them, and adapt them to their will, until this becomes the motor of the economy, the moulder of objective reality, which lives, and moves, and acquires the character of volcanic lava, which can be channelled where the will pleases and how the will pleases.[7]

Gramsci took up Labriola's attack on the positivist and Darwinian interpretations of Marx. Only a Marxism purged of any taint of determinism could avoid the descent into reformism. On the other hand, he did not want to fall into the opposite extreme of utopianism, based on an all-conquering will to power, similar to actualist fascism or syndicalism. When he was accused of 'Bergsonian voluntarism' at the 1917 conference of the PSI. in Florence[8], he was nearest to adopting this view, supporting Mussolini's calls for intervention in the war[9] and undoubtedly influenced by Gentile and Sorel.[10] However, unlike his fellow Torinese Piero Gobetti, he did not regard the Russian revolution and the emphasis on voluntarism, culturalism and autonomy as representing 'the negation of socialism and an affirmation and exaltation of liberalism.'[11] Gramsci learnt from Croce to be on his guard against 'Jacobinism' and 'cultural messianism', which 'always speak in abstractions, of evil, good, oppression, liberty, light, dark which exist absolutely, generically and not in concrete and historical forms such as economic and political institutions, within which society disciplines itself, and through or against which it develops . . .'[12]

To escape from what he correctly saw as the pitfalls of the idealist philosophy of action, Gramsci reaffirmed the orthodox Marxist thesis concerning the centrality of 'objective conditions of production and material goods' in determining changes, 'almost mathematically', of the sum of relations which 'regulate and inform human society' and the 'level of men's awareness . . .'[13]

Gramsci's incorporation of his earlier idealism within the conventions of historical materialism inspired much of the *Prison Notebooks*. An important factor of his new faith in *Capital* was the experience of the factory council movement in Turin from 1919 to 1920.[14] The *biennio rosso*, following the end of the war, was a period of unprecedented social unrest throughout Italy. Employers responded to the end of the wartime boom, as military contracts were withdrawn, with drastic cutbacks. Turin steelworkers, radicalized by the war, reacted by organizing their opposition around the factory staff associations (*commissioni interne*). The movement spread to other concerns, such as the Fiat car plant, and by-passed the reformist trade unions which were largely controlled by the PSI. The factory council movement, as it became known, led Gramsci to reappraise his view of Lenin and the Russian revolution. He saw it as a genuine transfer of power to the workers, believing the slogan 'All power to the Soviets' reflected Russian reality. Through the journal *L'Ordine Nuovo*, which he set up in April 1919 with Tasca (later ousted), Terracini and Togliatti, he became the main theorist of the movement. For Gramsci, the council's success derived from their having developed a proletarian consciousness on the 'real' basis of the 'objective' conditions of the relations of production. As a result, their action escaped the dilemma of being either damningly reformist or hopelessly utopian. Gramsci believed that capitalism had matured to the point at which the transition to communism could take place. However this would only occur when the proletariat had achieved a sufficient degree of awareness of these conditions and internal organization to be able to take this step for themselves.

According to Gramsci, this revolutionary education was being provided by the factory councils:

> The factory council is the model of the proletarian State. All the problems which are inherent in the organisation of the proletarian State, are inherent in the organisation of the Council. In the one and in the other the concept of citizen decays, and is replaced by the concept of comrade: collaboration to produce well and usefully develops solidarity, multiplies the bonds of affection and brotherhood. Everyone is indispensable, everyone is at his post, and everyone has a function and a post. Even the most ignorant and the most backward of the workers, even the most vain and the most 'cultivated' [civile] of the engineers ends up by convincing himself of this truth in the experience of the factory organisations: all end up acquiring a communist consciousness in order to understand the great step forward that the communist economy represents over the capitalist economy. The Council is the most suitable organ of reciprocal education and development of the new social spirit that the proletariat has succeeded in expressing . . . Working-class solidarity, which in the union develops in the fight against capitalism . . . in the council is positive, permanent, incarnated even in the most fleeting moments of industrial production, it is contained in the joyful awareness of being an organic whole, a homogeneous and compact system that through working usefully, and disinterestedly producing social wealth, affirms its sovereignty and realises its power and its freedom as creator of history.[15]

The councils, in Gramsci's eyes, overcame the divisions of the bourgeois state between capital and labour, giving the workers the responsibility and the self-discipline to work with each other for the benefit of all rather than just themselves.

Gramsci's interpretation of the councils was, to say that least, absurdly optimistic. As a model of the society of the future it had all the worst features of the 'organic' conception of the state, which regarded individuals as functional units of a greater whole. The individual was pigeon-holed with his or her role in the productive process, with no account given of its relation to the other aspects of human life. Nor did he contemplate the likely result of a greater awareness of social reality amongst factory operatives – namely an increased dissatisfaction with industrial labour. A boring and repetitive job remains such, no matter who one is working for. The only measure Gramsci suggested for evaluating this system was its greater efficiency. But this did not necessarily entail greater freedom or increased opportunities to enjoy the myriad elements which make life worthwhile. The absence of such considerations in any of Gramsci's writings must be taken into account when discussing the extent to which his communism avoids the pitfalls of Leninism. His advocacy of the councils, his belief that their success stemmed from their being largely spontaneous and democratic in nature, is often regarded as indicative of the essentially open nature of his political theory. But if the goal aimed for was unacceptably *simpliste* as a model of how societies work, then its implementation would have to be enforced and, in practice, entail a restriction of freedom.

The failure of the movement at the hands of the government and employers meant that Gramsci, unlike Lenin, was saved the problem of either denying his earlier views or considerably revising them. Instead he retained his faith in a 'productivist' communist future, implicit in the practices of capitalism. He had to admit, though, that the Turin workers were alone in their appreciation of this. A Gramscian style revolution involved asking how to spread this awareness amongst the entire Italian proletariat, particularly the peasants who formed the majority of the population – a task for which he increasingly regarded the PSI and union leaders as unsuited. As a result, he joined with other opponents of 'reformism' in setting up the PCI in January 1921. The party began to take on an important role in his thought as the instrument for preparing the working class for the eventual takeover of power. However, membership was not the preserve of an intellectual elite whose 'scientific' knowledge of the laws of history gave them the right to dictate the proletariat's 'real' interest to them. As we shall see, such a view was precluded by his understanding of Marxism, which he denied could be separated from the actual beliefs and practices of the masses or be turned into a number of abstract schemes. He maintained that the party could not become a group of isolated ideological purists, refusing to take part in elections or union activity for fear of being tainted with the sin of reformism.[16] This became ever more vital with the rise of fascism. Gramsci supported the policy of a united front between opposition parties with the broadest possible appeal, to counter Mussolini. He was the PCI's representative in Moscow from 1922 to 1923, and gained the Comintern's support for his ideas, replacing the dogmatic 'maximalist' Bordiga as

General Secretary in August 1924. However, despite Moscow's support, it is doubtful whether he would have retained their sympathy if he had not been arrested in November 1926.[17] He was already expressing doubts about the turn of events in Russia, and his opposition to Stalin's policy when in prison caused heated debates amongst fellow communist inmates. Had his brother not chosen judiciously to hide his real opinions from Togliatti and the PCI leadership in Russia, he would probably have been condemned or expelled by the party.[18]

Imprisonment by the fascist authorities thus probably saved Gramsci from similar treatment at the hands of Stalin. As it was, he had the opportunity to elaborate and rework his ideas into a distinctive Marxist philosophy. It is possible to identify four themes stemming from his political writings, which are further developed in the *Notebooks*:

i The critique of vulgar Marxism and its revision to accommodate the idealist concern with the importance of ideas and will in the creation of action.
ii The resilience of capitalism due to its ideological hold on the masses (hegemony).
iii The creation of an alternative communist culture, able to express accurately the interests of the working class, and its importance for a successful communist revolution.
iv The organization of the society of the future on the basis of the communist mode of production.

Each of these four themes will be examined in turn below.

### HISTORICAL MATERIALISM AND CROCEAN HISTORICISM

The central theme of the *Notebooks* was the relation of the socio-cultural superstructure to the 'objective' underlying processes of the economic base. Gramsci denied the positivist claim that the former was but the reflection of the latter. In polemic with Bukharin, he rejected the idea that Marxism provided a set of 'scientific' laws of economic development to which all human behaviour could be reduced as 'mysticism' or 'superstition'.[19] Against evolutionary Marxism he repeated Labriola's strictures that human begins stood outside natural processes, moulding them to their will. 'Thus man does not enter into relations with nature simply, because he himself is part of nature, but actively, by means of labour and technology.'[20] Moreover, not even specifically human action could be explained by law-like generalizations. Following Croce, he criticized the claim that the methods of the natural sciences should, or even could be extended to the study of society.

Two problems stood in the way of this. First, like Croce, he maintained that there were no 'bare facts' which could provide the exact data on which different theories could build. This was because the facts were themselves constituted by the interpretation given of them.

> The enquiry into a series of facts to find the relations between them presupposes a 'concept' that permits us to distinguish that series from other possible series: how can there take place a choice of facts, to be adduced as proof of the truth of one's own assumption, if one does not have a pre-existing criteria of choice? But what will this criteria of choice be, if not something superior to each single fact under enquiry?[21]

This is related to Gramsci's second and main objection to sociological laws – namely that social theories did not simply offer an account of the underlying mechanisms of society, but were part of how people understand and act in their society. Theory was inextricably linked to practice – there could be no theory of society distinct from how people conceive of it. The belief 'that every fluctuation of politics and ideology can be presented and expounded as an immediate expression of the structure', separated theory and practice and encouraged 'passivity' and 'mental laziness' amongst the masses. Far from being a value-free, 'scientific', theory of society, 'economism' was a return to theological modes of thought which negated the agent's freedom of choice and action:[22]

> The concept of 'objective' of metaphysical materialism seems to want to mean an objectivity which exists even apart from man, but when one affirms that a reality would exist even if man did not exist one is either speaking metaphorically or one falls into a form of mysticism. We know reality only in relation to man and since man is historical becoming, even knowledge and reality are a becoming, even objectivity is a becoming etc. . . .[23]

Theories did not simply offer knowledge of social processes, thereby providing a basis for more effective action. They informed human action in such a way that to clarify or extend the norms guiding present activity would have a commensurate effect on practice.[24]

Gramsci's attack on 'metaphysical materialism' bears witness to his early idealist leanings. Again following Croce, Gramsci believed that members of a particular society or group shared a common 'world view' which gave coherence to their beliefs and goals and sustained their collective practices.[25] However, he accused Croce of separating the concepts whereby the world could be understood from the experiences and situation of the men and women who used them. Croce did this by giving ideas an autonomous existence, regarding them as the products of the development of Spirit, rather than of the real life struggles of human beings in history. Croce's histories thus 'fall into a new and curious kind of "idealist" sociology, no less absurd and inconclusive than positivist sociology.'[26] According to Gramsci, Croce's mistake was much the same as Bukharin's – that of assuming a reality external to humanity, separate from its needs and purposes. Although formally correct, readers of the previous chapter will appreciate this does not accord with the weight Croce ascribed to the 'economic' moment in practice – a point which informed much of his historical writing and political judgements.

Thus far, Gramsci's criticisms of positivism and Crocean idealism parallel those made by Labriola and Gentile respectively. His arguments are significantly based on a reading of the 'Theses on Feuerbach' which, it will be remembered, were at the heart of Labriola's interpretation of Marx, and Gentile's theory of the unity of thought and practice in the 'humanisation of labour.'[27] However, Gramsci was satisfied by neither: Gentile was too idealist, and Labriola too positivist.[28] The problem, therefore, was 'how to escape solipsism and at the same time avoid the mechanistic conceptions implicit in the concept of thought as a receptive and ordering activity.'[29] To resolve this dilemma, he contended that some assumption was required of the 'objective' nature of our statements about reality. This was not an empirical hypothesis, based on an independent set of facts external to human consciousness because, for reasons rehearsed above, to establish the facts of experience, it was first necessary to settle on undisputed criteria for deciding what they were. The solution had to be epistemological, setting constraints on what made a belief rational or not. 'Objective', Gramsci wrote, 'always means "humanly objective", that which can correspond exactly to "historically subjective", that is objective would mean "universally subjective"'.[30]

As often occurs in reading the *Notebooks*, we need to employ a certain amount of intuitive feel to grasp Gramsci's meaning and piece together his scattered statements on any one topic. I interpret him as saying that through history human knowledge of the world was progressively refined and would be eventually unified in a single cultural system. The current contradictions and incommensurabilities between different systems of belief had a practical origin in the 'internal contradictions which tear apart human society'. The 'struggle for objectivity' was *ipso facto* part and parcel of the class struggle 'to free oneself from partial and fallacious ideologies' and arrive at 'the cultural unification of the human race'. Thus, 'what the idealists call "spirit" is not a point of departure but of arrival, it is the ensemble of superstructures moving towards concrete and objectively universal unification, and is not a unitary presupposition.'[31]

Gramsci has been interpreted as reversing the Marxian base – superstructure model, rendering the former subordinate to the latter.[32] Certainly his argument often apears perilously close to Gentile's – namely that only through humanity's progressive transformation of nature could a common language for understanding it be established. However, he rejected the idealist view that nature was entirely a creation of mind as militating against any inter-subjective communication. Consensus between different world-views could only be achieved by force. It was not enough that everyone held a belief for it to be true or rational. Rather, there must be further grounds of a practical nature, in some way traceable to empirical statements about the world which everyone could in principle agree on. Gramsci illustrated his argument with a famous example of Bertrand Russell's:

> What would North-South, East-West mean without man? . . . It is evident that East and West are arbitrary, conventional, that is historical, constructions . . . And yet these references are real, they correspond to real facts, they permit us to travel by land and by sea and to arrive exactly where one has decided to arrive, to "forsee" the future, to objectivise reality, to understand the objectivity of the external world. Rational and real identify with each other.[33]

The 'philosophy of praxis' differed from both idealism and 'mechanical materialism' in being predicated upon a theory of rationality which assumed that people could share the same empirical judgements in given situations and act upon them. Rationality was not just a matter of the coherence of the beliefs concerned, nor of consensus about their validity, but of their practicality. They gave us an orientation in the world, 'indissolubly connected to a certain organised (historicised) "matter" . . .'[34] Marxism did not provide knowledge of unchanging economic laws, but a criterion for judging and appraising beliefs with respect to the knowledge they rendered in a practical situation. Ideologies ceased to be 'mere individual illusions' and became 'a reality . . . objective and operative.'[35]

We are now in a position to understand Gramsci's interpretation of historical materialism. He denied that it consisted of 'the iron conviction that there exist objective laws of historical development, similar in kind to natural laws', although he understood the quasi-religious appeal of such a conviction.[36] This did not entail abandoning the notion of the objective world altogether, only of an external reality which existed apart from human knowledge of it. Nor did it prevent discussion of whether the theory people held of reality was the best one available to them in a given historical situation. The superiority of the 'philosophy of praxis' resided in its 'historicist' nature.[37] This was Gramsci's greatest debt to Croce. Crocean historicism was less idealist than Gramsci's criticisms make out. Whilst philosophically Croce saw everything in terms of Spirit, practically one could only judge in terms of success.

Gramsci's theory of rationality was closer to Croce's than he realized or wished to admit, although it was formulated with greater clarity. However, Gramsci saw Marxism as the true descendant of German idealism, taking the Preface to *A Contribution to the Critique of Political Economy* as his source. Gramsci paraphrased the salient passages thus:

1. Mankind only poses for itself such tasks as it can resolve; . . . the task itself only arises where the material conditions for its resolution already exist or at least are in the process of formation.
2. A social formation does not perish before all the productive forces for which it is still sufficient have been developed and new, higher relations of production, do not take their place, before the material conditions for their existence have been developed in the womb of the old society . . .[38]

These two points, frequently alluded to in the *Notebooks*, should be read together with the thesis, also drawn from Marx's Preface – 'that men become conscious (of the conflict between the material forces of production) on the ideological level of juridical, political, religious, artistic and philosophical forms.'[39] These two quotations contain the core of Gramsci's social philosophy. They show the essentially Marxist origins of his thought – the emphasis on 'material conditions' as the underlying reality of social formations. However, the base did not determine the superstructure – it provided the 'real' conditions which a 'rational' theory would correctly capture. This suggested that there were forms of consciousness which were irrational, and which it was the role of the Marxist intellectual to unmask.

### HEGEMONY AND THE CRITIQUE OF 'FALSE CONSCIOUSNESS'

The concept of hegemony was Gramsci's main contribution to political theory, and derived from his revision of orthodox Marxism. As we have seen, Gramsci did not reverse the traditional Marxist base–superstructure model. Instead he reinterpreted it in Crocean manner to mean that theory was the attempt to solve 'problems posed by the historical process'. Rational theories would be those which were adequate to the 'real' historical situation. This was not, as Croce argued, the product of a metaphysical entity, Spirit, but of the development of the forces of production.[40]

This posed the question of why capitalism survived when, as Gramsci believed, the social and economic pre-conditions existed for the transition to communism. He attributed its survival to the interrelatedness of base and superstructure in determining social change. He divided the latter into two levels:

> the one that can be called 'civil society', that is the ensemble of organisms commonly called 'private', and that of 'political society' or 'the State'. These two levels correspond on the one hand to the function of 'hegemony', which the dominant group exercises throughout society, and on the other hand to that of 'direct domination' or command, expressed through the State and 'juridical' government.

The two functions were connected. The first set of institutions obtained 'the "spontaneous" consent given by the great masses of the population to the general direction imposed on social life by the dominant fundamental group, this consent derives "historically" from the prestige (and consequent confidence) which the dominant group enjoys because of its position and function in the world of production.' The organs of 'State coercive power . . . "legally" enforce discipline' when consent failed.[41] Hegemony, therefore, referred to the ideological ascendency of one or more groups or classes over others in civil society. Capitalism continued to survive because the workers accepted its general outlook – the cultural dominance of the bourgeoisie made the resort to political force unnecessary to maintain their power. Thus the masses had to be freed from enthralment to the cultural hegemony of the capitalist classes before a successful challenge to the state could occur.

The importance Gramsci ascribed to cultural factors constituted a significant departure from the economism of classical Marxism. The ruling classes imposed their hegemonic vision through a whole variety of superstructural institutions, such as schools, the media, religion and the everyday practices people engaged in. People saw the world through ideologically distorted spectacles and thus a whole world view had to be challenged before a revolution would enlist mass support. As a result of this insight, he rejected the orthodox interpretation of ideology as an epiphenomenon of the base.[42] He referred to Marx's assertion that 'men gain consciousness of their tasks on the ideological terrain of the superstructures,' these being 'objective and operative'.[43] Whilst the economy was the motor of history, it could not itself produce radical political changes – 'the existence of the objective conditions is not in itself sufficient: one must "know them" and how to use them. And want to use them.'[44] Ideology fulfilled this function – it was 'the terrain on which men move, acquire consciousness of their position, struggle.'[45] Popular 'common sense' thinking always lagged behind economic changes. Revolt was easily contained because the masses were not fully conscious of what was wrong with their situation. Trade Unions, for example, tended to demand a greater share of the capitalist cake, presenting workers' grievances in terms of the aspirations of the dominant group, rather than aiming at a new way of organizing productive activity. Change could not come about by waiting for economic laws to 'bring about palingenetic events.' Nor would simple intransigence work, since this was incohate and unorganized and would simply result in a mindless Ludditism. Rejecting the strategies of both Turati and Bordiga, Gramsci insisted 'that there must be a conscious struggle predisposed to bring "understanding" of the exigencies of the economic position of the masses, which may conflict with the traditional leadership's policies.'[46] This involved Gramsci in three tasks: showing which properties rendered an ideology false, providing criteria for a true ideology; and developing a strategy for establishing it amongst the masses. This section will deal with the first two elements, the next with the third.[47]

We have already examined one property of forms of false consciousness identified by Gramsci – their epistemology. They presented themselves 'as a dogmatic system of eternal and absolute truths.'[48] Agents suffered from this form of delusion when they regarded their acts as the products of some natural or metaphysical process outside their control. Gramsci maintained that both Croce and Bukharin had committed this error, seeing human actions as the product of Spirit or nature respectively. As a result they inhibited agents from perceiving where their true interests lay.[49] This was related to the second identifying feature of erroneous ideologies –

their function in upholding or legitimizing unjust social institutions and practices. The hegemony of the ruling class was maintained by a false representation of its customs and power as inevitable – as God's will, or the product of some natural law. Catholicism was Gramsci's favourite example and he was fascinated by the history and organization of the Roman Church. He regarded Croce's philosophy as serving a similar function in legitimizing Giolittean Italy, albeit only to fellow intellectuals.[50]

Showing that an ideology functioned to support given power relations, rather than as an objective way of seeing the world, provided no reason for dropping it. This was the shortcoming of the Paretian, positivist critique of ideologies. Since, for positivists, all ideologies were more or less irrational or sham, and people simply acted as they did for more or less contingent reasons, there was no real benefit for the agent in revealing the illusion in the first place. Gramsci, on the other hand, wanted to demonstrate that the philosophy of praxis provided not only a more coherent way of looking at people's actions, but also a means of judging them, by providing knowledge of where their true interests lay. Marxism, as interpreted by Gramsci, '. . . is the historicist conception of reality which has liberated itself from every residue of transcendence and theology, even in their highest speculative incarnation, whilst Crocean idealist historicism still remains in the speculative – theological phase'.[51] Historical materialism was the 'expression of real historical development', that is the underlying economic base. In accord with the Marxian preface, Gramsci argued that a true ideology promoted the development of the forces of production.[52] This was in line with the productivism we noted in Gramsci's reflections on the factory councils, and his assertion that the proletariat's real interest was the maximisation of output – something which could only be achieved by workers' control of the means of production. This suggests that the main aim was simply to increase productive efficiency. Yet this did not have to involve the liberation of people's intellectual and creative talents – a system could become more efficient if it made them desire less by reducing them to the level of machines.

Gramsci considered this possibility in the notes on Taylorism and Fordism. Taylor's *The Principles of Scientific Management* (1911) put forward just such a scheme for producing a pliant work force, suited to the requirements of modern industry. Gramsci believed it would never be successful in Europe because, unlike in America, the workers were less imbued with the ethic of work for work's sake. It was a means to other goals, producing resentment when the cost was too high. Nor did he think that dull routine labour would turn operatives into automatons. On the contrary, the repetitive nature of factory tasks would release their brains to consider their situation and appreciate the injustice of their exploitation by the capitalist.[53]

However, this created more difficulties for Gramsci. The notion that human interests could be traced 'in the last analysis' to the requirements of the economy was appealing, because it seemed to provide an 'objective' standard for evaluating a given ideology. Unfortunately, for reasons Gramsci himself pointed out, the two could not be related in an unproblematic way. We cannot determine whether a society correctly or efficiently serves human interests without some idea of what they are, and the degree of satisfaction which is legitimate. A Christian, who subordinates everything to earning a place in heaven, will have different priorities from a capitalist, who measures success by the amount of money he has in the bank. Our interests depend upon the needs and wants we have. These are not immutable, but, as Gramsci showed, alter according to the particular theory we hold of them. Moreover, only the most naive utopian believes that all our desires can be satisfied. Some measure or procedure must therefore exist to adjudicate between conflicting or incompatible desires, even in a state of infinite material abundance. Gramsci recognised these problems, and for this reason stated that it was necessary first to decide what people's 'real' requirements were on the level of ideology. This made his argument somewhat circular, since the criteria for evaluating Marxist ideology were thus products of that same ideology.

Gramsci's dilemma was akin to Labriola's, whose work he admired and developed. Labriola had similarly argued that Marxism was only valid as praxis, but had failed to overcome his orthodox Marxist concern with the primacy of the economic factor. Gramsci developed this idea in a radical way. A doctrine proved its truth by its success, its ' "practical" efficacy.'[54] The best philosophy was therefore one which provided a complete orientation for the lives of everybody – which was 'totalitarian.'[55] This immediately gave rise to the worry that if a whole society could be completely deluded, then this 'delusion' would be true. Gramsci countered this objection by maintaining that no system could be totally successful unless it was in fact true to the prevailing historical conditions,

Mass adhesion or non-adhesion to an ideology is the real critical test of the rationality and historicity of modes of thinking. Any arbitrary constructions are pretty rapidly eliminated by historical competition, even if sometimes, through a combination of immediately favourable circumstances, they succeed in enjoying a certain popularity, whilst constructions which correspond to the demands of a complex and organic period of history always end up by imposing themselves and prevail even if their affirmation only occurs in more or less bizarre and heterogenous combinations.[56]

Gramsci drew the conclusion that even Marxism was 'an expression of historical contradictions' and hence 'perishable'.[57] Christianity and vulgar Marxism were not wrong in the abstract sense – they had played a historical role, but this had passed. This defence appears problematic, for it relied on a base line – a set of objective historical conditions – which we, using Gramsci as our guide, have already condemned as inadequate. He denied that a situation could ever arise where a false ideology could combine with a set of extremely repressive social institutions in such a way that all critical discussion of its false world view would be prevented.[58] But if a society were extraordinarily coercive, could it not enforce a distorted view of what counted as coercion, and hence be successful and 'true' in Gramsci's sense? The only way out of such a situation would be to hold to a view of eternal or transcendental truths, or pre-conditions for arriving at truth, such as he explicity rejected.

Gramsci's response to the above problem was that criticism could only come from within, and that the criteria for evaluating repressive conditions were always present, albeit in 'embryonic form', in the experiences of the agents' frustration and suffering. This produced a contrast between thought and action which 'is the expression of profounder contrasts of a socio-historic order.' It meant that a social group 'manifests in its acts' a different conception of the world from that which, for reasons of 'intellectual subordination', it articulated in words. What was required was a 'critical' theory which would enable the masses to build on this dissatisfaction. For disaffection with the world did not provide the grounds for rejecting it and opting for an alternative. People might be at fault, and their dissent without foundation – some reason had to be given explaining why the current ideology was wrong.[59] Gramsci's Marxian historicism claimed to provide this without falling into undue relativism: '[S]ince man is the ensemble of his conditions of life, one can quantitatively measure the difference between past and present, since one can measure the degree to which man dominates nature and chance.'[60]

The extent to which humanity could leave the realm of necessity and enter that of freedom made it possible to evaluate the options available at a given time. An ideology would be legitimate to the extent that it led to the maximum freedom for individuals. It was the capacity 'to transform the external world', that is 'to potentiate oneself or develop oneself', which defined what human beings were. The truth of Marxism was thus one of degree. Its claim was that it represented the best guide to emancipation available to agents at any one time.[61]

To recapitulate, Gramsci's argument was not that the economic base determined the superstructure, rather that it placed a constraint on what forms of consciousness were possible. Some ideologies were more restrictive than others, and do not allow individuals to become all they could be. The 'philosophy of praxis' was superior because it gave the masses 'the concrete means' to realize themselves:

> 1. by giving a determinate and concrete ('rational') direction to their own vital impulse or will; 2. by identifying the means which will make this will concrete and specific and not arbitrary; 3. by contributing to modify the ensemble of the concrete conditions for realising this will to the extent of one's own limits and capacities and in the most fruitful form.[62]

It created a new 'historical block' of structural and superstructural elements whereby individual should achieve their potential through the conscious transformation of their relations with each other and nature. It presupposed that discontent with the present already existed, even if only exiguously, and that it had a 'real' basis in the 'material pre-conditions' for social change.[63] Two related questions remained to be answered. First, how would this 'theoretical consciousness' be attained given the prevailing hegemony of false ideologies? Second, did Gramsci's social theory provide an adequate basis for the organization of a future society? These are the subjects of the next two sections.

## INTELLECTUALS AND THE PARTY:
## THE ORGANIZATION OF A NEW HEGEMONY

Nothing bears greater witness to Gramsci's debt to the native Italian political tradition than his writings on the role of intellectuals and the party in the creation of a new hegemony. He related this problem directly to the central theme of how to create a nation which would be united both politically and culturally.[64] Significantly, these two aspects predominated over class in his analysis, with Gramsci looking to a 'national-popular' movement to transform Italian life.[65] The new hegemony would not just involve a correct appraisal by

members of the proletariat of their class and economic interests –
although these were necessary preliminary stages. It was the
moment when '. . . one becomes aware that one's own corporate
interests, in their present and future development, transcend the
corporate limits of the purely economic class, and can and must
become the interests of other subordinate groups too'. It was 'the
most purely political phase', when economic and political aims
achieved an intellectual and moral unity, 'posing all the questions
around which the struggle rages, not on a corporate but on a
"universal" plane.'[66]

Gramsci contrasted his proposals for a new hegemony with the
unity that was actually achieved during and after the Risorgimento
by the liberals. The Italian state was created by the bourgeoisie's
Moderate Party, whose sole aim was to maintain their socio-
economic position by securing political power. They achieved this,
not via an intellectual and moral reform of the nation, but through a
system of power-broking, first with foreign nations, then with the
landowners, and finally with the workers. The resulting system of
trasformismo involved 'the gradual but continuous absorption,
achieved by methods which varied in their effectiveness, of the
active elements produced by allied groups – and even those which
came from the antagonistic groups . . .'[67] The other classes were
gradually emasculated as their leaders were enticed to join the ranks
of the ruling group. However, this process could not continue
indefinitely – the exploitative class interests of the bourgeoisie meant
that at a certain stage the 'spontaneous' consensus of the masses,
obtained by the prospect of joining the ruling elite, would be
replaced by the overt control and oppression of the workers and
peasants. Fascism represented this stage.[68] The hegemony proposed
by Gramsci was quite different – it incorporated other classes by
gaining their active support. This could only come about when the
dominant section rose above its 'corporate' interests to engage those
of the popular masses. The Jacobins in the French revolution
furnished him with his model. By acknowledging the needs of other
sectors of society

> not only did they organise a bourgeois government, i.e. make the
> bourgeoisie the dominant class – they did more. They created the
> bourgeois State, made the bourgeoisie into the leading, hegemonic
> class of the nation, in other words gave the new State a permanent
> basis and created the compact modern French nation.[69]

In contrast, the Mazzinian Partito d'Azione had succumbed to the
allure of joining with the Moderates in forming an intellectual/

political elite, and the revolutionary opportunity was lost. 'They said they were aiming at the creation of a modern state in Italy, and they produced a kind of bastard.'[70]

Gramsci's notion of hegemony had affinities with Croce's ethico-political interpretation of history. Gramsci's division of the super-structure into 'civil society' and 'political society' corresponded to the Crocean distinction between the ethical and economic/political moments of Spirit, and the order of primacy he gave them accorded with Croce's later formulation of his doctrine after 1924. Both shared the same historicist presupposition that ideas were rendered rational and real by forming part of the immanent development of history. Gramsci endorsed Croce's contention that philosophy entered the mass consciousness as a 'popular religion' rather than as a set of abstract logical axioms, so that it became an intrinsic part of all political practices. He even stated that it could not be class-based but must 'nationalise itself', agreeing with Croce that 'patriotism' was the most potent 'link by means of which the unity of leaders and led is effected.'[71] Yet in his stress on the function of language, education and the party in forging this moral unity, and his insistence that hegemony must be total – a complete union of theory and practice – he approached the spirit of Gentile. The latter element especially involved a criticism of Croce going back to the 'debate between philosophical friends' of 1913, when Gentile had berated Croce's lack of commitment and antipathy to 'definitive systems.' The idealism of his generation, as Gobetti's *Rivoluzione Liberale* illustrates, was often closer to actualism than Croce's 'olympian' religion of liberty. Gramsci's revisions of his Crocean inheritance had a lot in common with those made by his contemporaries, albeit from different political standpoints. Whilst many of these objections were well-founded, Gramsci committed the same error of dismissing the Crocean distinction as inherently conservative, failing to see its importance in establishing a critical dimension for historical and philosophical thought.[72] This had grave practical consequences, as we shall see when we examine his theory of society.

Gramsci's conception of hegemony was nevertheless unequivocally linked to his interpretation of Marx. Hegemony could only be successfully exercised by the 'fundamental' class, which performed the progressive function in the economy, developing the relations implicit in the base; '. . . for if hegemony is ethico-political, it must be economic, must necessarily be based on the decisive function exercised by the leading group in the decisive nucleus of economic activity.'[73] He accused Croce of failing to link the ethico-political moment to its real origins in the practical concerns of human beings in given historical conditions. Croce's political class were supposedly above narrow economic interests, their allegiance being to Spirit or historical development alone. His historicism was thereby weakened, remaining the preserve of an intellectual elite contemplating eternal truths incomprehensible to the majority. Moreover, it was also false, since putative eternal truths were simply the concerns of the ruling class presented as objective facts about the world.

Croce upheld this illusion by removing from his histories the great moments of change – the Renaissance, the French Revolution and the Risorgimento – 'when an ethico-political system dissolves and another is formed by fire and by steel; the moment in which one system of social relations disintegrates and falls and another asserts itself.' Whereas Catholicism successfully penetrated down to the lower strata of the community, Crocean idealism did not compromise. The bourgeoisie or 'middle rank' were the permanent and only active force in history, although their composition differed and broadened with time. Hegemonic change was always a 'passive revolution', the dialectic of 'conservation and revolution'. Members of the masses joined the ruler's ranks and were absorbed by a continual process of *trasformismo*. But this prevented them ever expressing their own interests, producing a disjunction between theory and practice which manifested itself in rebellious activity such as strikes and street violence. Croce therefore perpetuated 'the historical wrong of the ruling class', which had been to systematically prevent popular participation in decision making:

> He believes he's providing a philosophy and provides an ideology, he believes he's providing a religion and provides a superstition, he believes he's writing history from which the element of class has been exorcised and instead describes with great accuracy and merit the political masterpiece whereby a given class succeeded in presenting and having accepted the conditions of its existence and class development as a universal principle, as a conception of the world, as a religion, that is he describes the development of a practical means of government and domination.[74]

During the nineteenth century the Crocean variety of liberal reformism was able to gain the genuine allegiance of other classes. The bourgeoisie was ' "really progressive" i.e. [the social group which caused] the whole society to move forward, not merely satisfying its own existential requirements, but continuously augmenting its cadres for the conquest of new spheres of economic and productive activity.' Croce failed to realise that his 'ideology' was limited to a particular historical phase and class which must eventually change: 'As soon as the dominant social group has exhausted its function, the ideological bloc tends to crumble away; then "spontaneity" [passive consent] may be replaced by "constraint" in ever less distinguished and indirect forms, culminating in outright police measures and *coups d'etat.*'[75] The contemporary relevance of this passage is obvious. To attack Croce was to undermine the hegemony of the liberal class, for whom fascism was a last desperate rearguard action. An 'anti-Croce' was thus a pre-condition for attaining a truly philosophical, historical and hence political consciousness. However Gramsci did not reject all of Croce's philosophy – he reformed it, claiming to succeed where Croce had failed, to produce a philosophy which would be a genuine religious expression of the whole Italian people.[76]

Gramsci's famous remarks on the role of intellectuals in the organization of the party developed out of this critique of the liberal problematic of the political class. He admitted that the division of society into 'rulers and ruled' was a 'primordial fact.'[77] The distinction derived not only from the subordination of one class to another, but, as Mosca's pupil Michels had shown, existed even within workers' organizations. Gramsci accepted this situation as inherent in the division of labour and the social structure of capitalist society; that the party must lead the masses was therefore inevitable. However, his political elite would speak for the true historical class – the proletariat. Mosca and Croce's 'men of middling rank' could not mediate between conflicting groups in society, because they represented a declining class interest. Their claim to independence merely reflected the continued hegemony of bourgeois cultural values, despite their diminished socio-economic power. However, the proletariat constituted a universal class, and their triumph would produce the harmony of communist society. The attempt to unite liberalism and democracy was doomed to failure as a moral/cultural unit could only emerge with the abolition of class divisions and the consequent institution of 'true democracy.'

Gramsci distinguished two types of intellectual: 'traditional' and 'organic'. Members of the former group 'put themselves forward as autonomous and independent of the dominant social group'. Examples included self-styled 'detached' scholars like Croce and ecclesiastics, who expressed the values of surpassed modes of production. But their position was unsustainable; Croce might act like a 'lay Pope', but 'the most significant character' of his philosophy resided in 'his links with senators Agnelli and Benni'.[78] 'Organic' intellectuals, in contrast, acknowledged their relationship to a particular social group and 'give it homogeneity and an awareness of its own function not only in the economic but also in the social and political fields'.[79] Gramsci altered the sense of intellectual in this category to mean 'not those strata commonly described by this term, but in general the entire social stratum which exercises an organisational function in the wide sense – whether in the field of production, or in that of culture, or in that of political administration.'[80]

Gramsci likened the difference between 'traditional' and 'organic' culture to the contrast between Renaissance humanism and the Reformation. Croce was a modern Erasmus, whose anti-Catholicism and anti-Marxism had served the reactionary function of cutting the intelligentsia off from the bourgeois establishment. The Reformation had succeeded in penetrating down to the masses, providing them with a new world view and creating a unity 'between the bottom and the top, between the "simple" and the intellectuals'. This did not mean that a new culture simply emerged from production – it must actively challenge the 'common sense' traditional ways of thinking of the masses.[81] The 'new intellectuals' exercised' a 'directive' function, without becoming an elite group:

> [T]he need for contact between intellectuals and simple . . . is not in order to restrict scientific activity and preserve unity at the low level of the masses, but precisely in order to construct an intellectual-moral bloc which can make politically possible the intellectual progress of the mass and not only of small intellectual groups.[82]

The chief instrument for disseminating this new proletarian culture was the communist party, the 'collective intellectual'. Following Croce, Gramsci praised Machiavelli as the first to conceptualize politics as 'ethico-political' activity, which he reinterpreted as the transformation of the superstructure. The 'modern Prince' is not 'a real person',

> It can only be an organism, a complex element of society in which a collective will which has already been recognised and has to some extent asserted itself in action, begins to take concrete form. History has already provided this organism, and it is the political party – the first cell in which there come together germs of a collective will tending to become universal and total.[83]

The party was composed of three elements:

i a popular base of ordinary people
ii the leadership, which co-ordinated activity at a national level

iii 'an intermediate element which articulates the first element with the second and maintains contact between them not only physically but also morally and intellectually'.[84]

Gramsci's party was designed to include all the populace, not just an elite section of it. Unlike Lenin, he did not believe that party cadres should 'elaborate an independent ideology' without reference to what the workers, deluded by 'bourgeois ideology', actually thought themselves.[85] The 'educational relationship', which 'exists throughout society as a whole', was 'active and reciprocal, so that every teacher is always a pupil and every pupil a teacher'.[86] Ideologies were formed on the basis of movements and desires which were already expressed, usually inchoately, by the people, not on the basis of scientific laws of economic and social development.[87] The party brought together leaders and led 'organically', not 'mechanically'. Far from denigrating 'the spontaneous philosophy of the masses', Gramsci praised it. He condemned 'bureaucratic centralism' as the 'pathological manifestations' of a 'narrow clique' – a sign of 'the political backwardness of peripheral forces.'[88] In a passage clearly aimed at Stalinism he observes

A party's police function may be either progressive or regressive. It is progressive when it aims at keeping dispossessed reactionary forces within the bounds of legality and raising the backward masses to the level of the new legality. It is regressive when it aims at restraining the living forces of history and maintaining an outdated, anti-historical legality that has become a mere empty shell. When the party is progressive it functions 'democratically' (in the sense of democratic centralism), when it is regressive it functions 'bureaucratically' (in the sense of bureaucratic centralism). In the latter case the party is merely an executive, not a deliberating body; accordingly it is technically a policing organ, and its title of a 'political party' is not more than a mythological metaphor.[89]

Gramsci's desire, stemming from his interpretation of Marx, for a democratic party removed from the Russian model, has led many to regard him as advocating an alternative, 'Italian road', to socialism.[90] Although he noticed important differences between Russia and the West, these can in fact be interpreted as justifying Lenin's strategy as much as an Italian alternative. Whilst in Russia 'the state was everything and civil society was primitive and amorphous', in the West the state was 'merely an outer trench' behind which stood 'a powerful chain of fortresses and casemates' – the 'trench-systems' of civil society. Continuing the military analogy, Gramsci isolated two phases of the attack on bourgeois institutions – the 'war of position' and the 'war of manoeuvre'. The former was a protracted attack on the cultural superstructure, necessary in 'the more industrially and socially advanced states.' But this did not obviate the need, when the time was ripe, for a rapid and no doubt violent 'war of movement', or revolutionary action of the usual type, to topple the capitalist leaders when they too resorted to coercion to maintain their position.[91]

Whilst many aspects of the Italian communist party reflected Gramsci's precepts for its organization and activity in establishing a new hegemony,[92] its profession to be a parlimanetary party with commensurate ambitions was totally at odds with his theory. Indeed, in the light of the ultimate goal – the creation of a new type of society – such ambitions are in Gramscian terms completely misconceived. Many commentators have pointed to this to justify a Leninist reading of Gramsci. Given the conditions prevailing in Russia one would expect Gramsci to have endorsed Lenin's strategy of adopting revolutionary methods from the start. However, we have found their conceptions of the party and ideology to differ so fundamentally that Gramsci's Leninism might seem simply a product of his idealized picture of the Russian revolution. Yet a genuine ambiguity persisted in Gramsci's thought. He made the test of an ideology its success – and Lenin's revolution was undoubtedly successful. 'In these terms,' Gramsci remarked, 'one could say that Ilich advanced philosophy as philosophy in so far as he advanced political doctrine and practice.'[93] In historicist terms, a dictatorially imposed 'collective will' was as true as one 'spontaneously' accepted by the masses.[94] It remains to be seen whether the fault does not reside in the goal itself.

## THE NEW ORDER

Gramsci remained true to the orthodox Marxist vision of a future 'withering away of the state.' He describes this transition variously as 'the reabsorption of political society in civil society' and 'the disappearance of political society and the coming of a regulated society.' The coercive institutions and legal structures of 'political society' would disappear by degrees 'as even more conspicuous elements of regulated society (or ethical state or civil society) make their appearance.'[95] Gramsci shared the traditional Marxist antipathy to the liberal system of rights and justice as products of the capitalist system.[96] Like Marx, he believed that society could

cross the narrow horizon of bourgeois right. . . . In a more advanced
phase of communist society, when the enslaving subjugation of
individuals to the division of labour, and thereby the antithesis
between intellectual and physical labour, have disappeared; when
labour is no longer just a means of keeping alive but has itself become
a vital need; when the all-round development of individuals has
increased their productive powers and all the springs of wealth flow
more abundantly.[97]

For Gramsci, as for Marx, the *gemeinschaftlich* relations of the new
hegemony were built upon the overcoming of both natural and
artifically created scarcity through the productiveness of communist
society. This was the 'real' (economic) basis, where 'the premises
exist one hundred per cent', for a fully 'rational', and 'totalitarian',
conception of the world. It was the 'cathartic' moment – the creation
of a new 'historical block' when 'purely economic (or egoistic–
passional)' feelings were transformed into 'ethical' relations between
members of a new society. 'Necessity' would be exchanged for
'freedom', and the structure would cease to be 'an external force
which crushes man' and become 'an instrument to create a new
ethico-political form and a source of new initiatives.'[98]

Not surprisingly, many commentators have doubted the plausibility
of both the Marxist idyll and Gramsci's version of it. Gramsci
attributed the lack of 'spontaneous' fellowship between workers to
the alienating conditions of the capitalist mode of production. To
regard the legal and moral rules of 'political society' as other than
historically determined was an ideological error, falsely objectifying
a contingent repressive social situation. This assumption – that all
social conflict was ultimately class-based – presupposed a very
simple view both of human nature and the complexity of modern
society. Gramsci, here going beyond Marx, suggested that under
communism everyone would be aware of the interdependence of all
the functions each individual member performed, and moderate his
or her demands on others accordingly. By virtue of this 'total'
perspective, people could achieve a 'collective will . . . through
which a multiplicity of dispersed wills, heterogeneous aims, are
welded together with a single aim, on the basis of an equal and
common conception of the world.'[99] Yet how, in the modern world,
can people ever come to appreciate and give relevant weight to all
the myriad tasks performed by men and women in every aspect of
their lives? Surely they can only acquire a 'cultural-social unity' and
act as 'collective man' at the cost of greatly diminishing the
possibilities for self-development which Gramsci claimed to be
increasing. For it is conflict between different types of self-

fulfillment more than over scant resources which is likely to render justice and morality necessary to preserve individual freedom.[100]

Gramsci believed that the increasing power to produce goods would in the course of history be matched by greater freedom. In reaching this conclusion he made the mistake of confusing the choice of ends with the cognitive and practical means of attaining them – the union of theory and practice. The upshot of this confusion was to regard the success of a given political ideology as an indication of its truth. Whilst Gramsci can be cleared of any authoritarian intentions, his thought is undeniably amenable to such an interpretation, not because of what he said, but because to what he failed to tackle. In the aftermatch of fascism questions began to be raised as to whether practically, rather than philosophically, his theory could be implemented in anything but a totalitarian manner, a debate to which we shall turn in the next chapter.

# 8

# BOBBIO, DELLA VOLPE AND THE 'ITALIAN ROAD TO SOCIALISM'

Modern Italian social theorists sought to unify theory and action by working a revolution in the people's perception of the world, thereby changing their political practice. They believed a unity of conception and purpose amongst Italians would complete and transform the merely formal unification attendant on a common set of political institutions. Not surprisingly, resistance fighters maintained that the anti-fascist struggle represented a 'second Risorgimento', truer than the first and providing the moral regeneration and popular participation the former had lacked.[1] In this chapter I shall examine the dissolution of this problematic, and the abandonment of the aspiration to 'make Italians' in favour of creating the institutions of a workable democracy; taking as my example a debate in the early 1950s between a liberal political thinker, Norberto Bobbio, and various political and cultural spokesmen of the Communist Party. The debate neatly captured the central question of post-war Italy, namely whether the PCI could create a mass democracy without the difficulties that had bedevilled all prior attempts, and which had culminated in fascism. The discussion centred on two of the main topics of the Italian political tradition:

i the role of intellectuals
ii the relations between state and society

Norberto Bobbio was born in Turin in 1909. His liberalism, like Gramsci's communism, reflected the industrial problems of the north, and eschewed the metaphysical liberalism of Croce and the southern Hegelians. A constitutional lawyer by training, he attached great importance to the legal framework of politics and the protection it afforded the individual. He renewed interest in the

Italian positivist tradition, editing important volumes of the works of Cattaneo, Pareto and Mosca, and he drew inspiration from the English contractarians, having written seminal studies of Hobbes and Locke early on in his carer. He had belonged to the largely anglophile intellectuals' anti-fascist movement – the Party of Action – inspired by the 'liberal socialism' of Piero Gobetti and Carlo Rosselli, athough he confessed that he did not adopt this position until the 1940s.[2]

Bobbio's essentially social-democratic stance needs stressing, because the questions he raised belong to the classic themes of 'cold war liberalism'. The debates centred on the Marxist equation of culture with ideology, the Liberal redefinition of democracy as essentially representative rather than participatory, and their setting up of a dichotomy between liberal and totalitarian regimes centred on the criticism of Stalinism.[3] Whilst neither Bobbio, nor his interlocutors, escaped the limits imposed by the contemporary political climate, the mutual respect accorded by both parties distinguishes their discussion, and highlights its significance when compared with, for example, the slanging match between Aron, Merleau-Ponty and Sartre which took place at roughly the same time in France.[4] Indeed, the whole point of the exchange was to avoid adopting positions which merely mirrored the progressive political division of Europe into opposed, armed, ideological blocks.

Bobbio opened the debate with a provocative criticism of 'cultural politics'. He accused both 'diehard defenders' of the Western political tradition and its vehement opponents of betraying the fundamental duty of the intellectual

> to commit himself to illuminating with reason divergent positions, to put in discussion the pretensions of all of them, to resist the temptation for a definitive synthesis, or making an irreversible choice, to restore to men – each armed against the other with contrasting ideologies – faith in discussion, to re-establish both the right to criticism and respect for the opinion of others.[5]

The intellectual, he insisted, must cease to be a prophet or oracle and become an observer, who instead of precipitating an easy answer to problems, would remain perplexed by all solutions.[5] Bobbio applied this argument in an attempt to deflate both the anti-communism of cold war liberals, and the anti-liberalism of fellow-travelling left-wing intellectuals. He pointed out the self-contradiction of the liberals' defence of freedom of speech and their simultaneous denial of it to those who did not share their political sympathies. Likewise, he maintained that the wholesale rejection by the left of the practices and ideals of liberalism as 'bourgeois', and hence irrevocably corrupt, did not make sense given Marxism's undoubted debt to the liberal tradition. Rather than rushing into antagonistic and mutually exclusive camps, therefore, intellectuals of both sides should seek areas of contact and discussion within their common cultural inheritance:

> [T]he defenders of the liberal-bourgeois civilisation should reflect to what extent the new communist society is the inheritor of their conception of the world and history, and refuse to be drawn into the polemic against a revived 'barbarism', the defenders of the new communist society must reflect, much more seriously than they have up until now, on how far they should welcome, in making good their claim to build a new civilisation, the values contained within liberalism.[6]

Bobbio denied that his own position, of dialogue rather than conflict, implied that the intellectual should become apolitical. He claimed that he merely disavowed 'cultural politics' in order to make room for the 'politics of culture'. The former involved the 'planning of culture on the part of politicians'; the latter, in contrast, consisted of 'the politics of men of culture in defence of the conditions necessary for the existence and development of culture.'[7] Provision of a suitable environment for cultural activity of any kind required a respect for individual liberty. '[T]he politics of culture', he asserted, 'must be in the first instance a defence and encouragement of liberty, and thus of the strategic institutions of liberty.'[8] In making this point, Bobbio launched into a fierce criticism of the betrayal of what he regarded as a fundamental tenet of liberalism – namely tolerance – by its erstwhile defenders organized around bodies like the Italian Association for Cultural Freedom and journals such as *Preuves* and *Tempo Presente*. He argued that their *a priori* exclusion of communists from the rights of intellectual freedom, which they claimed to stand for, was a gross hypocrisy.[9] This line of attack is all the more comprehensible when one remembers that the elections of 1947 had secured the Christian Democrats a near absolute majority – the only time an Italian party has ever achieved this – largely as the result of a concerted anti-communist propoganda campaign aided by the Americans. The De Gaspari government had continued to prosecute this policy once in office, rendering them a natural target for Bobbio's objection that the manipulation of culture for political ends necessarily perverted it.

His arguments, however, clearly applied with equal force to the PCI, who at that time maintained a compromising support for the

Soviet Union, and were in any case committed to the Gramscian programme of establishing a new hegemony. Their attempt to harness culture to purely political ends had been evident in the *Politecnico* affair of a few years earlier. This independent communist periodical, edited by the novelist Vittorini, had come under fierce attack in 1946 from the PCI leader Togliatti, who condemned its lack of a coherent cultural policy as dilettante.[10] Vittorini's argument differed from Bobbio's, however, in adopting the Crocean view that culture existed in a sphere of its own, quite distinct from political concerns.[11] Indeed, when reflecting on the affair some years later, Vittorini admitted that his adherence to communism had always been motivated by an ideal of the creative power of the individual, rather than any coherent social and political doctrine.[12] We have already noted this element in Italian idealism – a posture which found its home in post-war Italy in the existentialism of Abbagnano and others. Bobbio, in contrast, was well aware of the disastrous consequences of adopting this as a political position, producing as it did the intellectual elitism we discovered in Croce and Gentile in particular. Although neither critics of the left nor the right seemed to appreciate it at the time, Bobbio's contention that a particular type of political commitment was required of the intellectual to protect the value of culture presented a challenge to all the diverse ways of relating culture and politics Italian theorists had traditionally adopted. He maintained that the intellectual's role was neither to create a new hegemony, nor to form a privileged class above the mêlée of everyday life. Rather this duty consisted of working towards the conditions necessary for any kind of cultural activity to take place. Bobbio equated culture with the pursuit of all those activities – art, science, leisure, human relationships – which render our lives worthwhile. However, he went beyond the Crocean equation of culture with human creativity and liberty through his awareness that its defence entailed a definite institutional and legal framework guaranteeing the individual's freedom from external interference. Croce's liberalism had been deficient in attempting to base politics entirely on the fostering of creative autonomy without considering the need for constraints and rights to protect each person's freedom of action. The PCI, he intimated, ran the risk of making a similar mistake.[13]

His debate with the PCI centred on which political system, the liberal or the communist, was best suited to facilitating human liberty and hence culture. The discussion was opened by Bianchi Bandinelli, in an article in the party journal *Società*.[14] He remarked, somewhat strangely given Bobbio's critique of cold war liberalism, that all culture was political and that the liberal claim to represent anything more universal than the capitalist system was a fraud. Since he illustrated this point with an American publication, *Confluence*, similar to those castigated by Bobbio himself, he must either have misunderstood or chosen or misrepresent Bobbio's case. As the latter remarked in his reply, Bandinelli's argument amounted to little more than the assertion that 'since everyone does it, so must we.'[15] This led Bobbio to open up a second, and extremely fruitful, aspect of the discussion – namely the extent to which communism was compatible with liberalism, human freedom and a healthy cultural life entailing similar safeguards under both types of regime. Behind this question inevitably lay the factual problem of whether the Soviet Union correctly reflected Marxist theory. If it did not, then there was no need for Italian communists to compromise themselves by adhering to the party cultural policy. It would be both possible and more coherent for them to defend individual liberty – 'the politics of culture' – whilst remaining communists.[16]

Bobbio returned to this theme in an important article on 'Dictatorship and democracy', in which he developed his ideas concerning the legal framework required for cultural freedom. He began by questioning Lenin's identification of the state with dictatorship, due to its origins as a means of class oppression. Two consequences, he argued, followed from this view. First, the distinction between liberal-democratic governments and dictatorships, such as the fascist regime in Italy, disappeared. Even if the Marxist thesis were accepted, the nature and application of class power differed demonstrably within the two types of polity. This confusion led to the second consequence – Lenin's claim that since dictatorial rule was inevitable prior to the transition to communist society, the 'dictatorship of the proletariat' in the Soviet Union was preferable to Western governments, because it marked a further stage on the road to socialism. Bobbio contended that this obfuscated the issue between liberals and communists. The class origins of state power did not enter the liberal critique of dictatorship; the question turned on what guarantees existed to prevent the abuse of that power, whoever held it. Just as the 'bourgeois' state could be either 'dictatorial' or 'liberal', so could a 'proletarian' government. The doctrine of the separation of powers, he remarked, might have originated with the rise of the bourgeoisie, but the constitutional techniques it inspired in order to assure the independent administration of justice were equally important for workers as for any other class. The complete subordination of law to politics by Soviet jurists, on the grounds that all authority emanated from the workers, failed to answer the liberal objection. For liberals also stressed that the source of power came solely from the people in civil society – the problem lay in how this power was exercised.[17]

Bobbio's thesis was rapidly taken up by Galvano della Volpe, probably the most original Marxist philosopher of post-war Italy.[18] He directly confronted the problem of whether the freedom secured within a socialist democracy, even of the Soviet type, was superior to that found in liberal parliamentary regimes in the West. In part this was unfortunate, since it tended to conflate an examination of Marxism was a defence of the Soviet Union. However, the grounds on which della Volpe mounted his counter-attack undoubtedly revealed weaknesses within Marxist political theory. He maintained that the purpose and basis of authority could not be distinguished from the methods used to control it, since the 'means' changed according to the 'ends' they served.[19] Della Volpe based his argument on a careful reading of Marx's 'Critique of Hegel's Doctrine of the State', a work only published in 1927, but which he had made of central importance in the development of his own brand of Marxism. He did not use this text to justify an Hegelian reading of Marx, but to stress the radical distinction between the two created by Marx's criticisms. Adopting Feuerbach's 'transformative method' Marx had accused Hegel of inverting subject and predicate, making the real subject of history – the empirical existing world – a manifestation of the Idea. Della Volpe believed this argument provided the key to understanding Marx's method generally, since, whatever the topic, he applied the same procedure to demystify the reification of abstract concepts into real entities.[20] Bobbio's purportedly universal rights derived, he claimed, from exactly this error.

Quoting from a number of early Marxian texts,[21] della Volpe maintained that rights arose from the contradictions of bourgeois society, dominated as it was by competitive individualism. In liberal theory the state existed to protect the essentially selfish, private interests of individual producers. The separation of powers and the need for rights, therefore, stemmed from the simultaneous estrangement of people from each other and from the community as a common bond. This state of affairs resulted from the division of labour and the stress on individual acquisitiveness and private property attendant upon the introduction of market relations in capitalism. The whole juridical and institutional framework of the state consisted of a hypostatization of the economic and social conditions of bourgeois life.[22] The liberal system of parliamentary representative democracy was an expression of this divide between the individualism of society and the universal standards of the public sphere required to regulate the conflicts arising within capitalism. However, citing Marx, della Volpe asserted this distinction no longer existed once society was linked by a unity of interests deriving from the social nature of production, of which politics formed a part:

> Then . . . the legislature is representative only in the sense that *every* function is representative. For example, a cobbler is my representative in so far as he satisfies a *social* need . . . just as every man is a representative of other men. In this sense he is representative . . . by virtue of what he *is* and *does*.[23]

The true concept of democracy is that espoused by Rousseau, and endorsed by Marx, of a participatory system based on popular sovereignty, aiming at producing the 'general will' of the people.[24] Marx presumed, and della Volpe blindly followed him in this, that with the abolition of the preconditions of private property and class warfare, individual and social ends would naturally coincide. When this occured, the 'civil liberty' of the bourgeois state would be replaced by the 'egalitarian liberty' of communism. The former, or *libertas minor*, 'consists of free economic initiative, security of property . . . and the relative moral liberties of conscience, religion, press etc.'. The second constituted 'a more universal liberty.' *Libertas maior* 'is the *right* of *everyone* to *social* recognition of his *personal qualities* and *capacities:* it is the truely *democratic* application of *merit:* that is the *social* potential of the *individual* and therefore of his personality.'[25]

Finally, della Volpe used the above to demonstrate, though purely in theoretical terms, the superiority of the Soviet system to the western. He based his remarks on Marx's brief comments on the transition to communism in the *Critique of the Gotha Programme*, using Lenin's approval in *State and Revolution* as evidence of their adoption within Russia.

According to Marx, in communism's lower phase, to which the Soviet Union corresponded in della Volpe's view, a purified form of bourgeois right persisted in which 'the right of the producers is *proportional* to the labour they do, the equality consists in the fact that measurement is *by the same standard*, labour.' In the transitional phase, equality, and hence liberty, was truely meritocratic, based on the personal contribution to the social product – a stage represented in Russia by Stakhanovism. Inequality, however, clearly still persisted, because the same standard was applied to people of unequal abilities and personal circumstances. Since 'right can never rise above the economic structure of a society and its contingent economic development', its disappearance would only be possible once the exploitation of human beings by each other became impossible. This would occur once the private ownership of the means of production, and the subordination produced by the division of labour, had been abolished in communism's final phase – an harmonious society of communal production, based on altruism and providing conditions of material abundance.[26] Drawing on Kelsen's approving remarks on the 1924 Soviet Constitution, della Volpe concluded that rights were recognized only to the extent that the competitiveness of capitalism required them. Their progressive diminution in Soviet law simply corresponded to the advances made by Russia towards the ideal communist society.[27]

If della Volpe's article reads today as a somewhat pedantic exposition of the main principles of Marxism, it undoubtedly had the virtue of making clear what Marx's position on these questions was – a matter of some difficulty given the obscurity of the relevant texts at that time. However, as Bobbio pointed out, the main thrust of the liberal argument had simply been put to one side.[28] He asked why freeing the individual from the servitude of the capitalist division of labour should obviate the problem of dissent and conflicts of opinion. Della Volpe lumped together two types of liberty under the category *libertas minor:* the economic – reflecting the capacity of individuals to do certain things; and the civil – regarding their rights to decide for themselves, free from state or other interference, what use they might make of their talents and goods. Freeing the masses from wage-slavery though, and thereby increasing their ability to act autonomously, did not remove the necessity for a legal right to make one's own choices – indeed, as Bobbio remarked, it implied such a right. Rights, in other words, reflected the divorce between politics and culture, thought from power, in a manner unrelated to the bourgeois separation of civil society and political state.[29]

Della Volpe had suggested these 'civil rights' would be unnecessary, because decisions in a communist society evolved from a truly democratic process, in turn made possible by a socialized economy in which the division between private and public interest no longer persisted. As Bobbio noted, this too involved a great deal of question begging. The rationale of democracy, he countered, involved the notion of free, autonomous individuals, each with an equal right to choose which kind of life was best. Even assuming that there no longer existed any limit on the resources available – surely an impossible aim – differences would still continue as to what forms of life were truly the best, as the enactment of any one form would potentially damage the interests of others. Of course, theorists of participatory forms of democracy would stress its inherent value in providing understanding and awareness of people's mutual wants and needs, so that agreement could be reacted on a number of common interests. Yet a technical limitation would arise in implementing this system in large-scale societies, where it would be impossible for everyone to come via discussion and personal contact to appreciate the demands of others. Differences of experience and hence of preferences, inevitable in any complex industrial society, would render unanimous agreement difficult to achieve without coercion, and so decisions would tend to be made by majoritarian vote. Moreover, questions of time and scale made the participation of all citizens in every decision itself an impossibility, so that the representative system could not be as easily dismissed as della Volpe presumed. Unless minorities had some protection of their liberties, rights in other words, then democracy could have oppressive consequences, since it was possible for the wishes of a particular group to be consistently outvoted by the rest. As democracy derived its *raison d'être* from the liberal notion of individual freedom, it could not in practice be illiberal by denying freedom of choice and remain democratic in anything but a merely formal sense. This, he observed, was precisely what had occured in the USSR – where elections were by universal suffrage, but a single party selected the list of candidates and effectively identified itself with the government.[30]

Concluding, Bobbio asked whether the very goal of a totally harmonious society, of egalitarian liberty or *libertas maior*, was compatible with individual freedom in any recognizable form. Della Volpe reiterated Viscinskij's claim that the foundation of authority 'is not bourgeois "civil society", but the proletarian organic mass of workers.' Following Marx, della Volpe contended that in communism's lower phase each producer received a reward comensurate to the labour he expended – an equal right which was still bourgeois in origin 'although principle and practice are no longer at loggerheads.' As we saw, he argued that this criteria had been met by the Stalinist policy of Stakhanovism, which he contrasted to the enforced competition of capitalism.[31] Yet why should the productivity of a particular coal miner be judged a more social indicator of merit than the ability to write symphonies (Shostakovitchism?) or to make money, or be any less competitive? The decision as to who contributed more would depend on the evaluation of the goods concerned – a matter in the Soviet case simply made by party fiat. The question of the legality and fairness of the 'means' would only disappear if the 'ends' had been decided in advance. 'Who', Bobbio challenged, 'was courageous enough to make such a choice?'

Della Volpe's argument suggested that a regulated economy would remove the advantages of personal gain, so that all labour contributed to the common welfare, rather than to that of the individual. If, during the transitional stage, not all the manifold abilities of human beings were realizable, producing inequalities by favouring some talents over and above others, then this would be transcended under communism, which had the means to ensure universal and equal maximal self-development amongst individuals. This presumed a great deal to work, since the fact of public ownership of the means of production would not abolish either the diversity or the differences in spheres and levels of achievement people could attain. How, for example, could one co-ordinate the multiplicity of attributes, needs, likes and skills that existed both between and within individuals? How could tasks be assigned without damaging somebody's interests or potential? Clearly such questions could only be solved by having principles of justice and rights to mediate between conflicting claims, specifying both social duties and spheres of personal freedom. Thus a conflict existed between Marxism's commitment to individual self-development and its stress on communal relations. As Bobbio pointedly remarked, 'what distinguishes the perfect human society from an organic society of insects . . . is freedom from interference by others,' for the very fact 'that freedom as autonomy cannot be separated from freedom as non-interference.' Moreover, if this is true of communism's last phase, it is all the more pertinent to the period of socialist transition.[32]

The above exchange had immediate practical consequences in the Italian context by providing criteria for evaluating the policies of the PCI. Since 1944 the Communist Party had proclaimed the necessity of following a democratic road to socialism, adapted to the social conditions of Italy.[33] As we have seen, they claimed, somewhat spuriously, the authority of Gramsci for this strategy of a 'war of position', as opposed to a violent 'war of movement'. Yet although they stressed their commitment to working through the existing institutions, participating in the drawing up of the Italian constitution in 1947, their appraisal of the inherent value of the main tenets of liberal democracy remained highly ambivalent. Togliatti's contribution to the discussion was therefore very significant.

Unfortunately, the circumstances of the pre-Khruschev era led Togliatti to begin by justifying the Soviet repression of 'the abstract formal liberties of a narrow privileged group, as the means to advancing millions of men towards the conquest of a new, rich and multiple personality.'[34] However, he then extended this argument to dispute Bobbio's contention that the democratic freedoms, now enjoyed in the West, had resulted solely from the extension of liberal rights to the masses. In reality, two related events characterized this development:

> The first is the rise and consolidation of new forms of association (such as the unions, for example) which embrace a greater number of men than were ever involved in voluntary associations before; the other is the new position of men relative to the economic facts at the base of their associative life. It might seem that the two facts are completely unrelated, or only linked because the unions are the most important of the new associations characteristic of the democratic period, called by their very nature to demand a regulation of the economy that liberalism consequently ignored or denied. The true link resides instead . . . in the coming to light of a new conception of the relations between men in society and this new conception, in its turn, is the consequence of the fact that new masses of human beings have been driven onto the stage of history, that is onto the stage of a real and conscious movement.
>
> The question of liberty, of its content, of its forms and of its limits, is completely conditioned by this movement.[35]

Togliatti's reply essentially encapsulated the central thesis of the PCI – that the democratization of society goes hand-in-hand with the gradual socialization of the economy via workers and state control of the means of production. In classic Italian fashion, the institutional question is subsumed under the issue of developing a new conscious-ness, adequate to changing social conditions. However, as Bobbio remarked, one could accept the bulk of Togliatti's argument and still legitimately raise the questions of how relations between individuals would be co-ordinated, and what degree of uncoerced individual choice would be left open. Togliatti, like della Volpe, used the language of autonomy to conflate two different types of freedom: that concerned with 'increasing opportunities', common to socialism, with the liberal desire 'to diminish the bonds' constricting individual action. 'The major political problem', Bobbio contended, 'is to discover whether they are asking . . . not only for different, but incompatible, things; that is to say, whether . . . [they] are two operations which can be performed together, and if so between what limits and under what conditions.'[36] Putting off such questions on the grounds that whilst all would be resolved in the perfectly harmonious society of the future, the nature of that community lies beyond present human knowledge, represented a dangerous moral blindness in theory, of which Marxist practice has all too frequently been culpable.[37] Reiterating his main criticism of della Volpe's argument, Bobbio noted that if one could easily reject liberalism as a set of privileges of the bourgeoisie, it was harder to do so once one considered it as 'the theory and practice of the limits on state power, above all in an epoch such as ours, in which so many omnipotent states have reappeared.'[38]

In spite of the PCI's reputation as a 'Western' parliamentary party, it has consistently side-stepped the issue of the compatibility of communism with so-called liberal freedoms. From his Naples address of 1944 on 'National Unity' to the 'Yalta Memorandum' of 1964, Togliatti's strategy of a 'progressive democracy' which transformed existing institutions from within by securing greater worker participation and giving them a new social content, remained substantially unchanged. Even after 1973, when it inaugurated the much vaunted policy of a 'historical compromise', the PCI continued to be ambivalent about the nature of the future communist society. Bobbio challenged them once again to explain which institutional arrangements could replace those of representative democracy, and still preserve a pluralistic and free society.[39] 'After all the water (and blood) which has passed under the bridges of history', he claimed, it was 'unforgivable' to repeat scholastically Lenin's statements on the Soviets and Marx's on the Paris Commune, and elevate them into a political theory.[40] The problem of 'who governs' could still not replace the central difficulty of 'how' government was conducted.[41]

Although Bobbio's later articles formed part of a socialist attempt to undercut the PCI's electoral advances during the 1970's, they enjoyed much greater approval amongst left-wing intellectuals than his earlier polemic. Lucio Colletti, della Volpe's star pupil, had criticized the social-democratic tendencies of the party during the 1960s on largely orthodox grounds.[42] Now he too bemoaned 'the *weakness* and sparse development of political theory in Marxism.'[43] As Bobbio ruefully observed, the ensuing debate was directed less against himself, and more between different factions of the communist left as to how far others had 'erred' in admitting the justice of his remarks.[44] The party, however, brought these debates to an end by reasserting the validity of their 'third way', different from both the social-democratic path and the revolutionary, Leninist, model adopted in Russia – '[T]he defence and development of democracy today', wrote Berlinguer, the new leader, 'can only happen via the struggle to overcome capitalism, in this sense the workers' struggle for democracy has a precise class content. Here is the difference between us and liberal or social-democratic views.'[45] In other words, politics was a matter of class divisions – abolish them and the necessity for the political sphere 'withers away'.

In a number of recent articles, Bobbio has developed his own alternative strategy for the fusing of liberalism and socialism,[46] based on an intricate analysis of the relations between state and civil society.[47] In brief, Bobbio's thesis is that socialists must adopt the formal framework of liberal democracy, but extend it to occupy additional social spaces to just local and national elections for various legislative bodies. The workplace, health and education authorities etc. . . . must also come under democratic control. He distinguishes this proposal from the usual leftist call for a return to the classical model of participatory democracy, which he believes is unworkable in modern society. Democracy must rather be representative in form and social in situation. At the same time, he distinguishes his conception of democratic socialism, which seeks the democratic control of society, from social democracy, which he regards as the forced attempt to incorporate a social input into democratic procedures. Three themes therefore dominate the essays:

i the critique of participatory democracy
ii the analysis of the liberal theory of democracy
iii the explanation of possible ways for its extension throughout society as a whole

I shall examine each of these in turn below.

*i.* Bobbio argues that the participatory model of democracy, e.g. of Rousseau, is unsuited to modern atomistic society. Drawing on later pluralist versions of Mosca's work, particularly those of Schumpeter and Sartori, he maintains that the competitive model of different parties vying for the people's vote is much more realistic. Bobbio gives four main reasons for this:

a The modern ethos is individualistic, so that no amount of rational argument will bring about an all-embracing general will.
b This cultural orientation is reinforced by the diversification of modern industrial society, which makes it harder to form common interests.
c Direct democracy can never mean that the people vote on each and every issue after a prolonged discussion of all the elements involved – there simply would not be enough hours in the day.

The only solution would be to mandate delegates to vote in specified ways. The difficulty here is that we belong to too many diverse groups – e.g. as workers, parents, city dwellers etc. . . . – for this proposal not to either shade into the competitive model by degrees, or result in the false attribution of certain 'real interests' to the people as a whole.

d The increased complexity of modern society makes people ill-informed judges of their own interests, so that representatives can serve us better than we can ourselves.[48]

*ii.* Given these conditions, Bobbio believes the liberal model of representative democracy to be much more realistic. This is characterized by the 'rules of the game' which establish by whom and by what procedures collective decisions are taken. Representative democracy, he argues, presupposes the social reality of modern society – viz. that it is made up of self-seeking individuals. The appeal of the competitive model is thus that it mirrors the market mechanisms which regulate exchanges between individuals in society.[49] The basic framework for its successful operation is the protection of the individual given by those liberal political rights which guarantee freedom from external interference. However, he argues that the classical liberal equation between economic and political liberty is inadequate. The liberal assertion of individual rights was made against monarchical regimes and the vested interests of the landed aristocracy. To use these arguments, as contemporary neo-liberals do, against democratically elected governments and programmes for social justice is inappropriate. In other words, there is now a conflict between liberalism's view of the social agent and its notion of the political agent, which is ultimately untenable. The former assumes a meritocratic notion of desert, suitable to the classical liberal conception of the market; the latter argues that each individual is entitled to equal respect regardless of his or her abilities – two conceptions which plainly conflict with each other.[50]

*iii.* For Bobbio, the solution to the liberal dilemma lies in reconciling the individualist premises of liberalism with notions of distributive justice. This leads him to reflect on the new neo-contractarians.[51] He attacks Nozick for defending only economic freedom, and admires Rawls' attempt to produce a social contract theory which can establish the conditions for political liberty as well. However, he regards the establishment of social rights as only a preliminary to the extension of democratic control to all areas of society. Just as the political rights of freedom of expression and assembly, and to the vote regardless of sex, creed or colour established the basis for parliamentary democracy, so social rights provide the precondition for democratic control of the various aspects of social life.[52] Bobbio believes this is made necessary by the very features of modern society which render direct democracy unworkable. The diversification and specialization of industrial societies have led to the concomitant growth of agencies outside our control – bureaucracies, technocracies, international corporations. These constitute so many 'invisible powers' which subtly influence our everyday life and which no amount of parliamentary legislation can adequately control. Representative democracy on the competitive party model should therefore be extended to these new areas as well.[53]

Bobbio's thesis clearly reflects the political debates and experiences of modern Italy. As he notes, someone who lived the first half of his life under fascism can appreciate that a 'bad democracy (and ours is pretty bad) is always preferable to a good dicatatorship (and Mussolini's dictatorship was certainly better than Hitler's) . . .'[54] His desire to provide a workable theory of democracy is further reinforced by his belief that the struggle for a democratic and non-violent ordering of human affairs is the only means of preventing the universal devastation of a nuclear war. An international politics based on the threat of mutual destruction parallels the use of violence by dictators and terrorists to resolve domestic issues.[55]

However, if nobody can doubt the worthiness and importance of Bobbio's ideas and aims, there are a number of problems with his arguments. Surprisingly for the student of Pareto and Mosca, he does not fear the inherent elitism of the competitive model, and the possibilities it offers for the domination of politics by particular party oligarchies. Nor is it clear how his proposals for the extension of democracy could avoid the inflation of political activity, demanded by programmes for increased participation, or the creation of the spectre of the 'total' citizen, perpetually voting at different meetings, which he criticizes so effectively. Finally, and most importantly, Bobbio's model assumes that allegiance to the 'rules of the game' will be relatively unproblematical, deriving from the pursuit of our interests. Like Machiavelli, Pareto and Mosca, he believes that our social duties can only be realistically based on self-interest.[56] However, if this provides the principal reason for adhering to the system, then a strong temptation exists to 'free ride' whenever possible. If one has the money, or the political power, to support or avoid the penalties for breaking the law, then one will have no qualms about doing so. The Rawlsian argument – that one will imagine the possibility of being worse-off than one actually is – seems in practice to carry little weight for those ready to use their position or wealth for their personal advantage. Recognition of the constitutive principles of democracy involves some understanding of people's obligations to each other. This is unlikely to emerge from an individualist conception of politics based on rights and interests.[57] It depends upon an appreciation of the intrinsic, rather than instrumental, value of certain common goods for human beings generally, regardless of whether or not one desires them personally.

The 'politics of culture', to return to the theme of his earlier book, provided more than a set of agreed rules. As Bobbio noted himself, it consists of a general outlook, which 'mediates' between conflicting interests by allowing us to appreciate the validity of the wants and desires of others.[58] However, *pace* Bobbio, this cannot be taught by intellectuals, but only learnt through the social experiences of everyday life. Thus the argument has come full circle, for 'making citizens' and 'creating the state' are two inseparable and complementary processes. In the conclusion I wish to tentatively examine the problems this fact poses for relating social theory to political practice in the modern world.

# 9

## CONCLUSION

### *Social theory and political action*

Italian social theory has always had an undeniably pronounced political import. Even those theorists, like Pareto and Mosca, who claimed that they merely offered objective descriptions of human behaviour, did not refrain from drawing appropriate policy conclusions for a 'realistic' politics from their findings. The idealist school engaged in the apparently more modest task of making Italians aware of the social and cultural processes which formed and bound them together. Yet this appeal to a common heritage and identity was done with the express purpose of creating a political community, united by unique national forms of self-understanding. Finally, Marxist theorists, particularly Gramsci, sought to go beyond both the objectivist and the relativist positions by showing how we might formulate an immanent critique of our current beliefs and attitudes and gradually move towards a more self-conscious grasp of the forces and processes affecting our lives.

Clearly this trichotomous division of the types of social theory found in the Italian tradition is somewhat over-schematic. Pareto, for example, was well aware of the influence of ideals on political behaviour, just as Croce conceded the causal properties of certain contingent social and economic factors in fashioning systems of belief. However, the emphasis within each thinker can be attributed to one of these three modes of thought. These alternative approaches to the study of society have significant similarities to the three kinds of social theory dominant today: the positivist, the hermeneutic and the critical schools of thought.[1] They provide three different ideal types which relate social theory to political practice in correspondingly different ways.

Positivists, in the Paretian mould, seek universal laws of human behaviour analogous to those predicated of matter in natural science. They adopt an empiricist epistemology and search for the constant causal factors – Pareto's residues and derivations – which are either hidden within, or deducible from, human action. Knowledge of these mechanisms provides the political scientist with an accurate guide for obtaining certain specific goals via the manipulation of the appropriate elements.

Hermeneutic thinkers, in contrast, deny the possibility of objective social knowledge. They point out that human beliefs are not constant, but change through time. These variations cannot be credited to external factors, because our responses are themselves a function of the set of beliefs we hold. Human practices are constituted by the various systems of values and culturally specific meanings we adhere to. Knowledge of any society must therefore be relative to the subjective understandings its members have of it, with no special status beyond the particular historical context.

Lastly, critical theorists accept that the effects of the social and economic facts of human existence are mediated through the complex of self-understandings that agents have of themselves. However, they reject the conservatism implicit within the hermeneuticist positions. They maintain that we can develop alternative and more critical viewpoints from which we can all appraise our possibilities for action, from within whatever cultural tradition we happen to belong. As we saw with Gramsci, this possibility for criticism need not depend upon a transcendental notion of what constitutes human real interests. Instead he attempted a dialectical synthesis of the two approaches outlined above. He examined the various instances of systematic distortions in the agents' understanding of their actions, as manifested by the contrast between their overt beliefs and the tacit regulative norms underlying many of the practices they take for granted. He could not reveal this disparity without appealing to independent empirical evidence regarding certain constant features of human activities.

Before considering the plausibility of any of these methods of enquiry, I want to outline briefly those factors which led to social theory having such a tremendous political importance, not only in Italy but in the modern world generally. As recent Italian history exemplifies, the main explanation relates to the problem of providing modern citizens with rational and legitimate reasons for their political allegiances.[2] With the general demythologizing of authority, we, in the west at any rate, can no longer accept God's will or natural law as the ground of our obligations. Social bonds increasingly appear as the products of history and tradition, having no basis other than the unplanned network of human custom. Fuelling this increasingly self-conscious attitude towards the conventions and laws which regulate human affairs are the expanded horizons offered by greater social mobility, better communications and the extension of education. Whilst agricultural societies are relatively stable and localized, industrial and post-industrial technological societies require a flexible and educated workforce able to adapt to the vagaries of an international market. These processes undermine the socializing institutions, like the extended family and distinctive national patterns of life, upon which communitarian allegiances were based in the first place. Thus an enhanced sense of the provisional nature of our intersubjective understandings goes hand-in-hand with the dissolution in reality of these older social bonds and the decline of the political and economic environment which generated them.

The collapse of traditional patterns of behaviour has created new political demands to provide the emerging novel social roles with a legitimate standing. Areas of everyday life which were previously governed by norms accepted unreflectively by the populace, like the status of women, now require legislation to gain approval in their changed form. Our relations and obligations towards others in matters such as care of the sick and elderly, or racial and sexual discrimination are increasingly the object of public debate and policy rather than convention. Similarly, as the economy has grown ever more specialized, complex and international, public regulation has become more necessary to cope with pockets of deprivation and to maintain the fairness of market exchanges.

Thus the same factors favouring an enhanced self-consciousness amongst the populace of Western nations have led to the need for greater politicization and public control of social life. Little wonder that these conditions should have spawned a number of grand social theories, all claiming to replace the systems of belief of the past as the legitimizers of our attitudes, our actions and our political rights, goals and duties. How plausible, then, are the above three candidates for this role?

Undoubtedly the Paretian response has achieved the most favour from governments and politicians. Best characterized as the carrot and stick approach, it consists of finding the right balance of incentives and coercion to lead individuals to support the public interest. The key to its successful operation resides in the claim to have discovered certain universal and invariant truths of human psychology. In my analysis of Pareto's theory I made three main criticisms, which stand against any similar account.[3]

   *i*  Pareto made the mistake of elevating a way of looking at the world, which was largely local in both time and place, into an unavoidable and all-pervasive mode of human behaviour. Despite the historical scope of his study, his main concern was to describe and explain the corrupt political practices of contemporary Italian politics and to interpret almost any other event in their terms. As a result, he had a disastrously impoverished view of the possible range of moral attitudes.

*ii* The type of behaviour encouraged by Pareto's parsimonious conceptual scheme ultimately led to his endorsement of the demagogic tactics of Mussolini. He responded to the sudden variety of conflicting claims for legitimacy outlined above by regarding them all as aspects of human self-interest. The successful government derived its power from knowing how to harness these base motives with the right balance of smooth talking and bribery and the use of force to keep recalcitrant elements in order. By denying the possibilities for people to co-ordinate themselves according to reflectively held shared norms, Pareto left open no alternative to manipulation as the source of social order. For if self-interest provided the only rational source of political obligation, then the public interest would increasingly require enforcement to prevent free riding. Only widespread acceptance of an official ideology, backed by the coercive power of the law-enforcing agencies, would prevent resentment growing up when, inevitably, people's private plans were thwarted. Dissatisfaction could be reduced by deliberately favouring certain groups and marginalizing the others, but greed would render any coalition a temporary affair whilst the partners sought more favourable arrangements. Totalitarian control of all aspects of society was alone capable of stemming the rise of discontent and calls for change.

*iii* These two weaknesses of Pareto's approach were compounded by the very manner in which he related theory and practice. His adoption of the methodology of the natural sciences as his model for social enquiry committed him to an instrumentalist view of politics. Just as explanations in the natural sciences take the form, if event $E$ occurs in situation $S$ then $X$ will result with a probability of $P$ – so, he believed, social theories could provide general laws of human activity with a certain predicitive power. Leaving aside the question of the feasibility of this characterization of social science, it plainly invited the adoption of manipulative political practices on the part of those who adopted it. As 'scientific Marxists' of the Leninist stamp, for example, amply illustrate, social theories of this type purport to provide a superior knowledge of social processes which justify the wholesale coercion of the masses into 'rational' ways of acting.

The chief moral and empirical objection to the instrumentalist view, as the idealists pointed out, is its dismissive attitude towards the understandings and values held by the agents themselves.[4] Insight into the laws of human behaviour must take precedence over the intentions of the actors themselves. If the social scientist does not make this assertion, then the task of building up a neutral causal theory of action will be impossible, for beliefs differ in certain crucial respects from the data of natural science. First they are indeterminate – as Pareto discovered, people give a bewildering variety and often inconsistent number of reasons and descriptions of a similar set of actions. Second, these different interpretations of what Collingwood called the 'outside' of a given action,[5] can radically effect how agents ultimately respond to it. The success of general lawlike explanations in the natural sciences depends upon the possibility of explaining all material changes from the first three minutes onwards according to the same concepts and processes. Human beings, however, adopt divergent and often incommensurable conceptual schemes, which in turn define the sort of people they conceive themselves to be and constrain the type of acts they perform. It is a function of this diversity that almost any complex historical event will be the subject of numerous rival accounts of comparable plausibility. Moreover, disagreement over how to explain these events will run parallel with a broad consensus about their 'outside' detail, like the time and place they occured. What differs are the 'inner' motivations of the participants and the difficulty of bringing all of them under a single covering law or set of laws.

Finally, the aspiring social scientist's problems are compounded by the openness of human affairs. The determining factors can be mutliplied almost endlessly. Momentous historical events have been attributed to causes ranging from the length of Cleopatra's nose to the invention of the wheel. It would be impossible to account for occurrences such as these in advance. Mark Antony's aesthetic sense belongs to an unknown chemistry, his meeting with Cleopatra was a chance encounter. Similarly, prior to the existence of the wheel it would be impossible to imagine its influence on future history, since one could not predict its impact without actually inventing it. But human life is constantly bound up with individual predilections, contingency and conceptual innovations which radically change the patterns of our lives.[6] These interactions are so complex and unplanned that to provide a scheme capable of taking all of these into account plainly defies our ingenuity. This problem need have nothing to do with the sheer scale of the enterprise – though I cannot imagine how this could be overcome – the difficulties arise from the impossibility of guessing the moves both of ourselves and others given a potentially infinite number of variables. Contingency, linked with our ability constantly to change the conceptual framework within which we view and interpret events and our responses, makes the search for constant factors a Sisyphean task, as indeed the 'monstrous' bulk of Pareto's volumes confirms.

Of course, social life does not appear to us in as anarchistic and disjointed a manner as the above account suggests. Interaction with others assumes that we all *do* have a reasonable insight into what other people intend by their words and actions, built upon numerous, largely unconscious, shared meanings. Our lives gain coherence and comprehensibility through engaging in various practices which coordinate our actions with those of others. A particular society is characterized by the roles and activities it contains, and we partly identify individuals through these. Marriage, for example, involves the partners in certain attitudes and duties which structure their behaviour and the responses of friends and acquaintances towards them. As marriage declines as an ideal this creates difficulties both for couples and society at large in deciding what exactly is required of them. Frequent reference is made to the traditional roles which provide a touchstone for criticism, the development of new types of conduct and a provisional source of stability and common understanding.

Croce appropriately defended liberalism by writing a history revealing the origins and nature of the ensemble of practices and beliefs underlying liberal institutions. Yet the weakness of this approach was immediately apparent. To provide a coherent picture of liberalism he had to return to the nineteenth century, and paint an idealized picture of the era of bourgeois hegemony between 1815 and 1914. As Gramsci pointedly remarked, neither the struggles of the French revolution nor the collapse of the First World War were allowed to disturb the calm and apparent stability of liberal Europe. The difficulty of making a given set of human practices authoritative is that they are liable to change and disappear. The central questions of social and political theory turn on finding criteria which enable us to decide upon the validity or otherwise of the institutions and rules which govern us. A bland appeal to the authority of practices as such is no help in their evaluation or revision. The vacuousness of this tactic became plain when Croce was forced to voice his criticism of the present by advocating a hopelessly anachronistic return to the methods of the past.

Croce's insistence that we need to understand the 'inside' of events and social relations by entering into the thoughts and motivations of the actors involved highlights many of the inadequacies of positivist social science. But it does not give us much of an alternative.[7] For example, he never addressed the problem of 'false consciousness' and the possibility that participants might be mistaken in their understanding of their behaviour. An historian can often explain past actions in terms of factors and concepts unknown or even unintelligible to the agents. This poses an important question concerning the limits of the social scientist's understanding compared with those of the people studied.

Croce never made it clear how we might assess rival interpretations, and seemed oddly content to assert that Spirit speaks through us all in a cunning, if unknowable, manner. A fideist belief in the inherent order and benign nature of history provides scant consolation when faced with the palpable reality of anarchy and violence. As we saw, not even Croce remained happy with it. Indeed, the constant, and often compromising, revisions that the years between 1914 and the 1940s required of his historicist endorsement of practices ultimately led him to move towards a neo-Kantian position which could provide transcendental grounds for the criticism of the present.

Gentile's 'actualism' demonstrated one possible consequence of only looking at the internal aspect of practices at a time when their legitimacy was widely doubted. The inherent relativism of this approach, and the lack of criteria for adjudicating between different interpretations, made force the only possible arbiter between the inevitable conflicts between different individuals. If the nature of practices were to become so disputed that they could not longer be regarded as authoritative, in the way Croce had desired, then there would be no basis for intersubjective understanding at all. By following this line of argument to its most extreme conclusions, Gentile was forced to reverse the Hegelian thesis that customs and norms create the state, and make the state the subject of history.

Gramsci attempted to avoid both the instrumentalism inherent to empirical social theories and the conservatism of the idealist approach. He argued that the search for empirical correlations and the necessity for the interpretation and understanding of human practices were not distinct and incompatible types of inquiry, but were both important for the investigation and the changing of social and political life. He drew attention to the fact that the norms and patterns governing human behaviour could represent responses to prevailing material conditions of which the agents were not themselves aware. The causal impact of the development of productive forces on the possible forms of social structure could not be ignored. Similarly, causal explanations could not replace a concern with motives and intentions. For example, Gramsci noted that the solidarity of the working class was constantly undermined by the assimilation of the more advanced group into the ruling elite. Like Pareto and Mosca, he accepted that low levels of activism could often be causally explained by the deliberate strategy of politicians or factory bosses, who offered material incentives to the more articulate amongst the workers, leading them to reject their class roots. But to explain the effectiveness of this strategy required an understanding of the motivations of the workers and the reasons for their falling for this ploy. The hegemony of the bourgeoisie in part turned upon the manner in which the working class had internalized the values and beliefs of their oppressors, and came to willingly uphold the very system which oppressed them. But appreciating that a particular society could only function on the basis of certain shared ways of seeing the world did not rule out a causal explanation in terms of certain prevailing social conditions. For people would not necessarily be liberated from the source of their oppression merely by recognizing it as such. When tacit consent failed, then fascism revealed the strength of simple coercive action.

Gramsci's theory claimed to provide the masses with knowledge about how they might change themselves by making them aware of the causal processes underlying their repression. This endeavour ran the risk of collapsing into the instrumentalist model examined earlier. Pareto and Mosca failed to appreciate how a set of causal patterns might be subverted by our knowing about them. If the workers learn they are being offered bonuses to decrease their union activity, their attitude towards them might change and their behaviour alter accordingly. But a positivist might nevertheless claim that as long as the social conditions which create these false ideologies prevail, then people have no valid reason for dropping them. Such was the substance of Mosca and Pareto's critique of socialism – that the operative laws of human society, the ineradicable inequalities of ability, wealth and power, made it an unrealizable ideal. They argued that people would only accept the socialist alternative when the necessary conditions were present. This could not occur unless someone who knew the necessary causal factors producing this situation possessed sufficient power to manipulate the relevant elements needed to bring it into being.

Lenin, in *What is to be Done?*, used an anlogous argument to justify the seizure of power by a vanguard elite, and the creation of the conditions which would produce the desired behaviour on the part of the masses. Prior to the establishment of true socialism, he argued, the party must rule in the people's name, since they would remain subject to numerous false ideologies which would distort their perception of their real interests.[8] Gramsci appeared to reject a great deal of this strategy. He stressed how the critique of false ideologies developed out of contradictions within the masses' own self-understandings, which were indicative of the discrepancy between their real needs and those imposed or suggested by the prevailing world-view. Gramsci's party had an educative rather than a directive role and worked towards a time when the gap between the reality of the social order and the illusory ideas which attach people to it would reach crisis proportions, culminating in a spontaneous revolution.

It is nevertheless doubtful how successfully Gramsci transcended the difficulties we have noted with the positivist and the idealist schools. Part of his defence against instrumentalism was the claim that only mass adherence to a given set of practices could guarantee their validity. But this could always be the product of ideological distortion and political manipulation. Nor did he spell out the objective social institutions which would permit the reflective and unconstrained activity he aimed at. Clearly notions of truth, freedom and justice were involved but, like many in the Marxist tradition, he put off detailed discussion of these terms on the grounds that communism represented that social state where such concepts became redundant. This produced a certain circularity in his argument, since the critique of the present depended on bringing into being a set of social conditions which would render his motivating ideals valid.

Gramsci's theory remains incomplete as long as his description of the material conditions required for human freedom to flourish remain obscurely defined. For it is only the practicality of such a situation coming about which can justify action towards it. This requirement has been a constant theme of Norberto Bobbio's work. He criticizes Marxism for failing to develop its conception of the future communist ideal in a way which is relevant to popular political action in the present – the means cannot be separated from the ends. It is not sufficient, he argues, to change people's perceptions and social arrangements – the manner in which they are altered is just as important. The indeterminate nature of the Marxist goal accounts for the underdeveloped discussion of Marxist political methods –

even in as sophisticated a thinker as Gramsci. Bobbio at last tackles the question of what institutional arrangements are needed for people not only to change their social set-up but to *choose* to do so. Politics – the provision of a forum whereby social theories can compete with each other for peoples attention – remains indispensable.

If social theory advances and informs political practice, it requires a political framework within which to operate. Substituting social theory for politics involves subverting the self-understandings of ordinary people and adopting the instrumentalist perspective of the expert.[9] But no social theory can legitimately claim to do this, since the scientific pretensions of inquiry into human affairs are, for reasons outlined above, severely limited as no perfect understanding of the causal processes affecting human lives is possible. Practices embodying authoritive social theories no longer command universal allegiance, if they ever did so. Prime Ministers gain their authority from the approval of electors, not divine right. Although politicians frequently maintain there is no alternative to their policies, we have good reason to doubt this claim. The limits of social theory mean that we need mechanisms which allow us to weigh up competing theories and enable us to reject some and accept or modify others without fear of repression. Bobbio invokes the 'rules of the game' of liberal democratic politics as providing the minimal basis for uncoerced rational co-operation between autonomous individuals. Democracy as a political practice implies accepting the inadequacies of social theory.

Democracy, however, must be valued for more than the instrumental efficacy Bobbio praises. Its value inheres in the educative nature of democratic practices. Bobbio is unduly dismissive of civic virtue, regarding it as unrealistic in present societies. But surely the cynicism inspired by calls upon public duty derives not from the inherent unworkability of such schemes so much as the lack of the social preconditions necessary for their operation. Bobbio argues that social rights frequently precede the creation of political rights. However, dissaffection with democracy commonly stems from the continued inegalitarian nature of society, which creates large differentials in the amount of political power wielded by different individuals, and places a disproportionate share of the cost of public projects on the less well off. He is right to assume that self-interest undermines civic duty, but wrong to suggest any political system – least of all democracy – can dispense with it.

We seem faced with a paradox. Social theory has eroded the traditional shared meanings creating our obligations to each other, but cannot recreate or replace them. Inequalities can no longer be accepted as 'natural' or divinely ordained, yet by what criteria are they to be abolished? Clearly one cannot ignore the problem of motivating people to adhere to particular political arrangements. The minimal democratic rules Bobbio outlines – the ability to make relatively free choices of candidates and issues on a roughly equal basis with other voters, and to abide by majority decisions made in this way – imply rather different social arrangements from those which exist today. How can people be encouraged to accept the necessary changes?

The only plausible solution, denied in principle by Pareto and Mosca and only equivocally accepted by Bobbio, is through the experience of democracy itself. For to engage in even a 'bad democracy', as Bobbio describes contemporary Italy, is to be made aware of these inequalities and to move towards the reform of society in a direction which makes free discussion possible. Democracy, in other words, has as its rationale the discovery of common goals by debate and reflection, enabling the various theories of social existence to join with, be modified by, and change the everyday understanding of ordinary citizens. One could say it represents the politics of a community of social theorists.

Within a democratic community we gain confirmation of our subjective aspirations and perceptions through the assent of our fellow citizens. We escape imprisonment without our own consciousness – incapable of distinguishing reality and illusion – by interaction and discourse with others and the gradual development and refinement of a public language. Our sense of ourselves is intersubjectively grounded and leads to an awareness both of the interrelatedness of social life and a respect for individual autonomy stemming from the irreducible separateness of persons. No single individual can style him or herself as the impersonal instrument for the realization of the best possible outcome. We must seek to determine whether our actions are right or wrong solely from the point of view of our position in the world and our relations with others. Our primary concern becomes the character of our actions *vis-à-vis* the rights and requirements of other people, rather than the state of the world as a whole – the justification of our acts is interpersonal rather than administrative. Through exploring the nature and quality of our relations with others we are led to reappraise both ourselves and our situation and to change them in a non-manipulative manner. This is the essence of democratic politics.[10]

Italian social analysts sought to substitute their theories of society for the disparate self-understandings of ordinary Italians. The success of any one of their projects would have rendered the need for politics redundant – but no social theory can legitimately claim to fill this role. Instead of seeking comprehensive explanations of human affairs, the task of social and political theorists must be the rather different one of creating the political conditions for social theories to be developed and challenged. Exploring this question takes up beyond the boundaries of the present study.[11]

# GLOSSARY

This glossary contains notes on a number of the Italian terms, politicians and minor political theorists most frequently mentioned in the text.

*Amendola, Giovanni, (1882–1925)* Philosopher, journalist and politician, he achieved early fame as a contributor to Papini's *Leonardo*. An admirer of William James, he developed his own brand of mystical pragmatism. In later years he began to use these ideas in the service of a more radical 'democratic' liberalism. As a political jouranlist and deputy he opposed the corrupt practices of successive administrations and later was a prominent critic of fascism. He led the walkout from parliament of independent liberals ('the Aventine succession') after Matteotti's assassination, only to fall victim to a fascist attack himself.

*Crispi, Franscesco, (1819–1901)* Born in Sicily, he initially held Mazzinian sympathies and was a member of Garibaldi's 'Thousand'. Once in parliament he became increasingly reactionary. His ministries, from 1887 to 1891 and from 1893 to 1896, combined an aggressive foreign policy with repressive measures at home. Although he gained Italy her first overseas possessions, notably Eritrea, his patriotic fervour met its Waterloo when the disastrous defeat of Adowa (March 1896) brought the abortive attempt to annex Abyssinia to an end.

*Depretis, Agostino, (1813–87)* Leader of the Left at the time of the fall of the Right, he successfully held prime ministerial office from 1876 to his death in 1887. He introduced the clientelistic tactics known as *trasformismo*, which led to the demise of the two 'historical' parties. By forestalling parliamentary defeat by timely resignation and the remolding of coalitions, he successfully weathered eight ministries and established the pattern for future Italian governments.

*Gobetti, Piero, (1901–26)* Son of a Turin grocer, he was an extraordinarily precocious intellect, founding his first review, *Energie Nuove*, in 1918 at the age of 17. Although much influenced by Gramsci and the *Ordine Nuovo* group, he remained a socialistic liberal rather than a communist. In 1922 he set up a weekly, *La Rivoluzione Liberale*, which took over from *La Voce* as an eclectic meeting point for social and cultural criticism. In 1925 he was forced into exile, dying in Paris of bronchitis and heart failure.

*Gioberti, Vincenzo (1801–52)* Born in Turin, he was ordained a priest in 1825. A philosopher, he aimed to rally the Papacy to the nationalist cause. In 1843 he wrote *Del Primato Morale e Civile degli Italiani (Of the Moral and Civil Superiority of the Italians)*, which had a great influence on the liberal catholic, neo-Guelph supporters of Pius IX. His hope that the Church would take an active political stance proved illusory. He headed the Piedmontese government from December 1848 to March 1849, when he retired, condemned by the Papacy for his politics and his philosophy.

*Giolitti, Giovanni, (1842–1928)* The major Italian statesman of the period, he first entered politics in 1884 as a member of the Left. He served as Minister of Finance under Crispi in 1889, forming his first ministry in 1892. Between 1903 and 1921 he headed four more ministries, lasting eleven years in all, longer than any other elected Italian Prime Minister. He attempted to 'put Marx in the attic' by undermining support for the socialists with a number of social and electoral reforms. He remained nevertheless a conservative liberal and cynics interpreted these measures as manoeuvres to remain in power. This is slightly unfair since he was perceptive enough to oppose colonial expansion and entry into the First World War, both of which contributed to his fall from office. His response to fascism was more one of withdrawal than of overt criticism. His weakness was a symptom rather than a cause of the failure of the liberal party.

*Historical Left and Right* The so-called 'historical' parties descended from the two main groupings at the end of the Risorgimento. The Mazzinian republican 'Party of Action' became the opposition 'Left', the ruling 'Right' descended from the 'Moderate Party' led by Cavour and inspired by the neo-Guelph liberal catholics and the neo-Hegelians. After the Right's fall from power, in 1876, the two parties began to merge, due to Depretis' use of *trasformismo* and the rise of the new liberal, socialist, catholic and ultimately fascist parties.

*Mazzini, Giuseppe, (1805–72)* Born in Genoa in 1805, he was the theorist of Italian republicanism and established, in 1831, the revolutionary society 'Young Italy'. He sought to unite Italy through a mass insurrection brought on by encouraging a religious patriotism amongst the people. He left Italy after the failure of the 1848 revolutions and the fall of the Rome Republic in 1849. In 1853 he founded the *Partito d'Azione*, its aims symbolized by its motto 'Dio e popolo' (God and the people). Its supporters ultimately formed the 'Left' after unification. Mazzini was never fully reconciled to the House of Savoy, and sponsored numerous abortive conspiracies until his death in 1872.

*Moderate Party* Formally constituted in 1848, it grew out of the neo-Guelph movement inspired by Gioberti and Balbo. From 1849 it was led by D'Azeglio and Cavour and became the 'Right' in the Italian parliament after unification. The party of the neo-Hegelians, it held power until 1876 and was later idealized by Mosca, Croce and Gentile.

*Papini, Giovanni, (1881–1956)* Like Prezzolini, he was a self-taught cultural spokesman of great influence, largely as a result of his Florentine review *Leonardo* (1903–8). Originally a pragmatist with Nietzschean overtones, his thought consisted of an uneasy mixture of elitism, nationalism, mysticism and realism. Trying to sustain this mixture led him first into futurism, then, around 1918, to Catholicism and finally made him a keen fascist and almost an establishment figure, whose *Life of Christ* became a massive best-seller.

*PCI (Partito Communista Italiano)* The Italian Communist Party was founded in 1921 when a left wing faction, including its first three leaders, Bordiga, Gramsci and Togliatti, split with the Socialist Party. After 1953 it became the main opposition party, gradually increasing its percentage of the vote from 22.6 per cent in 1953 to 30.4 per cent in 1979.

*Prezzolini, Giuseppe, (1882–1982)* An autodidact, he had a profound influence on Italian culture before the First World War. He edited the review *Leonardo* (1903–5) with Giovanni Papini, later founding the influential *La Voce* (1908–14). A Crocean with syndacalist sympathies, he succeeded in gathering together a large number of diverse contributors of all points of view. An inveterate non-conformist and critic, his sympathy for fascism was short-lived and he ultimately went to America to teach and write his memoirs. He ended his long life as a self-styled Voltairean figure, writing polemical pieces from his home in Lugarno, Switzerland.

*PSI (Partito Socialista Italiano)* The Italian Socialist Party was founded in 1892. Two different wings established themselves from the start, the radical 'intransigents' led by Enrico Ferri, and the larger group of moderate reformists headed by Filippo Turati, the eventual leader of the party. In 1921 the party finally split and a separate Communist Party was formed. After 1953 it suffered severe electoral losses to the PCI and has attempted ever since to regain support by opposition to it and alliance with other centre parties. This policy has recently proved tremendously successful under its current leader, and the present Prime Minister, Bettino Craxi, although its percentage of the vote remains around 11 per cent, compared with 14.2 per cent in 1958, its highest poll since the 1948 election.

*Risorgimento* Meaning 'Resurrection', it is the term usually applied to the nineteenth-century movement for national unification. It had the following four phases:

i 1815–47, the period of moral and intellectual preparation
ii 1848–9, when there were a number of abortive republican revolutions and disillusionment with the liberal Papacy
iii 1850–61, the period of Cavour and political unification under Piedmont and the House of Savoy, and the liberation of the south by Garibaldi
iv 1861–70, the final phase of consolidation, with the acquisition of Venetia in 1866 and the occupation of Rome in 1870.

Nationalists regarded the movement incomplete until Italy obtained the

Trentino in 1919. Since all the hopes and aspirations of the first phase remained unfulfilled, both fascists and resistence fighters frequently spoke of a 'second Risorgimento' of moral regeneration to complete the political settlement obtained by the first.

*Rosselli, Carlo, (1899–1937)* A social scientist, he was instrumental in the development of 'liberal socialist' ideas on the reformist wing of the Socialist Party. Opposition to Mussolini after 1922 led to his editing a number of clandestine socialist weeklies, which ultimately caused his arrest by the fascist authorities in 1927. In 1929 he escaped to France, where he founded a new anti-fascist organization 'Giustizia e libertà' ('Justice and liberty'), which sought to promote a liberal democratic form of socialism. On June 9th 1937 he and his brother Nello were assasinated in France by fascists.

*De Ruggiero, Guido, (1888–1948)* Born in Naples, De Ruggierio was the most important of the third wave of southern Hegelians. A pupil of Gentile's actualism, he did not follow him into fascism, and took over as the main contributor on philosophy to Croce's *La Critica*. An anglophile, his *History of European Liberalism* (1924) was translated by R. G. Collingwood. Its Italian reprint, in 1941, ultimately led to his arrest by the fascists. From June to December 1944 he was Minister of Education in the Bonomi adminstration.

*Salvemini, Gaetano, (1873–1957)* Historian and reformist socialist, he campaigned vigorously for the reform of parliament and the relief of the south. His journal, *L'Unità*, argued that general equality between north and south remained to be fought for. An outspoken critic of political corruption, his pamphlet *Il Governo della Malavita* denounced the Giolitti regime. A deputy from 1919–21. he went into exile in 1925, ultimately becoming professor of history at Harvard University.

*Togliatti, Palmiro, (1893–1964)* A founder member of the PCI, taking over as leader from Gramsci after his imprisonment. During the war he remained in Russia, and essentially towed the Stalinist line. However, on returning to Italy in 1944 he began to sketch out an independent 'Italian road' to socialism, suited to the conditions of the West – a strategy which made him less radical than Nenni's socialists. This new moderation was evident in his vote, in the 1947 constituent assembly, in favour of the inclusion of the Lateran Treaties into the constitution, thereby securing the favoured position of the Catholic Church. During the Cold War, his party was excluded from government but continued to grow spectacularly. He advocated a strategy of 'progressive democracy', socializing society from the bottom up, to cope with this situation. After 1956, the party increasingly distanced itself from Russia, and Togliatti formulated a doctrine of 'polycentrism', which stressed that different nations would follow distinct lines of development towards socialism. These ideas were best framed in the famous 'Yalta Memorandum', written shortly before his death, which became a key text of the Eurocommunist movement.

*Trasformismo* The term used to describe the merging of the 'historical' Left and Right parties of the post-Risorgimento era after 1876. It then came to denote the means whereby coalitions between different factions were formed by 'transforming' erstwhile opponents into allies by the use or abuse of government patronage.

*Turati, Filippo, (1857–1932)* A founder member of the PSI and leader of the 'gradualist' or 'minimalist' wing of the party, and editor of the journal *Critica Sociale*. A firm believer in socialist unity, he maintained a precarious hold on the party until 1904. Thereafter the more radical 'maximalist' wing, led first by Ferri and later by Nenni, came increasingly to dominate, despite several left-wing successions – notably the syndicalists (1908) and the communists (1921). He nevertheless refused to join Bissolati's reformist socialist party which split from the PSI in 1912. His willingness to join with other parliamentary parties to oppose fascism led to his expulsion in 1922. Imprisoned by Mussolini, he was spirited away to France by Rosselli in 1926, where he eventually died.

# NOTES

BIBLIOGRAPHICAL NOTE

Since translations of the Italian works examined here are, when available, both uneven and not always readily accessible, all references are to the originals and all English renditions of quotes from foreign languages are my own. A short bibliography at the back of the book lists the main works, translations and English and Italian commentaries on each theorist.


*1. Introduction*

1 G. Carducci, 'Discorso al popolo nel teatro nuovo di Pisa' (1886), in *Confessioni e Battaglie*, first series, (Bologna, 1917), p. 481.
2 G. Prezzolini, *Amendola e 'La Voce'*, (Florence, 1973), p. 28.
3 G. Amendola, 'Il Convegno Nazionalista', *La Voce*, II, (1910), p. 51.
4 Ibid.
5 E. Garin, *Cronache di Filosofia Italiana, 1900–1943*, 2 vols, (Bari, 1955) and A. Asor Rosa, 'La Cultura, Dall'Unità a Oggi', *La Storia d'Italia* IV, ii, (Turin, 1975) and N. Bobbio, *Profilo Ideologico del Novecento Italiano*, (Turin, 1986) provide such a history.
6 The subsequent remarks on my general approach will no doubt reveal my indebtedness to the methodological writings of Q. Skinner, particularly 'Meaning and Understanding in the History of Ideas', *History and Theory*, VIII, (1969), pp. 3–53, ' "Social Meaning" and the Explanation of Social Action', in Patrick Gardiner (ed.) *The Philosophy of History*, (Oxford, 1974), pp. 106–27, 'Some Problems in the Analysis of Political Thought and Action', *Political Theory*, XXIII, (1974), pp. 277–303; and the Preface to *The Foundations of Modern Political Thought*, 2 vols (Cambridge, 1978), I, pp. ix–xv. For a full bibliography, and a sympathetic account of his writings, see James Tully, 'The Pen is a Mighty Sword: Quentin Skinner's Analysis of Politics', *British Journal of Political Science*, XIII, (1983), pp. 489–509.
7 Q. Skinner, ' "Social Meaning" of social actions', pp. 111–15.

8 In addition to the work of Skinner cited in note 6, especially 'Meaning and Understanding', p. 53, see A. MacIntyre, *A Short History of Ethics*, (London, 1967), pp. 1–4.

9 E.g. J. Femia, *Gramsci's Political Thought*, (Oxford, 1981), p. 19.

10 Quotations and emphasis from J. Femia, *Gramsci's Political Thought* pp. 19–20. I should add that dissent from his introduction does not mar my admiration for the rest of his book.

11 For a general survey of the politics, and the economic and social problems of post-unification Italy, see M. Clark, *Modern Italy, 1871–1982*, (London, 1984), pp. 12–90, from which this and the next paragraph are drawn.

12 Gaetano Salvemini, quoted in M. Clark, *Modern Italy, 1871–1982*, p. 63.

13 A. Gramsci, 'Alcuni temi della questione meridionale', in *La Questione Meridionale*, eds F. de Felice, V. Parlato, 3rd edn, (Rome, 1982), pp. 131–60.

14 S. Spaventa, *Dal 1845 al 1861: Lettere, scritti, documenti*, ed. B. Croce, 2nd edn, (Bari, 1923), pp. 148, 149.

15 S. Spaventa, *La Politica della Destra*, (Bari, 1909), p. 29. Compare with G. W. F. Hegel, *Lectures on the Philosophy of World History: Introduction, Reason in History*, trans. H. B. Nisbet, with an introduction by Duncan Forbes, (Cambridge, 1975), p. 52. See S. Onufrio, ' "Lo Stato Etico" e gli hegeliani di Napoli', *Nuovi Quaderni del Meridione*, VI, (1968), pp. 76–90, 171–88, 271–87, 436–57, 466–92, and VII, (1969), pp. 64–78, 196–214 for a full discussion of how their views on this topic varied.

16 F. De Sanctis, 'Zola e *L'Assomoir*' (1879) in *Saggi Critici*, ed. L. Russo, 3 vols, (Bari, 1979), p. 336.

17 A. C. De Meis, *Il Sovrano. Saggio di filosofia politica con riferenza all'Italia*, (1868), ed. B. Croce, (Bari, 1927), p. 71. The most complete study of the Neapolitan Hegelians is G. Oldrini, *La Cultura Filosofica Napoletana dell '800*, (Bari, 1973) and his useful anthology *Il Primo Hegelismo Italiano*, (Firenze, 1969).

18 See especially his *La Filosofia Italiana nelle sue Relazioni con la Filosofia Europea con note e appendici di documenti*, (1862) ed. G. Gentile, 3rd edn, (Bari, 1926).

19 F. De Sanctis, *Storia della Letteratura Italiana* (1872–3), 2 vols, ed. B. Croce, 5th edn, (Bari, 1954).

20 S. Spaventa, *La Politica della Destra*, p. 199.

21 S. Spaventa in his speech of 24 June 1876 on the nationalization of the railways, the debate which led to the fall of the Right, in *Discorsi Parlamentari*, (Roma, 1913), pp. 419–20.

22 B. Spaventa, *Principii di Etica* (1869), ed. G. Gentile, (Naples, 1904), pp. 155–60. See the discussion in S. Onufrio, 'Lo "Stato Etico" ', pp. 449–57, on Bertrando, and pp. 466–92 for Silvio's view quoted n. 21 above. Compare with G. W. F. Hegel, *Philosophy of Right*, trans. T. M. Knox, (Oxford, 1952), para. 260. On this debate, and its extension by Croce and Gentile, see R. Bellamy, 'Croce, Gentile and

Hegel and the doctrine of the ethical state', *Rivista di Studi Crociani*, XX, (1983), pp. 263–81.

23 F. De Sanctis, *Storia della Letteratura*, II, pp. 435–6.

24 P. Villari, 'Ciò che gli Stranieri non Osservano in Italia', in *Le Lettere Meridionale ed Altri Scritti sulla Questione Sociale in Italia*, (Florence, 1898), pp. 183–4.

25 See his fundamental essay 'La Filosofia Positiva e il Metodo Storico' (1866) in *Saggi Critici*, ed. G. Battelli, (Lanciano, 1919), and the study *Niccolo Machiavelli e i suoi tempi*, (Firenze, 1877–82).

26 R. Ardigò, *La Formazione Naturale nel Fatto Del Sistema Solare*, (1877) *Opere* II, (Padua, 1889), pp. 129, 189, 350, 258 ff.

27 R. Ardigò, *La Morale dei Positivisti*, (1879) in *Opere* III, (Padua, 1900) pp. 422–5.

28 R. Ardigò, *Psicologia come Scienza Positiva*, (Mantova, 1870), *La Scienza dell' Educazione*, (Padua, 1893).

29 E.g. R. Ardigò, *La Morale dei Positivisti*, p. 404, E. Ferri, *La Sociologia Criminale*, (Turin, 1884), C. Lombroso, *L'Uomo Delinquente* (Turin, 1878).

30 Cf. pp. 59–60.

## 2 Vilfredo Pareto

1 This dual picture of Pareto is presented even by Joseph Schumpeter, *Ten Great Economists: From Marx to Keynes* (New York, 1951), pp. 131–42, who stands alone amongst economists in considering both aspects of Pareto's work. S. E. Finer's 'Introduction' to his selection of Pareto's *Sociological Writings*, (Oxford, 1966) provides the best and most balanced account of the development of his theory, but is largely limited to an exposition of its main elements in abstraction from his political commitments.

2 E.g. F. Borkenau, *Pareto*, (New York, 1936); R. Aron, 'La Sociologie de Pareto', *Zeitschrift fur Sozialforschung*, VI, (1937), pp. 489–521; H. Stuart Hughes, *Consciousness and Society*, (Brighton 1979), pp. 260–1.

3 Here I follow on from the pioneering article of S. E. Finer, 'Pareto and Pluto – Democracy: The retreat to Galapogos', *American Political Science Review*, LXII, (1968), pp. 440–50.

4 See notes 2 and 3 above.

5 V. Pareto, *Lettere ai Peruzzi, 1872–1900*, ed. T. Giacalone-Monaco, 2 vols, (Geneva, 1984), I, (292), 25 August 1874, (33), 1 November 1872.

6 Pareto 'Suffragio Universale', *L'Italiano – Gazzetta del Popolo*, 12 November 1872, in *Écrits Politiques*, 2 vols., ed. G. Busino, (Geneva, 1974), I *Lo Sviluppo del Capitalismo*, pp. 47–51.

7 Pareto's concern with this problem can be seen in the third of his 'Letters from Italy', written for the American journal *Liberty*, VI, (1889), pp. 7–8, in *Écrits Epars*, ed. G. Busino, (Geneva, 1974), pp. 30–5. Outlining the findings of the studies on the south, he concluded: 'Such facts reveal

a very serious state of things, and our statesmen take a heavy responsibility upon themselves in not paying heed to them; perhaps the day will come when the *bourgeois* will pay dear for their indifference and cruelty to the poor.' (p. 35).

8 Pareto, *Riflessioni e Ricerche*, ed. T. Gialacone–Monaco, (Padua, 1966), p. 45.

9 Pareto, 'Se convenga fissare per legge un minimo al salario guadagnato e un massimo alla ricchezza speculata', *Atti della Reale Accademia Economico-agraria dei Georgofili di Firenze*, Series, IV, IX, (1886), pp. 103–30 in *Écrits Politiques*, I, p. 192.

10 Pareto, *Lettere ai Peruzi, 1872–1900*, II (1247), 16 February 1886, p. 623.

11 Pareto, 'Se convenga fissare', p. 205.

12 'Socialismo e Libertà', *Il Pensiero Politico*, February and April 1891, pp. 227–37, 421–41, in *Écrits Politiques*, pp. 376–409.

13 Ibid., p. 400.

14 Pareto, 'Letters from Italy, III', p. 31.

15 Pareto, 'Socialismo e Libertà', p. 401.

16 Pareto, *Correspondance, 1890–1923*, ed. G. Busino, 2 vols, (Geneva, 1975), I (30), 31 December 1891, p. 175.

17 Pareto, 'Socialismo e Libertà', pp. 384, 387.

18 Pareto, 'Le Sorti Future Della Parte Liberale', *L'Idea Liberale*, 28 August and 4 September 1892, in *Écrits Politiques*, I, p. 550.

19 Pareto, *Cours d'Économie Politique*, 'Il Resumé,' pp. 1–2.

20 Ibid., paras 686–9.

21 'L' Italie économique,' *Revue des deux mondes*, 15 October, 1891. The episode led to the police breaking up meetings against protectionism addressed by Pareto, and ultimately produced an enquiry into the governments policies. See De Rosa's note in *Lettere a Maffeo Pantaleoni, 1890–1923*, ed. G. De Rosa, (Geneva, 1984), pp. 134–9, 143 for full details.

22 Pareto, *Cours*, paras 1054–5.

23 Pareto, 'Liberali e Socialisti', *Critica Sociale*, 1 September 1899, in *Écrits Politiques*, II, p. 323.

24 E.g. Pareto, 'Le péril socialiste', *Journal des Économistes*, May 1900; in *Libre – echangisme, Protectionnisme et Socialisme*, ed. G. Busino, (Geneva, 1965), pp. 322–39 and 'Un applicazione di teorie sociologiche', *Rivista Italiana di Sociologia*, July 1900, in *Écrits Sociologiques Mineurs*, ed. G. Busino, (Geneva, 1980), pp. 178–238. This latter article contains all the main elements of his mature sociology.

25 Pareto, 'Il Nuovo Indirizzo della Politica Liberale', speech to the Camera dei Deputati, 4 February 1901, in *Discorsi Parlamentari*, 4 vols, (Roma, 1953–6), II, pp. 629, 633.

26 Pareto, 'Gli scioperi e il Ministro Giolitti', *La Vita Internazionale*, 20 July 1901, and 'Un poco di fisiologia sociale', ibid., 5 September 1901, in *Écrits Politiques*, II, pp. 356–64, 365–73.

27 Pareto, *Les Systèmes Socialistes*, 2 vols, (Paris, 1902), I, p. 2.

28 Ibid., II, pp. 389–90, 393.
29 Ibid., I, pp. 6–15, 34–41.
30 Ibid., I, pp. 15, 21–2, 24–5.
31 Ibid., II, pp. 380–4.
32 Ibid., I, pp. 132–3.
33 Ibid., I, 58–62.
34 Ibid., II, pp. 454–6.
35 Ibid., II, p. 416–9.
36 Ibid., I, p. 38.
37 R. Wohl, *The Generation of 1914*, (London, 1980), chapter 5.
38 Pareto, 'L'aristocrazia dei briganti', *Il Regno*, I, (1903) in *La Cultura Italiana Attraverso le Riviste*, vol. II, pp. 455–60.
39 Pareto, 'La borghesia può risorgere?', *La Cultura*, II, pp. 467–8.
40 Pareto, *Cours*, II, 394–5.
41 Ibid., p. 469.
42 As he wrote to Pantaleoni on 16 May 1898 – 'In Italy, dear friend, there is nothing that either you or I can do. There aren't even four cats who share our opinions . . . In Italy there are but three parties: 1. the thieves who govern. 2. the socialists. 3. the clericals – I don't want to go along with any of them. Thus I'm contenting myself with pure science and I advise you to do the same.' (Pareto, *Lettere a Pantaleoni*, II, (358), p. 196.)
43 Pareto, 'Il crepuscolo della libertà', *Rivista d'Italia*, February 1904, in *Écrits Politiques*, II, p. 408.
44 *Lettere a Pantaleoni*, II, (310), 11 November 1897, p. 121; (533), 2 February 1906, p. 457.
45 *Correspondence*, II, (1037), 5 April 1917, p. 958.
46 See N. Bobbio, 'Introduzione alla Sociologia di Pareto', in *Saggi sulla Scienza Politica in Italia*, (Laterza, Bari, 1971), pp. 52–5, for an analysis of the different aspects of the *Trattato*'s 'monstrosity'.
47 *Trattato Sociologia Generale*, ed. N. Bobbio, 2nd Italian edn 1923, (Milano, 1964), para. 850.
48 Ibid., para. 150.
49 Ibid., paras 149, 151.
50 B. Croce, 'Sul Principio Economico. Due Lettere al Prof Pareto', *Giornale degli Economisti*, 1900, reprinted in *Materialismo Storico ed Economia Marxistica*, 3rd edn economica, (Bari, 1978), pp. 209–28. Pareto always remained respectful of Croce, maintaining him to be 'a great philosopher like Plato, Kant, Hegel etc. . . .' Gentile, on the other hand, was a 'great bore . . . who would be banned should they prohibit the use of morphine.' (*Correspondence*, II, (1190), 6 July 1921, p. 1069.)
51 Pareto, *Trattato*, paras 84–5, 867–70.
52 Ibid., para. 889.
53 Ibid., para. 888.
54 Ibid., para. 2412.
55 Ibid., paras 2025–6, 2227.
56 Ibid., para. 2178.
57 Ibid., paras 2237–39, 2274–8.

58 Ibid., paras 2053–9.
59 Ibid., paras 2230–6, 2279.
60 Ibid., paras 825–7, 2466 note 1.
61 Ibid., para. 2410.
62 Ibid., paras 2444, 2480 and note, 2484 and note.
63 Ibid., para. 2422.
64 Ibid., paras 2421, 2423.
65 For a forceful criticism of Pareto in this vein see P. Winch, *The Idea of a Social Science*, (London, 1958), pp. 95–111.
66 Pareto, *Trattato*, para. 1843.
67 Ibid., paras 2060, 2067 ff.
68 Ibid., paras 2128–39.
69 Pareto raises this difficulty himself in *Trattato* paras 2133–7, 2140–6.
70 I am grateful to David Beetham for underlining this point in his comments on an earlier draft.
71 Ibid., paras 12–13, 69–72.
72 Ibid., paras 1864–8.
73 Ibid., paras 1608–9.
74 Ibid., para. 2480 and notes and *La Trasformazione della Democrazia* (1920), in *Écrits Sociologiques Mineurs*, pp. 949–50.
75 Pareto, *Trasformazione* pp. 955–63.
76 Pareto, 'Il Fascismo', (1922), in *Ecrits Sociologiques Minerus*, pp. 1078–89. Pareto noted, in a letter to Pantaleoni, that fascism confirmed the breakdown in authority he had predicted in *Trasformazione*. (*Lettere a Pantaleoni*, III, note 704, 2 May 1921, 279–80.)
77 Pareto, *Trattato*, para. 1843; Pareto, *Trasformazione*, pp. 923–4.
78 Pareto, *Trasformazione*, note 697, 26 November 1920, pp. 273–4, Pareto, 'Il Fascismo'.
79 Pareto, *Lettere a Pantaleoni*, n. 708, 17 June 1921, pp. 285–6.
80 Ibid., n. 733, 23 December 1922, p. 320.
81 Pareto, *Trasformazione*, p. 927.
82 *Correspondance*, II (1249), 11 October 1922, p. 1106.
83 Ibid.
84 Ibid., n. 1261, 13 November 1922, p. 1114.
85 Ibid., n. 1263, 19 November 1922, p. 1116.
86 Ibid., n. 1309, 23 March 1923, p. 1141.
87 Ibid., n. 1280, 5 January 1923, p. 1126. Pareto even quotes the famous concluding passage of the Florentine's work; seeing his own book as containing the material to give rise to a man 'prudente e virtuoso', able to revitalize the nation.
88 A Lyttleton, *Italian Fascisms: From Pareto to Gentile*, (London, 1973), p. 22.

### 3 Gaetano Mosca

1 E.g. W. G. Runciman, *Social Science and Political Theory* (Cambridge, 1963), p. 64; Arthur Livingston, 'Introduction', G. Mosca, *The Ruling Class*, trans. H. D. Kahn (New York/London, 1939), pp. xxxvii–ix.

2 For details of this feud see the fundamental study by James H. Meisel, *The Myth of the Ruling Class: Gaetano Mosca and the 'Elite'* (Ann Arbor, 1958), pp. 169–83.

3 This group was composed of Pasquale Villari, Giustino Fortunato, Sidney Sonnino and Leopoldo Franchetti. For a discussion of the question see M. L. Salvadori, *Il Mito del buongoverno, La questione meridionale dal Cavour a Gramsci* , 2nd edn (Turin, 1963), and the useful anthology edited by R. Villari, *Il Sud nella Storia d'Italia* (Bari, (1961).

4 Quoted in Norman Lewis, *The Honoured Society* (London, 1964), p. 35. Evidence of the survival of these methods can be found in Judith Chubb, *Patronage, Power and Poverty in Southern Italy* (Cambridge, 1982).

5 P. Turiello, *Governo e Governati in Italia: Fatti* (1882), 2nd edn (Bologna, 1889), p. 28.

6 E.g. Benedetto Croce, 'Review of G. Mosca, *Elementi di Scienza Politica'*, *La Critica* XXI (1923), pp. 375–6; Arthur Livingston, 'Introduction', pp. xiv, xxxviii.

7 G. Mosca, *Sulla Teorica dei Governi e sul Governo Rappresentativo*, in *Ciò che la Storia Potrebbe Insegnare: Scritti di Scienza Politica* (Milano, 1958), p. 30.

8 Mosca, *Elementi di Scienza Politica* in Giorgio Sola (ed.) *Scritti Politici* (Turin, 1982), vol. II, pp. 720–37.

9 Mosca, *Teorica*, p. 34.

10 Ibid., p. 42.

11 Ibid., pp. 38–40.

12 Ibid., p. 44.

13 Ibid., p. 49.

14 Ibid., pp. 49–50, 51–2.

15 Ibid., p. 51.

16 Ibid., p. 53.

17 Ibid., p. 47.

18 Ibid., pp. 154–8.

19 Ibid., pp. 272–3.

20 Ibid., p. 275.

21 Ibid., pp. 276–7.

22 Ibid., pp. 277–8.

23 G. Salvemini, *Scritti sulla Questione Meridionale* (Turin, 1955), p. 48.

24 Mosca, *Teorica*, pp. 278–80.

25 Ibid., pp. 280–2.

26 Ibid., p. 284. The *camorra* is the Neapolitan branch of the Mafia.

27 Ibid. p. 284.

28 Ibid., pp. 286, 296–300.

29 Ibid., pp. 290–6.

30 Ibid., p. 289.

31 Ibid., p. 289.

32 Ibid., p. 291.

33 Ibid., pp. 306–7.

34 Ibid., p. 308.
35 P. Bachrach, *The Theory of Democratic Elitism* (London, 1972) pp. 10–17, correctly identifies Mosca as a precursor of the pluralist theories of Schumpeter, Dahl and Lasswell (whose work Mosca knew), and provides a critique from the viewpoint of classical participatory theories of democracy.
36 *Teorica*, pp. 310–19.
37 Ibid., p. 319.
38 Ibid., p. 320.
39 Ibid., p. 321.
40 Ibid., p. 326.
41 Ibid., p. 323.
42 An editor of the Italian equivalent of Hansard.
43 For details of this project see A. Ginzburg Rossi-Doria, 'A Proposito del Secondo Ministero Di Rudini', *Studi Storici*, X (1968), pp. 404–12.
44 Mosca, *Elementi* I, p. 608.
45 Ibid., pp. 621–3.
46 Ibid., p. 628.
47 Ibid., p. 669.
48 Ibid., Chapter VII.
49 Ibid., pp. 828–30.
50 Ibid., pp. 594–7.
51 Ibid., p. 645.
52 Ibid., pp. 645–9.
53 Ibid., pp. 649–53.
54 Ibid., p. 679.
55 Ibid., p. 681 note h.
56 Ibid., pp. 684–5.
57 See in particular *Le Costituzioni Moderne* (Palermo, 1887).
58 Mosca, *Elementi*, I, p. 684.
59 Ibid., pp. 689–91.
60 Ibid., pp. 692–3, 694, 696–7.
61 Ibid., p. 698.
62 Ibid., p. 699.
63 Ibid., p. 925.
64 Ibid., pp. 873–926.
65 Ibid., p. 699.
66 Ibid., p. 700 note b.
67 Ibid., pp. 543–4.
68 Mosca, 'Effetti Practici del Suffragio Universale', 16 June 1911, *Corriere della Sera*, in A. Lombardo (ed.), *Il Tramonto dello Stato Liberale* (Catania, 1971), p. 138.
69 Mosca, 'Il Concetto Moderno della Libertà Politica', 8 August 1911, *Corriere della Sera*, in *Il Tramento dello Stato Liberale*, p. 155.
70 Mosca, 'Il Suffragio Femminile in Italia', 18 March 1907, *Corriere della Sera* in *Il Tramonto dello Stato Liberale* p. 107.
71 Mosca, 'Feudalismo Funzionale', 19 October 1907, *Corriere della Sera*,

Ibid., pp. 199–203; 'Il Pericolo dello Stato Moderno', 27 May 1909, *Corriere della Sera*, Ibid., pp. 211–17.

72 Mosca, 'Stato Liberale e Stato Sindacale', 20 January 1925, *Rinascita Liberale*, in *Partiti e Sindacati Nella Crisi del Regime Parlamentare* (Bari, 1949), pp. 302–15.

73 Mosca, *Elementi*, II, p. 1015.

74 Ibid., pp. 1004–5.

75 Ibid., pp. 1039–41.

76 Ibid., pp. 1020–4.

77 Ibid., pp. 1022–3.

78 Ibid., pp. 1024–31.

79 Ibid., pp. 995–1002, 1096–103.

80 Mosca, 'Stato Liberale e Stato Sindacale', pp. 305–6.

81 Mosca, *Elementi*, II pp. 1098, 1116.

82 J. Lively, 'Pluralism and Consensus', in P. Birnbaum, J. Lively and G. Parry, *Democracy, Consensus and Social Contract*, (London, 1978), pp. 185–202.

83 Mosca, *Elementi*, I. pp. 659, 679.

84 P. Bachrach, *The Theory of Democratic Elitism*, pp. 1–9.

85 Mosca, *Elementi*, II, pp. 1001–2.

86 Ibid., pp. 1103–12.

87 Ibid., pp. 1102–3.

88 Ibid., Avvertenza, p. 1120.

*4 Antonio Labriola*

1 J. V. Femia, 'Antonio Labriola: A Forgotten Marxist Thinker', *History of Political Thought*, II (1983), p. 557, gives details of this simultaneous praise and neglect in the standard histories of Marxism.

2 The standard Italian account is Luigi Dal Pane, *Antonio Labriola nella Politica e nella Cultura Italiana*, 2nd edn (Turin 1975) which forms the basis for L. Kolakowski's chapter 'Antonio Labriola: An Attempt at an Open Orthodoxy', in *Main Currents of Marxism* vol. 2, trans. P. S. Falla (Oxford, 1978), pp. 175–92. I too draw heavily on Dal Pane's work.

3 G. Berti, 'Bertrando Spaventa, Antonio Labriola e l'hegelismo napoletano', *Società*, X (1954), pp. 406–30, 583–607, 764–91.

4 B. Croce, 'Antonio Labriola, Ricordi', *Marzocco* IX, (7) 14 February 1904, republished in A. Labriola, *Scritti vari editi e inediti di filosofia e politica, raccolti e pubblicabi da B. Croce* (Bari, 1906), p. 499.

5 A. Labriola, *Lettere a Engels* (Rome, 1949), (I), April 1890, p. 2.

6 B. Spaventa, *La Filosofia di Gioberti*, vol I (Napoli, 1863), pp. 92 ff.

7 B. Spaventa, *Esperienza e Metafisica* (Tornio, 1888), p. 138.

8 G. B. Vico, *La Scienza Nuova* (1744) ed. F. Nicolini, (Bari, 1974), para. 331.

9 B. Spaventa, *La Filosofia Italiana nelle sue Relazioni con la Filosofia Europea* in *Opere*, vol. III. ed. G. Gentile (Firenze, 1972), pp. 526–7, 528–30, 536–7.

10 S. Landucci, 'Il giovane Spaventa fra hegelismo e socialismo', *Annali dell'Istituto Feltrinelli*, I (1963), 647–707, and G. Berti, 'Bertrando Spaventa'.

11 A. Labriola, *La Dottrina di Socrate secondo Senofonte, Platone ed Aristotele* (1871), in *Opere*. vol. II, ed. L. Dal Pane (Milano, 1961), p. 139.

12 A. Labriola, *Della Libertà*, in *Opere*, vol. III, p. 42.

13 A. Labriola, *I Problemi della Filosofia della Storia in Scritti Filosofici e Politici*, vol. I (Torino, 1973), pp. 7–8, 15, 20–1.

14 Dal Pane, *Antonio Labriola*, chs IV–VI.

15 B. Croce, 'Ricordi', p. 500.

16 The opinion of Engels that 'Alles sehr gut', communicated to Croce in a letter of 8 July 1895, is partly reproduced in B. Croce, 'Come nacque e come morì il Marxismo teorico in Italia (1895–1900) – Da lettre e ricordi personali', in *Materialismo Storico e Economia Marxistica* 3rd edn economica (Bari, 1978), p. 260. Plekhanov reviewed the French edition of the *Essays* in *Novoie Slovo* (1897), n. 9. Lenin in a letter of 23 December 1897 (reproduced in *Rinascita X* (1954), p. 184) asked his sister Anna to translate them into Russian.

17 As he wrote in the preface of *Della Libertà Morale*, 'I make no vow to close myself up in a system as if in a kind of prison'. He repeated the remark in an attack on the positivist Marxism of De Bella in an open letter to Turati, published in *Critica Sociale* and reproduced in letter II of *Talking about Socialism and Philosophy*.

18 The standard edition of these works is Croce's edition of 1906, reissued with a long introduction by Eugenio Garin – A. Labriola, *La Concezione Materialistica della Storia* (Bari, 1965) – to which all references are made.

19 Loria's principle work was *Les Bases Economiques de la Constitution Sociale* (Paris, 1893), an enlarged French edition of an earlier (1886) Italian work. Enrico Ferri was a criminologist who linked crime to economic conditions and heredity. His best known book, *Socialismo e Scienza Positiva. Darwin – Spencer – Marx* (Rome, 1894), was bitterly attacked by Labriola, notably in an open letter to Turati of 5 June 1897, reprinted in *Discorrendo*, in *La Concezione* pp. 243–4. His worries about the contamination of Marxism by positivism and Darwinism is revealed in the following letter to Engels: 'Make sure, I pray you, that our good friends of Berlin don't make fools of themselves. *Vorwarts* (n. 217) praises to the heavens the entry into socialism of Professor Enrico Ferri, already a deputy for seven years, follower of the doctrine of Lombroso and a signal charleton like Loria.' *Lettere a Engels* (LXXII), 18 September, 1893, p. 123.

20 Labriola, *Lettere a Engels*, (IX), 30 March 1891, pp. 13–14. He regarded the praise of Loria as particularly indicative of this mental decay, adding 'You'll see . . . in the fifth issue of *Critica Sociale* – to which many [socialists] contribute, including my namesake [Arturo Labriola] – how Candelari substitutes Loria for Marx as the discoverer of that principle

[the materialist conception of history]'. Labriola is referring to R. Canderlari, 'Democrazia e socialismo' in *Critica Sociale*, 30 March 1891.

21 Labriola, *Del Materialismo Storico* in *La Concezione*, p. 78.

22 Ibid., p. 129.

23 Ibid., pp. 94–5.

24 'History is the work of man in so far as man can create and improve his instruments of labour, and with these instruments can create an artificial environment whose complicated effects react later upon himself and which by its present state and its successive modifications is the occasion and condition of his development. There are, then, no reasons for carrying back that work of man which is history to the simple struggle for existence.' Ibid. p. 76.

25 Ibid., pp. 78–87.

26 Labriola, *Discorrendo*, pp. 216–17.

27 Ibid., pp. 226–7.

28 Ibid., p. 204. The view of Engels as more 'determinist' and 'Darwinian' than Marx is not universally accepted, e.g. J. L. Stanley and E. Zimmerman, 'On the Alleged Differences between Marx and Engels', *Political Studies*, XXXII (1984), pp. 226–48, as against T. Carver, 'Marx, Engels and Dialectics', *Political Studies*, XXVIII (1980), pp. 353–63, and L. Kolakowski, *Main Currents*, I, pp. 399–408, which I largely follow. Labriola clearly wanted to distinguish Marxism from Darwinian and other strongly determinist accounts on the grounds, adduced by Kolakowski to Marx, 'that nature . . . is an extension of man, an organ of practical activity' (p. 401). Possibly his appeal to Engels suggests that the latter's 'naturalism' was more ambiguous or critical than commentators like Kolakowski and T. Carver, 'Marx, Engels and Scholarship', *Political Studies* XXXII, (1984), pp. 247–56, maintain.

29 Remarks to Croce in a letter of 17 May 1895, reproduced in B. Croce, 'Come nacque e come morì', p. 256.

30 Labriola, *Del Materialism Storico*, p. 70. The coherence of the Base/ superstructure distinction, classically criticized by J. Plamentaz, *Man and Society*, 2 vols (London, 1963), II, pp. 274–92, has recently received a powerful defence in G. A. Cohen, *Karl Marx's Theory of History: A Defence* (Oxford, 1978). For lingering doubts, which I share, see S. Lukes, 'Can the base be distinguished from the superstructure?', in D. Miller and L. Siedentop (eds), *The Nature of Political Theory* (Oxford, 1983), pp. 103–19. Lukes surprisingly argues that his negative conclusion does not affect the explanatory power of Marxism (pp. 119–20). I follow L. Kolakowski, *Main Currents*, I, pp. 335–46, in believing that it does.

31 Labriola, *Da un secolo all'altro*, in *La Concezione*, p. 345.

32 'Our doctrine does not pretend to be *the intellectual vision* of a grand plan or design, but is only a method of research and conception. Marx did not speak of his discovery as a *guiding thread* by chance', Labriola, *Del Materialismo Storico*, p. 85.

33 Ibid., pp. 115–17. This constitutes a problem within Marxism generally, see S. Lukes, 'Marxism, Morality and Justice', in *Marx and Marxisms*, ed. G. H. R. Parkinson (Cambridge, 1982), 195–265. I discuss its consequences for the theory and practice of the Italian Communist Party in the concluding chapter.

34 Labriola, *Discorrendo*, p. 256.

35 Ibid., p. 179.

36 Ibid., p. 286.

37 Ibid., p. 287.

38 G. D. H. Cole, *A History of Socialist Thought* (London, 1956), vol. III, part III. *The Second International 1889–1914*, pp. 709–43 is the best short account of Italian socialism in this period. Also useful for the ideological debates at this time is A. Asor Rosa, 'La Cultura', *Storia D'Italia* IV (ii) (Turin, 1975), pp. 1000–42.

39 'The expansionist movement of nations has its deep reasons in economic competition . . . Italy cannot remove itself from these developments of states which bring with them a development of peoples. If it did, and it could do it, in reality it would remove itself from the universal circulation of modern life; and remain *backward* in Europe'. A. Labriola, 'Il ritardo storico della borghesia italiana e le vie dell'espansione coloniale', interview published in *Giornale d'Italia*, 13 April 1902.

40 F. Turati, 'Dichiarazioni necessarie. Rivoluzionari od opportunisti?', *Critica Sociale*, XIV (1900), in M. Spinella et al. (eds), *La Critica Sociale*, collanda di periodici italiani e stranieri, 2 vols (Milano, 1959), I, p. 111.

41 Letter to Croce 9 October 1895, reproduced in 'Come nacque e come morì', p. 286. See also Ibid., pp. 270–1.

42 G. Sorel, Preface to A. Labriola, *Essais sur la Conception Materialiste de l'Historie* (Paris, 1897).

43 B. Croce, 'Sulla forma scientifica del materialismo storico.' (1896), in *Materialismo Storico*. p. 9.

44 Ibid.

45 B. Croce, Preface to K. Marx, *Rivoluzione e Controrivoluzione o il 1848 in Germania* (Roma 1899), in *Pagine Sparse*, series I, ed. G. Castellano, vol. I (Napoli, 1919), p. 315.

46 B. Croce, 'Sulla forma scientifica', in *Materialismo Storico*, p. 18.

47 B. Croce, 'Sul principio economica. Due Lettre al Prof. V. Pareto.' (1900), *Materialismo Storico*, pp. 209–30, and 'Il guidizio economico e il giudizio tecnico. Osservazioni a una memoria del Prof. Gobbi' (1901), *Materialismo Storico*, pp. 231–40. See especially pp. 219, 239.

48 B. Croce, 'Le teorie storiche del Prof. Loria.' (1896), *Materialismo Storico*, pp. 21–51.

49 B. Croce, 'Sulla forma scientifica.', p. 15.

50 G. Sorel, *Réflexions sur la Violence*, 2nd edn (Paris, 1910), p. 161.

51 B. Croce, 1899 preface to *Materialismo Storico*, p. xi.

52 B. Croce, 'Cristianesimo, Socialismo e Metodo Storica', review of G. Sorel *Le Système Historique de Renan* (1906), in *La Critica*, V (1907),

317–30. It was later used as a preface to the Italian edition of Sorel's *Reflexions on Violence* (1909).

53 Ibid.

54 Labriola, letter to Croce of 25 Dec 1896, in Croce 'Come nacque e come morì', p. 279.

55 A. Kulischioff, quoted in G. Arfe, *Storia del Socialismo Italiano (1892–1926)* (Turin, 1965), p. 83.

56 B. Croce, 'Per la interpretazione e la critica di alcuni concetti del Marxismo.' (1877), in *Del Materialismo Storico*, p. 104.

57 Letters to Croce of 8 October 1898 and 17 November 1989, in Croce, 'Come nacque e come morì', pp. 286–7.

58 Labriola was particularly dismayed to learn '. . . that Kautsky has refused to publish some articles in which Bernstein refers to your writings (Croce) and mine', letter to Croce of 17 November 1898, ibid.

59 Labriola, *Discorrendo*, p. 181.

60 Labriola, 'A Proposito della Crisi del Marxismo', review of Th. G. Masaryk, *Die Philosophischen und Sociologischen Grundlagen den Marxismus – Studien ur Socialen Frage* (Wien, 1899), in *Rivista Italiana di Sociologia*, III (1899), reproduced in *La Concezione*, p. 171.

## 5 Benedetto Croce

1 P. Gardiner, *The Nature of Historical Explanation* (Oxford, 1961), p. 46. This is how his ideas are usually interpreted by analytical philosophers, e.g. M. Mandelbaum, *The Problem of Historical Knowledge* (New York, 1938), whose criticism of Croce's philosophy was reviewed with some amusement by Croce himself in B. Croce, *La Critica*, XXXVII, (1939), p. 313. An attempt at greater mutual understanding can be found in W. H. Walsh, *An Introduction to Philosophy of History* (London, 1951), and Croce's review in *Quaderni della Critica*, VI (1951), pp. 193–4. I am grateful to the late Professor Walsh for his comments on an earlier version. The fullest accounts in English are by R. G. Collingwood, *The Idea of History* (Oxford, 1978), pp. 190–204, H. Stuart Hughes, *Consciousness and Society* (Brighton, 1979), pp. 200–29, and H. White, *Metahistory* (Baltimore/London, 1983), pp. 375–425. My own analysis is influenced by three classic Italian studies – F. Chabod, 'Croce Storico', *Rivista Storica Italiana*, LXIV (1952), pp. 473–530; Pietro Rossi, 'Benedetto Croce e lo Storicismo Assoluto', *Il Mulino* VI, (1957), pp. 322–54; and G. Galasso, 'Croce Storico', *Croce, Gramsci e altri Storici*, 2nd edn (Milano, 1978) – and the approach urged by G. Sasso in 'Per un 'interpretazione di Croce', *Passato e Presente nella Storia della Filosofia*, (Bari, 1967), pp. 69–151, especially p. 133.

2 I examine Croce's politics and its relation to his philosophy of history in greater detail in 'Liberalism and historicism, Benedetto Croce and the political role of Idealism in Italy c. 1890–1950', A. Moulakis (ed.), *The Promise of History* (Berlin/New York, 1985), pp. 69–119.

3 See H. Stuart Hughes, *Consciousness and Society*; C. Antoni, *Dallo*

*Storicismo alla Sociologia* (Florence, 1940), and Croce's review in *La Critica*, XXXVIII, (1940), pp. 302–3 for a discussion of those links.

4 B. Croce, *Contributo alla Critica di Me Stesso* (1915), in *Etica e Politica* 2nd edn economica (Bari, 1973), pp. 322–3, and E. Garin, 'Appunti sulla formazione e su alcuni caratteri del pensiero Crociano', *Intellettuali Italiani del XXe Secolo* (Roma, 1974), pp. 3–31.

5 For bibliographical and further details of this debate, dating it from 1883 rather than Windelband's 1894 rectoral address as is usual, see M. Ermarth, *Wilhelm Dilthey: The Critique of Historical Reason* (Chicago, 1978), pp. 186–97.

6 Croce, 'La storia ridotta sotto il concetto generale dell'arte (1893), reprinted in *Primi Saggi*, 2nd. edn (Bari, 1927), pp. 23, 36, 39.

7 Croce, *La Critica Letteraria* (Roma, 1894), pp. 118–19, 71.

8 Croce, 'Intorno alla filosofia della storia' (1894), *Primi Saggi*, pp. 67–8.

9 Croce, 'Sulla forma scientifica del materialismo storico' (1896), a review of A. Labriola *Del Materialismo Storico, dilucidazione preliminare* (Roma, 1896), reprinted in *Materialismo Storico ed Economia, Marxista*, 3rd edn, economica (Bari, 1978), p. 9.

10 Croce, *Estetica come scienza e linguistica generale*, (Milano/Palermo/Napoli, 1902), pp. 3, 11, 51, 63.

11 Ibid., pp. 131–3.

12 G. Prezzolini, 'L'Uomo-Dio' *Leonardo*, I (1903), pp. 3–4. See also Prezzolini, 'La Critica', *Leonardo*, I (1906), p. 362. On this period of Croce's career see E. E. Jacobitti, *Revolutionary Humanism in Modern Italy* (New Haven/London 1981), and R. Bellamy, 'Liberalism and historicism', pp. 72–4.

13 Croce admitted this later in his *Storia D'Italia dal 1871–1915*, 3rd edn economica (Bari, 1977), pp. 232–3, and this thesis is sustained by E. E. Jacobitti, *Revolutionary Humanism*, and E. Garin, *Cronache di Filosofia Italiana 1900–43*, 2nd edn, 2 vols (Bari, 1966), I, p. 226.

14 Croce, 'Leonardo, riviste di idee a.I ott. – dic 1906', *La Critica*, V (1907), pp. 67–9.

15 See the debate between Croce and Papini in 'La *Logica* di Benedetto Croce', *Leonardo*, III (1905), pp. 170–80.

16 Croce formally recognized his debt many times, first in the 'Postilla' to the second edition (1909) of his *Logica come Scienza del Concetto Puro*, 2nd edn economica (Bari, 1971), pp. 194–5, and in his *Contributo alla Critica di Me Stesso*, p. 349. This can now be documented in their correspondence examined below and in G. Sasso, *Benedetto Croce: La Ricerca della Dialettica* (Napoli, 1975), pp. 897–906, and in chapter 1 of my unpublished PhD, 'Liberalism and Historicism – History and Politics in the Thought of Benedetto Croce' (Cambridge, 1983).

17 E.g. Croce's letter to Gentile in A. Croce (ed.), *Lettere a Giovanni Gentile 1896–1924* (Milano, 1981), 287, 24 November 1906, and Gentile's letter to Croce in S. Giannantori (ed.), *Lettere a Benedetto Croce* (Firenze, 1974), II (361), 23 November 1906.

18 Croce's letter quoted in E. Garin, 'Appunti sulla formazione e su alcuni

caratteri del pensiero crociano.', p. 6. I have examined Croce's book on Hegel in, 'What is Living and What is Dead in Croce's Interpretation of Hegel'. *The Bulletin of the Hegel Society of Great Britain,* IX (1984), pp. 5–14.

19 Croce *Ciò Che è Vivo e Ciò Che è Morto nella Filosofia di Hegel* (1906), in *Saggio su Hegel,* 4th edn (Bari, 1948), pp. 128, 62–6, 90–1, 48.

20 Gentile's review of *Die Philosophie im Beginn des Zwanzigsten Jahrhunderts,* Festschrift für Kuno Fischer hgb. von W. Windelband, was eventually published in *La Critica,* V (1907), pp. 146–51.

21 Croce, *Lettere a Gentile* (289), 14 December, 1906.

22 Croce, review of F. Masci, *Filosofia, Scienza, Storia della Filosofia* (Napoli, 1902), *La Critica,* I (1903) pp. 68–71.

23 Croce, *Lettere a Gentile,* (291), 18 December 1906.

24 G. Gentile, *Lettere a Benedetto Croce,* (371), 29 December 1906.

25 Croce, *Lettere a Gentile,* (294), 31 December 1906, (295), 5 January 1907.

26 As Croce put it in his last friendly judgement on Gentile's mature system, whilst he sought 'il mondo in Dio', Gentile pursued 'Dio nel mondo', Croce, review of G. Gentile, *Sistema di Logica come Teoria del Conoscere,* in *La Critica,* XXII (1924), p. 52.

27 Croce, *Logica,* pp. 121–31, 84–93.

28 Croce, *Teoria e Storia della Storiografia* (1915), 2nd edn (Bari, 1920), pp. 3–17.

29 Ibid., pp. 87–93.

30 Croce, 'L'individuo e l'opera' (1925), in *Etica e Politica,* 2nd edn economica (Bari, 1973), p. 99.

31 Croce, *La Filosofia della Pratica: economia ed etica,* (1909), 2nd edn (Bari, 1915), pp. 174–5.

32 Compare Croce's *La Pratica,* pp. 167–77; *La Filosofia di G. B. Vico* (Bari, 1911), chapter X, 'La Provvidenza'; and 'Il concetto del divenire e l'hegelismo', *La Critica,* X (1912). pp. 294–310.

33 Croce, *La Pratica,* p. 165.

34 Ibid., p. 175.

35 'La moralità della dottrina dello Stato come potenza', *La Critica,* XIV (1916), pp. 158–9.

36 I develop this argument further in 'Croce, Gentile and Hegel and the doctrine of the ethical State', *Rivista di Studi Crociani,* XX (1983), pp. 263–81.

37 Croce, *The Idea of History,* pp. 213–17, 199, where he cites *Teoria,* pp. 118–19.

38 Croce, *Teoria,* chapter I. Croce's view (or possibly lack of a view) of historical objectivity can be found in his review of Mandelbaum's *The Problem of Historical Knowledge:*

> One comment (on p. 56) had me laughing heartily in which the author, recalling that I rejected the assertion of a Nazi writer who offered a photograph of Melos' Venus as the 'portrait of a German

lady' remarks, sarcastically, that if my 'need' which leads me to deny such a thing, is 'more profound and more effective than that of the Nazi writer, is a point which only the Absolute, and not Signor Croce, can answer', in which the comic figure is not me, but the Absolute, understood as some Signor Absolute, outside or above us. It would be vain to remind Signor Mandelbaum that in the Absolute, as in God, 'vivimus et movemur et summus'. (*La Critica*, XXXVII, (1939) p. 313)

According to Croce both interpretations belong to spirit's development and in the cosmic sense are therefore equally valid. Compare this with the idealist interpretation of historical explanation of M. Oakshott – *Experience and its Modes* (Cambridge, 1978), pp. 86–167, and 'The Activity of being an Historian', in *Rationalism in Politics* (London, 1962), pp. 137–67 – which distinguishes historians' history from a view of the past related to present needs.

39  R. G. Collingwood, 'Croce's Philosophy of History', *Hibbert Journal*, XIX (1921), pp. 263–78. Collingwood's own views presuppose a wider metaphysical context than is often realized, which at the time of his famous essay 'Human nature and history' (1936) was very close to Gentile's actualism. This led him into difficulties analogous to Gentile's, often passed over by commentators from the analytical school. For a corrective see L. Strauss, 'On Collingwood's Philosophy of History', *The Review of Metaphysics*, V (1951), pp. 559–86. For Croce's view of Collingwood, see 'In commemorazione di un amico inglese, compagno di pensiero e di fede', *Quaderni della Critica*, II (1946), pp. 60–73.

40  The debate consisted of three articles, two by Croce and one by Gentile, in *La Voce* of 1913, reprinted in A. Romano (ed.), *La Voce, 1908–1914* (Torino, 1960), pp. 595–605, 630–8, and 608–25 respectively.

41  Croce, *Teoria*, p. 153.

42  Ibid., p. 133.

43  Ibid.

44  The contemporary relevance of these questions is brought out in a recent collection of essays – *Philosophy in History*, (eds) R. Rorty, J. B. Schneewind and Q. Skinner, (Cambridge, 1984). My own analysis is indebted to the editors' introduction and the chapters by C. Taylor, A. MacIntyre, Q. Skinner and L. Kruger, asd well as much of the previous work of the first three authors on the philosophy of the social sciences.

45  Croce, *Contributo alla Critica di Me Stesso*, pp. 349–50.

46  Croce, 'Il risveglio filosofico e la cultura italiana' (1908), *Cultura e Vita Morale*, 3rd edn (Bari, 1955), pp. 10–11.

47  For the historical background to this change see R. Bellamy, 'Liberalism and Historicism', pp. 85–92. Croce's changing view of fascism can be seen in the four following newspaper articles, *Giornale D'Italia*, XXIII, (256), 27 October 1923; *Corriere Italiano*, III (28), 1 February 1924:

*Giornale D'Italia*, XXV, (164), 9 July 1924, Ibid., XXVI (103), 1 May 1925.

48  Croce, 'Il nuovo concetto della vita', *La Critica* XIV (1916), p. 324.
49  Croce, 'Storia economico – politica e storia etica-politica', *La Critica*, XXII (1924), pp. 334–41.
50  Croce, *Lectures on the Philosophy of World History: Introduction*, trans. H. B. Nisbet (Cambridge, 1975), p. 71.
51  The development of Croce's 'metapolitical' conception of liberalism can be seen in the following articles: 'Liberalismo', *La Critica*, XXIII, (1925), 125–8; 'La concezione liberale come concezione di vita', ibid. (1927), *Etica e Politica*, pp. 235–43; 'Liberismo e liberalismo', ibid., pp. 263–8.
52  Croce, 'La Protesta Contro il "Manifesto degli intellettuali fascistici" ', *La Critica*, XXIII (1925), pp. 310–12.
53  Croce, *La Storia come Pensiero e come Azione*, 4th edn, economica (Bari, 1978), pp. 33–4.
54  G. Gentile, 'La distinzione crociano di pensiero e azione', *Giornale Critico della Filosofia Italiana*, XXII (1941), pp. 274–8; A. Gramsci, *Il Materialismo Storico e la Filosofia di Benedetto Croce* (Turin, 1948), pp. 172–7. This criticism is shared by most commentators on Croce, even those sympathetic to much of his philosophy, e.g. the studies of G. De Ruggiero, C. Antoni, E. Garin and N. Bobbio, to name the most prominent and influential. However, as will be shown below. The distriction between theory and action is the saving grace of Croce's philosophy which ultimately prevented its degeneration into mere ideology.
55  Croce, *Storia del Regno di Napoli* (Bari, 1925), pp. 167, 174–5, 176, 204, 218, 240–1, 254–75.
56  Croce, *Storia dell' Età Barocca in Italia* (Bari, 1929), pp. (Bari, 1929), pp. 6–7, 10–11, 41–3, Croce later explicitly developed this thesis in 'La Crisi Italiana del' 500 e il Legame del Rinascimento col Risorgimento', *La Critica*, XXVII (1939), pp. 401–11. It was a historical tradition which both right and left sought to appropriate. See S. Woolf, 'Risorgimento e Fascismo, *Belfagor*, XX (1965), pp. 71–91 and A. Garosci, 'Primo e Secondo Risorgimento', *Rivista Storica Italiana*, LXXIV (1963), pp. 27–40.
57  Croce, 'Storia economico-politica e storia etico-politca'. *La Critica*, XXII (1924) pp. 338–9.
58  Croce's review of G. Mosca, *Elementi di Scienza Politica*, 2nd edn (Tornio, 1923), *La Critica*, XXI (1923), pp. 374–8.
59  A. Gramsci, *Il Materialismo storico e la Filosofia chi Benedetto Croce*, pp. 229–33.
60  This thesis is even more prominent in a preliminary study for his histories, 'Contrasti d'Ideali Politici in Europa dopo il 1870', *Etica e Politica*, pp. 251–63.
61  Croce, *Storia d'Italia*, pp. 8, 227–8.
62  Ibid., p. 238.

63 Ibid., p. 267.
64 Ibid., pp. 8–9, 239–40, and 'Principio, ideale, teoria della libertà (1939), *Elementi di Politica*, 8th edn (Bari, 1974), pp. 107–25.
65 Croce clearly had his idealized picture of Giolitti in mind in the following passage:

> Concrete liberal institutions are created from time to time by political genius inspired by liberty or (what is the same thing) liberal genius furnished with political prudence. To keep this genius alive in a people is the supreme duty, but it cannot be expected that the majority can cultivate it consciously, since it requires depth of feeling and power of intellectual synthesis only found in the ranks of the elect, of the legions devoted to the ideal.
> ('Principio, ideale, teoria della libertà', p. 125)

66 Croce, 'Fede e Programmi', *La Critica*, IX (1911), pp. 390–6.
67 The continuity in Croce's view of democracy is evident from his following articles: 'È necessario una democrazia?', *Unità*, I (7), 27 January (1912), p. 26; 'Principio, ideale, teoria della libertà', pp. 124–5; 'Intorno al Tocqueville', *La Critica*, XLI (1943), pp. 54–6; 'Revisione filosofica dei concetti di "Libertà" e 'Giustizia" ', *La Critica*, XLI (1943), pp. 276–84.
68 G. De Ruggiero, review of *Storia d'Italia*, in *Rivista Storica Italiana*, XLVI (1929), p. 312. I examine De Ruggiero's attempt to devise a liberal theory on actualist principles in a forthcoming article in the *Historical Journal*.
69 P. Rossi, 'Benedetto Croce e lo storicismo' p. 348, a view shared by F. Chabod and G. Galasso.
70 Croce, *Storia d'Europa nel Secolo Decimonono*, 4th edn economica (Bari, 1981), pp. 304–6.
71 Croce, 'Sulla situazione politica', *Giornale d'Italia*, XXIII (256), 27 October 1923.
72 Croce, *Storia d'Europa*, p. 316.
73 Ibid., p. 316.
74 *La Storia Come Pensiero*, p. 238.
75 Ibid., p. 151.
76 I am indebted to S. S. Wolin, 'Max Weber: Legitimation, Method and the Politics or Theory', *Political Theory*, IX (1981), pp. 401–24, for this interpretation of Weber.
77 For Croce's substantial agreement with Weber on this point see his review of the Italian translation of Weber's 'Science as a vocation' in *Quaderni della Critica*, IV (1948), pp. 93–5. Croce had drawn attention to the relevance of Weber's *Protestant Ethic and the Spirit of Capitalism* for the understanding of modern liberalism in a review of E. Troeltsch, *Der Historismus und Seine Uberwindung*, *La Critica* XXV (1927), p. 115, and develops it himself in his *Storia d'Europa*, pp. 11, 23.
78 Croce, 'La grazia e il libero arbitrio', *Ultimi Saggi*, 2nd edn (Bari, 1948), p. 301.

79 Croce, 'Una Pagina Sconosciuta degli Ultimi Mesi della Vita di Hegel', *Indagini sul Hegel e Schiarimenti Filosofici* (Bari, 1952), pp. 10–11.

80 Particularly important are Croce's articles 'La fine della civiltà', *Quaderni della Critica*, II (1946). pp. 1–7: 'L'Anticristo che è in noi', *Quaderni della Critica*, III (1947), pp. 66–70; 'Intorno al "Magismo" come età storica', *Quaderni della Critica*, IV (1948), pp. 53–63; and his review of E. de Martino, *Il Mondo Magico – Prolegomeni a una Storia del Magismo* (Turin, 1948), *Critica*, pp. 79–80 (both examined below) and the essays collected in B. Croce, *Storiografia e Idealità Morale* (Bari, 1950). This is the thesis of N. Abbagnano, 'L'Ultimo Croce e il Soggetto della Storia', *Rivista di Filosofia*, XLV (1953), pp. 300–13, whose argument is largely followed below.

81 These remarks draw on the criticisms of P. Winch, *The Idea of a Social Science* (London, 1958) and his 'Understanding a Primitive Society', *American Philosophical Quarterly*, I (1964), pp. 307–24; by A. MacIntyre, 'The Idea of a Social Science', *Against the Self-Images of the Age* (London, 1971), pp. 211–29; M. Hollis, 'Reason and Ritual', *Philosophy*, XLIII (1967) pp. 231–47; and Q. Skinner, ' "Social Meaning" and the Explanation of Social Action', *Philosophy, Politics and Society*, fourth series, (eds) P. Laslett. W. G. Runciman, and Q. Skinner (Oxford, 1972), pp. 136–57.

## 6 Giovanni Gentile

1 G. Gentile, 'Intorno all'Idealismo Attuale. Ricordi e confessioni' (1913), reprinted in *Saggi Critici*, seria seconda (Florence, 1927), p. 12.

2 Gentile, 'Il Metodo dell'Immanenza' (1912), *La Riforma della Dialettica Hegeliana* (Florence, 1975), pp. 221–5.

3 G. Hegel, *Lectures on the Philosophy of World History Introduction: Reason in History*, trans. H. B. Nisbet (Cambridge, 1975), pp. 52–3. See also Hegel, *Phenomenology of Spirit*, trans. A. V. Millar (Oxford, 1979), paras 5, 90, 785, 800, 808. I owe this interpretation of Hegel's relationship to Kant to R. C. Solomon, 'Hegel's Epistemology', *American Philosophical Quarterly*, XI (1974), pp. 277–89.

4 Gentile, 'Origine e Significato della Logica di Hegel' (1904), *La Riforma*, pp. 69–96; 'Il Metodo dell'Immanenza', ibid., pp. 225–9.

5 Gentile 'La Riforma della Dialettica Hegeliana e Bertrando Spaventa' (1912), *La Riforma*, pp. 27–65; B. Spaventa, *La Filosofia Italiana nelle sue Relazioni con la Filosofia Europea con note e appendici di documenti*, ed. G. Gentile, 3rd edn (Bari 1926) pp. 28–9, 122 ff, 130 ff, 203, and the comments of I. Cubeddù, *Bertrando Spaventa* (Firenze, 1964), pp. 51–4.

6 Gentile, 'Il Metodo dell'Immanenza', p. 232.

7 Gentile, *Teoria Generale dello Spirito Come Atto Puro* (1915), 3rd edn (Bari, 1920), p. 16.

8 B. Spaventa, *La Filosofia Italiana*, pp. 233–4.

9 Gentile's principal works on the philosophy of education are: *Sommario*

*di Pedagogia come Scienza Filosofica*, 2 vols (Bari, 1913–4); and *La Riforma dell'Educazione: Discorsi ai Maestri di Trieste* (Bari, 1920). In addition there are three volumes of various *Scritti Pedagogici* which make up vols XXXIX–XLI of the complete works.

10 Gentile, 'La Filosofia della Prassi' (1899), in *La Filosofia di Marx* (Florence, 1974), pp. 72–4, 82.

11 Gentile, 'Una Critica del Materialismo Storica' (1899), in *La Filosofia di Marx* p. 55. See the analysis of E. Garin, largely followed here, in *Cronache di Filosofia Italiana*, 2nd edn (Bari, 1975), vol. I, pp. 213–15.

12 Gentile, *Teoria Generale*, pp. 81–4, 91–2.

13 Gentile, *I Fondamenti della Filosofia dell Diritto* (1916), 2nd edn (Rome, 1923), p. 8.

14 Ibid., pp. 63–4.

15 Ibid., pp. 64–7, 69.

16 Gentile, *La Riforma Dell'Educazione*, pp. 24–6.

17 *Phenomenology of Spirit*, paras, 582–95.

18 B. Croce, 'Intorno all'Idealismo Attuale' (1913), *Conversazione Critiche*, serie seconda (Bari, 1924), pp. 72–3, 75–6. A remarkably similar criticism is made by H. Marcuse, *Reason and Revolution: Hegel and the Rise of Social Theory*, 2nd edn (London, 1954), pp. 402–9.

19 Gentile, 'La Colpa Commune', *Resto del Carlino*, 25 January 1918, reprinted in Gentile, *Guerra e Fede: Frammenti Politici* (Naples, 1919), pp. 79–83.

20 Gentile, 'L'Invincibile', *Resto del Carlino*, 3 July 1918, reprinted in *Guerra e Fede*, pp. 315–8.

21 The idealist/realist distinction forms the basis of Gentile's book *La Riforma dell'Educazione*, especially chapter IV, and even there it is related to the problems of a national revival, set chapter I. He condemns Nitti and the liberals as 'realists' in an article 'Realismo e Fatalismo' of 1920, reprinted in *Che Cosa è il Fascismo* (Florence, 1925), pp. 243–58, and it became a standard feature of his later anti-liberal polemics, e.g. *Origini e Dottrina del Fascismo*, 3rd edn (Rome, 1934), pp. 10, 15–20.

22 Gentile, *La Riforma dell'Educazione*, pp. 181–6.

23 H. S. Harris, *The Social Philosophy of Giovanni Gentile* (Urbana, 1960), pp. 155–67.

24 Gentile, *La Riforma Dell'Educazione*, pp. 1–16.

25 Ibid., pp. 32–47, 58–9, and Gentile, *Sommario di Pedagogia*, vol. II, pp. 37–44.

26 Letter to Mussolini, reprinted in Gentile, *Scritti Pedagogici*, III (Milan, 1932), pp. 127–8.

27 Gentile, 'Il Fascismo e la Sicilia', speech at Palermo, 31 March 1924, reprinted in *Che Cosa è il Fascismo*, p. 50.

28 Ibid., pp. 50–1. See also his article 'Il Contenuto Etico del Fascismo' (1925), in *Che Cosa è il Fascismo*, pp. 9–39, especially p. 36.

29 E.g. Gentile, *I Profeti del Risorgimento Italiano* (Florence, 1923) p. ii; and 'Risorgimento e Fascismo', in *Memorie Italiane e Problemi della Filosofia e della Vita* (Florence, 1936), pp. 116–17. These volumes as a

whole provide the most complete account of Gentile's version of the Risorgimento.

30 Gentile's preface to C. Cavour, *Scritti Politici Nuovamente Raccolti* (Rome, 1925), reprinted in *Che Cosa è il Fascismo*, pp. 179–96. This was deeply resented by liberals, e.g. G. De Ruggiero's review 'Nuova Letteratura Cavouriana', *Pagine Critiche*, 1 August 1926, reprinted in *Scritti Politici 1912–26*, ed. R. De Felici (Bologna, 1969), pp. 658–67; and B. Croce's comments in 'Contro la Troppa Filosofia Politica', *La Critica*, XXI (1925), pp. 126–8. Croce's remarks drew Gentile's reply that, whether he knew it or not, he was a 'Fascist without the black shirt' ('Il liberalismo di B. Croce' (1925), *Che Cosa è il Fascismo*, p. 154), a remark which ended their friendship for ever. The dialogue between them nevertheless continued, and as H. S. Harris points out, Croce is at the foreground of Gentile's later works as well, *Social Philosophy of Giovanni Gentile*, pp. 19–22, 221–3, 224–39.

31 Gentile, *Che Cosa è il Fascismo*, pp. 29–33, 41–63, 65–94; Gentile, *Origini e Dottrina del Fascismo*, pp. 50–1.

32 Gentile, *Philosophy of Right*, paras 189, 260, 301, 302. See the commentary of C. Taylor, *Hegel* (Cambridge, 1975), pp. 438–49; and R. Plant, *Hegel – an introduction* 2nd edn (Oxford, 1983), chapter 7, and R. Bellamy, 'Hegel's Conception of the State; *Political Science*, forthcoming.

33 This was the substance of Croce's ciriticism in 'Politica in "Nuce" ', *La Critica*, XXII, (1924), pp. 129–54, especially pp. 132–8.

34 *Origini e Dottrina del Fascismo*, pp. 36–7. Both Gentile and Gramsci were 'totalitarian' in a philosophical sense as implying a 'total' conception of human activity. Neither successfully removed its current pejorative connotations.

35 Gentile, *Genesi e Struttura Della Società* (Firenze, 1943), Avvertenza.

36 Ibid.

37 Ibid., pp. 13–14.

38 Ibid., p. 15.

39 Ibid., p. 33.

40 Ibid., p. 35–9.

41 Ibid., p. 37.

42 Ibid., pp. 39–40.

43 Ibid., p. 42.

44 This point is made by G. R. G. Mure in his review of the book in *Philosophical Quarterly*, I (1950), pp. 83–4. My own account is indebted to Mure's masterly analysis. I have dwelt on the problems and the alternatives to Gentile's views in R. Bellamy, 'Croce, Gentile and Hegel and the doctrine of the Ethical State', *Rivista di Studi Crociani*, XXI (1984), pp. 67–73.

45 I owe this conception of the idealist approach to politics to G. R. G. Mure's classic article, 'The Organic State', *Philosophy*, XXI (1949), pp. 205–18.

46 V. Arangio-Ruiz, 'L'Individuo e lo Stato', *Giornale Critico della Filosofia Italiana*, VII (1926), pp. 132–50.

47 Gentile, 'Postilla' to 'L'Individuo e lo Stato, *Giornale Critico*, VII (1926), p. 152.
48 Gentile, *Genesi e Struttura*, pp. 71–87, 111–12.
49 Ibid., pp. 61–6, 114.
50 Ibid., pp. 106–11.
51 Ibid., p. 40.
52 Gentile, 'L'Istituto Nazionale Fascista di Cultura' (1925), reprinted in *Fascismo e Cultura*, (Milan, 1928), p. 62.
53 Gentile, *'L'Enciclopedia Italiana* e il fascismo' (1926), *Fascismo e Cultura*, pp. 110–15. G. Turi, 'Il Progetto dell'*Enciclopedia Italiana*: l'Organizzazione del consenso fra gli intellettuali', *Studi Storici* (1972), pp. 93–152, shows him to have been largely true to his word, asking for contributions from the best qualified, regardless of their political sympathies.
54 Gentile, 'L'Immanenza d'azione', (1942), reprinted as an appendix to *Genesi e Struttura*, p. 173.
55 Gentile, *Dottrina Politica del Fascismo* (Padua, 1937) p. 19.

## 7 Antonio Gramsci

1 A. Gramsci *Lettere dal Carcere*, new edn by S. Caprioglio and E. Fubini, (Turin, 1965), (21), 19 March 1927, pp. 58–9.
2 G. Tamburrano, *Antonio Gramsci* (Lacaita, 1963); G. Fiori, *Vita di Gramsci* (Bari, 1966); J. M. Cammett, *Antonio Gramsci and the Origins of Italian Communism* (Stanford, 1967); A. Davidson, *Antonio Gramsci: Towards an Intellectual Biography* (Merlin: London, 1977).
3 Gramsci, *Il Grido del Popolo*, 29 January 1916, *Scritti Giovanili (1914–18)*, in *Opere*, vol. VIII (Turin, 1958), pp. 22–6.
4 Gramsci, *Avanti!*, 24 November 1917; Gramsci, *Il Grido*, 5 January, 1918, *Scritti Giovanili*, pp. 149–53.
5 Gramsci, 'Un Anno di Storia', *Il Grido*, 16 March 1918, *Scritti Giovanili*, p. 197.
6 Gramsci, 'Misteri della Cultura e della Poesia', *Il Grido*, 19 October 1918, *Scritti Giovanili*, p. 327.
7 Gramsci, 'La Rivoluzione contro il *Capitale*', p. 150.
8 Gramsci, *Quaderni del Carcere*, Edizione critica dell' Istituto Gramsci, ed. Valentino Gerratana, 4 vols (Turin, 1975), II, p. 1395 (*Il Materialismo Storico e la Filosofia di Benedetto Croce (M.S.)*, in *Opere* vol. II (Turin, 1949), p. 20) and A. Davidson, *Antonio Gramsci*, pp. 87–9. N.B. Since the new critical edition of the *Notebooks*, containing all of Gramsci's notes in the order he wrote them and with full scholarly apparatus, is still less widely known than the original Einaudi edition of 1947–51, I shall give references to the latter, where possible, as well.
9 E.g. Gramsci, letter to *Il Grido*, 31 October 1914, in G. Ferrata and N. Gallo (eds), *2000 pagine di Gramsci*, 2 vols (Milan, 1964), I, pp. 179–80 and A. Romano, 'Antonio Gramsci tra Guerra e Rivoluzione', *Rivista Storica del Socialismo*, I (1985), p. 413.

10 Gramsci, 'Il Socialismo e la Filosofia Attuale', *Il Grido*, 19 January 1918, cited in L. Paggi, *Antonio Gramsci e il Moderno Principe* (Rome, 1970), p. 21; and Gramsci, 'L'Uomo Più Libero' *Avanti!* 25 May 1917; *Sotto La Mole (1916–18)*, *Opere* vol. X (Turin, 1960), pp. 315–16.

11 Gramsci, 'Rassegna di Questioni Politiche', *Energie Nova*, 25 July 1919; P. Spriano (ed.), *Scritti Politici*, *Opere* vol. 1 (Turin, 1960), p. 151.

12 Gramsci, 'La Politica del "Se" ', *Il Grido*, 29 June 1918; *Scritti Giovanili*, p. 271; see also Gramsci, 'Il Nostro Marx', *Il Grido*, 4 May 1918, Ibid. pp. 217–21.

13 Gramsci, 'La Conquista dello Stato', *L'Ordine Nuovo*, 12 July 1919, in *L'Ordine Nuovo (1919–20)*, *Opere* vol. IX (Turin, 1954), p. 16.

14 For a full account of these events and their implications for Gramsci's Marxist theory see P. Spriano *L'Occupazione delle Fabbriche* (Turin, 1964); G. Williams, *Proletarian Order: Antonio Gramsci, Factory Councils and the Origins of Italian Communism 1911–21* (London, 1975); M. Clark, *Antonio Gramsci and the Revolution that Failed* (New Haven and London, 1977).

15 Gramsci, 'Sindacati e Consigli', *L'Ordine Nuovo*, 11 October 1919, *Ordine Nuovo*, p. 37.

16 Gramsci, 'L'Organizzazione, Base del Partito,' *La Construzione del Partito Communista, (1923–6)*, *Opere* vol. XII (Turin, 1972), pp. 272–6.

17 Davidson, *Antonio Gramsci*, pp. 239–42.

18 Fiori, *Vita di Gramsci*, pp. 291–3; A. Leonetti, *Note su Gramsci* (Urbino, 1971), pp. 191–209.

19 Gramsci, *Quaderni*, II, pp. 1415–16, (*M.S.*, pp. 141–2).

20 Ibid., p. 1345, (*M.S.*, p. 28).

21 Ibid., III, p. 1926, (*M.S.*, p. 156).

22 Ibid., II, pp. 1428–30 (*M.S.*, pp. 126–7).

23 Ibid., p. 1416, (*M.S.*, pp. 142–3).

24 Ibid., pp. 1485–6, 884–5 (*M.S.*, pp. 25–7, 32).

25 Ibid., p. 1330 (*M.S.*, p. 21).

26 Ibid., pp. 1241, 1402–3 (*M.S.*, pp. 217, 134).

27 The 'Theses on Feuerbach' were important in Gramsci's early Marxism, as in the following passage, replete with Gentilian language, calling for a return to 'the genuine doctrine of Marx . . . for whom man and reality, the instrument of labour and will, are not distinct, but identified in the *historical act.*', 'La Critica Critica' *Il Grido del Popolo*, 12 January 1918, *Scritti Giovanili*, p. 154).

28 Labriola had been praised by Gramsci in an early article in *Avanti!* 29 January 1918 'Achille Loria e il Socialismo', *Scritti Giovanili*, pp. 162–3. In the *Notebooks* he is called 'the only man who has attempted to construct the philosophy of praxis scientifically.' *Quaderni*, II, pp. 1507–8 (*M.S.*, p. 79).

29 Ibid., p. 1485 (*M.S.*, p. 22).

30 Ibid., pp. 1415–6 (*M.S.*, p. 142).

31 Ibid.

32 E.g. G. Tamburrano, *Antonio Gramsci*, p. 212; Norberto Bobbio,

'Gramsci e la concezione della società civile', *Gramsci e la Cultura Contemporanea*, 2 vols (Rome, 1969) I, p. 90. Gramsci's idealism is put in perspective by J. Femia, *Gramsci's Political Thought* (Oxford, 1981), chapter 3, to whose work I am indebted.

33  Gramsci, *Quaderni*, II, p. 1419 (*M.S.*, p. 144).

34  Ibid., p. 1492 (*M.S.*, p. 44).

35  Ibid., p. 1319 (*M.S.*, pp. 236–7).

36  Gramsci, *Quaderni*, III, p. 1612; *Note sul Machiavelli, sulla Politica, e sullo Stato Moderno (Mach.)*, in *Opere*, vol. V (Turin, 1949), p. 36.

37  Gramsci, *Quaderni*, II, p. 1437 (*M.S.*, p. 159).

38  Ibid., II, p. 1422 (*M.S.*, pp. 129–30), and III, p. 1579, (*Mach*, p. 41). Compare with K. Marx, 'Preface' to *A Contribution to the Critique of Political Economy*, in *Early Texts*, trans. R. Livingstone and G. Benton (Harmondsworth, 1975), p. 426.

39  Gramsci, *Quaderni*, II, pp. 1249, 1492 (*M.S.*, pp. 39–44) and I., p. 455.

40  Ibid., II, pp. 1507–8, 1487 (*M.S.*, pp. 79–80, 93).

41  Ibid., III, pp. 1518–9, (*Gli Intellettualli e L'Organizzazione della Cultura (Int.)*, in *Opere* vol. III (Turin, 1949), p. 9).

42  Gramsci, *Quaderni*, II, p. 871 (*M.S.*, p. 96).

43  Ibid., I, p. 436–7, II, p. 1319 (*M.S.*, pp. 236–7).

44  Ibid., II, ibid., p. 1338 (*M.S.*, p. 35).

45  Ibid., II, p. 869 (*M.S.*, p. 48).

46  Ibid., III, p. 1612 (*Mach.*, p. 37).

47  C. Mouffe, 'Hegemony and Ideology in Gramsci' in C. Mouffe (ed.), *Gramsci and Marxist Theory* (London, 1979), pp. 168–204 is invaluable for this topic, although less critical than the present author. My own interpretation draws inspiration from the discussion of ideology in R. Geuss, *The Idea of a Critical Theory* (Cambridge, 1981).

48  Gramsci, *Quaderni*, II, p. 1489 (*M.S.*, p. 95).

49  Ibid., pp. 1428–33 (*M.S.*, pp. 124–8).

50  Ibid., pp. 1375–95, 1232–4, 1270–1 (*M.S.*, pp. 3–20, 198–200, 232).

51  Gramsci, *Quaderni*, I, pp. 454–5; II, p. 1492 (*M.S.*, pp. 44–5).

52  Ibid., I, p. 37 (*Mach.*, p. 297).

53  Ibid., pp. 2146–7, 2141, 2161–2, 2171–2 (*Mach.*, pp. 317, 327–8, 337–8).

54  Ibid., II, pp. 893–4 (*M.S.*, p. 23).

55  Ibid., p. 1051 (*M.S.*, p. 39).

56  Ibid., pp. 1392–3 (*M.S.*, p. 18).

57  Ibid., pp. 1488–9 (*M.S.*, pp. 94–5).

58  Ibid., pp. 1379–85, (*M.S.*, pp. 6–11).

59  Ibid.

60  Ibid., p. 1337 (*M.S.*, p. 35).

61  Ibid., p. 1338 (*M.S.*, p. 35).

62  Ibid.

63  Ibid., p. 1057 (*Mach.*, p. 82).

64  On this topic see E. Garin 'Gramsci e il problema degli intellettuali', in his *Intellecttuali del XXe Secolo* (Rome, 1974), pp. 289–342.

65  Gramsci, *Quaderni*, II, p. 1398 (*M.S.*, pp. 120–1).

66 Ibid., III, p. 1584 (*Mach.*, pp. 45–6).
67 Ibid., p. 2011 (*Il Risorgimento (R.)*, in *Opere* vol. IV (Turin, 1949), p. 70).
68 Ibid., III, pp. 2012–13 (*R.*, p. 72).
69 Ibid., p. 2208 (*R*, pp. 85–6).
70 Ibid., p. 2053 (*R*. p. 94).
71 Ibid., III, p. 1729 (*Mach.*, p. 115), II, p. 1084. Croce, review of G. Mosca, *Elementi di Scienza Politica*, La Critica, XXI (1923), pp. 374–8.
72 G. Solari, 'Aldo Mautino nella Tradizione Culturale Torinese da Gobetti alla Resistenza', in A. Mautino, *La Formazione della Filosofia Politica di Benedetto Croce*, 3rd edn (Bari, 1953), pp. 75–7; P. Gobetti, 'I miei conti con l'idealismo attuale' (1923), in *Scritti Politici*, pp. 441–8; Gramsci, *Quaderni*, II, pp. 1240–1, 1315–7 (*M.S.*, pp. 215–16, 240–2).
73 Gramsci, *Quaderni*, III, p. 1591 (*Mach.*, p. 31).
74 Gramsci first sketched out those ideas in a work he was writing at the time of his arrest, 'Alcuni temi della questione meridionale', *La Questione Meridionale*, eds F. Felia and V. Parlato (Rome, 1966), especially p. 150. This, as he outlined to his sister-in-law (*Lettere*, (21), 19 March 1927, p. 58) was developed in the *Notebooks*, from which the quotes in the text are taken. *Quaderni*, III, pp. 1557–61, pp. 2037–9; II R. 1226–9, 1229–32, 1237, 1240–1, 1296; (*Mach.*, pp. 6–8, 97–8; *M.S.*, pp. 192–4, 195–7, 204, 216–17, 227, 229). See also *Lettere*, (263), 2 May 1922, p. 616.
75 Gramsci, *Quaderni*, III, p. 2012 (*R.*, p. 72).
76 Ibid., II, pp. 1225–6, 1232–4 (*M.S.*, pp. 190–1, 198–200).
77 Ibid., III, pp. 1752–4 (*Mach.*, pp. 17–18).
78 Ibid., p. 1515 (*Int.*, p. 5), and *Lettere*, (210), 7 September 1931, p. 451.
79 Ibid., p. 1514 (*Int.*, p. 3).
80 Ibid., pp. 1516–17 (*Int.*, p. 6), p. 2041, (*R.*, p. 100 n.1).
81 Ibid., I, p. 401 (*Int.*, p. 38); III, pp. 1857–64; II, pp. 1221–2, 1293–4, 1304 (*M.S.*, pp. 84–9, 186, 224–31, 248).
82 Ibid., II, pp. 1384–5, 1381–2 (*M.S.*, p. 11, 8–9).
83 Ibid., III, p. 1558 (*Mach.*, p. 5).
84 Ibid., pp. 1733–4 (*Mach.*, pp. 23–4).
85 V. Lenin, *What is to be Done?*, in K. Marx, F. Engels, V. Lenin, *On Historical Materialism* (Moscow, 1972), pp. 388–92.
86 Gramsci, *Quaderni*, II, p. 1331 (*M.S.*, p. 26).
87 Ibid., p. 1397 (*M.S.* p. 120).
88 Ibid., III, pp. 1633–5 (*Mach.*, pp. 76–7).
89 Ibid., pp. 1691–2 (*Mach.*, p. 26).
90 E.g. Tamburrano, *Antonio Gramsci*, pp. 173–6, 284–97. This issue is most fully discussed in J. Femia, *Gramsci's Political Thought*, ch. 6, with whose account I largely agree. For an alternative, Leninist reading of Gramsci, see C. Buci-Glucksmann, *Gramsci et L'Etat* (Paris, 1975).
91 Gramsci, *Quaderni*, I, pp. 122–3, III; pp. 1612–13; II, pp. 865–7 (*Mach.*, pp. 62–3, 66–8).
92 These are pointed out by M. Clark and D. Hine, 'The Italian

Communist Party: between Leninism and Social Democracy?', in D. Childs (ed.), *The Changing Face of Western Communism* (London, 1980), pp. 112–46.
93 Gramsci, *Quaderni*, II, p. 1250 (*M.S.*, p. 39).
94 These worries are stressed by A. Garosci, 'Totalitarismo e Storicismo nel pensiero di Antonio Gramsci', *Pensiero Politico e Storiografia Moderna* (Pisa, 1945), pp. 239–40. The charge of totalitarianism is also made, less subtly, by T. R. Bates, 'Antonio Gramsci and the Bolschevization of the P.C.I.', *Journal of Contemporary History*, XI (1976), p. 116. A. S. Sassoon's comment, 'that Gramsci's contribution to a debate on democracy has to a large extent been neglected . . . because he gives us little indication of the precise *form* of the new State', (*Gramsci's Politics* (London, 1980), p. 227), pinpoints the deficiency, absence even, of his political theory, not its strength as she claims. This is considered at greater length in the next section and the concluding chapter.
95 Gramsci, *Quaderni*, I, p. 662; II, p. 801, 763–4 (*Mach.*, pp. 94, 130, 132), p. 882, (*M.S.*, p. 75).
96 S. Lukes, 'Marxism, Morality and Justice', *Marx and Marxisms*, ed. G. H. R Parkinson (Cambridge, 1982), pp. 195–265.
97 K. Marx, 'Critique of the Gotha Programme', in *The First International and After*, ed. D. Fernbach (London, 1975), pp. 346–7.
98 Gramsci, *Quaderni*, II, pp. 1051–2 (*M.S.*, pp. 39–40).
99 Ibid., pp. 1330–1 (*M.S.*, p. 26).
100 S. Lukes, 'Taking Morality Seriously', *Morality and Objectivity*, ed. T. Honderich (London, 1985), pp. 105–9.


8 *Bobbio, della Volpe and the 'Italian Road to Socialism'*

1 A. Garosci, 'Primo e secondo risorgimento', *Rivista Storica Italiana*, LXXIV (1962), pp. 27–40.
2 Bobbio provides a fascinating account of his intellectual formation in 'Cultura vecchia e politica nuova' (1955), in *Politica e Cultura* (Turin, 1955), pp. 195–210.
3 A. Arblaster gives a clear characterization of Anglo-American 'cold war liberalism' in *The Rise and Decline of Western Liberalism* (Oxford 1984), pp. 309–332. Bobbio expresses analogous views to I. Berlin in *Four Essays on Liberty* (Oxford, 1969), which date from the same period.
4 For an examination of these issues, which has greatly aided my understanding of the relations between Marxism and liberalism, see S. Lukes, *Marxism and Morality* (Oxford, 1985) and A. E. Buchanan, *Marx and Justice: The Radical Critique of Liberalism* (London, 1982).
5 N. Bobbio, 'Invito al colloquio' (1951), *Politica e Cultura*, pp. 18–19.
6 Ibid., p. 31.
7 Bobbio, 'Politica culturale e politica della cultura' (1952), *Politica e Cultura*, p. 37.
8 Ibid., p. 38.
9 Ibid., pp. 43–6.

10 P. Togliatti, 'Politica e Cultura', *Il Politecnico*, September-December 1946, pp. 33–4.

11 E. Vittorini, 'Politica e Cultura. Lettera a Tolgliatti', *Il Politecnico*, Jan-March, 1947, p. 35.

12 E. Vittorini, 'Le vie degli ex-communisti', *La Nouva Stampa*, 6 September 1951.

13 See Bobbo's articles 'Dialogo tra un liberale e un communista' (1952), *Politica e Cultura*, pp. 84–99; 'Croce e la politica della cultura' (1953), ibid., pp. 100–20; 'Intellettuali e vita politica in Italia' (1954), ibid., pp. 121–38; and 'Benedetto Croce e il liberalismo' (1955), ibid., pp. 211–68.

14 B. Bandinelli, 'Confluenze e dissolvenze', *Società*, VIII (1952), pp. 278–89.

15 Bobbio, 'Difesa della libertà' (1952), *Politica e Cultura*, p. 49.

16 Ibid., pp. 51–7.

17 Bobbio, 'Democrazia e dittatura' (1954), *Politica e Cultura*, pp. 148–59.

18 G. della Volpe, 'Communismo e democrazia moderna' (1954), *Rousseau e Marx*, 2nd edn (Rome, 1957), pp. 45–56. N.B. Subsequent editions contain revised versions of this article, which reflect changes in della Volpe's views. For his final reply to Bobbio, see the important appendix to the fourth (1964) edition. A complete, if somewhat turgid, overview of his life and work, which included important contributions to Marxist aesthetics and the philosophy of history, is provided by J. Fraser, *An Introduction to the Thought of Galvano della Volpe (1895–1969)* (London, 1977). For a discussion of his political theory, see D. Zolo, *Stato Socialista e Libertà Borghesi* (Bari, 1976), pp. 77–106.

19 Della Volpe, 'Communismo e democrazia moderna', p. 47.

20 Della Volpe, *Logica come Scienza Positiva* (Riumti: Rome, 1956); K. Marx, 'Critique of Hegel's Doctrine of the State' (1843), in *Early Writings*, trans. R. Livingstone and G. Benton Harmondsworth, 1975, pp. 57–198. For a careful and critical reading of Marx's text see K. -H. Ilting, 'Hegel's concept of the state and Marx's early critique', in Z. A. Pelczynski (ed.), *The State and Civil Society: Studies in Hegel's Political Philosophy* (Cambridge, 1984), pp. 93–113. Ilting shows the deficiencies of Marx's criticisms, and *inter alia*, its inadequacy to provide the basis for an alternative theory of politics in the manner attempted by della Volpe and Lucio Colletti. Similar remarks are made by D. Forbes in his 'Introduction' to G. W. F. Hegel, *Lectures on the Philosophy of World History: Introduction* (Cambridge, 1975), pp. xxx-xxv.

21 Principally the 'Critique of Hegel's doctrine of the State', 'The Civil War in France', and 'Critique of the Gotha Programme', all translated by him in K. Marx, *Opera filosofiche giovanili*, trad. it. di G. della Volpe (Roma, 1950).

22 Della Volpe, 'Communismo e democrazia moderna', pp. 47–8. Compare K. Marx, 'On the Jewish Question', *Early Writings*, p. 230:

> Not one of the so-called rights of man goes beyond egoistic man, man as member of civil society, namely an individual withdrawn

into himself, his private interest and his private desires and separated from the community. In the rights of man it is not man who appears as a species-being. On the contrary, species-life itself, society, appears as a framework extraneous to the individuals, as a limitation of their original independence. The only bond which holds them together is natural necessity, need and private interest, the conservation of their property and their egoistic persons.

Della Volpe was clearly simply transcribed this passage in presenting his case against 'bourgeois' rights. See also the Marxian 'Preface', in *Early Writings*, especially p. 425, as always a crucial text for Italian Marxism.

23 K. Marx, 'Critique of Hegel's Doctrine of the State', as quoted in della Volpe, 'Communismo e democrazia moderna' p. 49. For this passage see Marx, *Early Writings*, p. 189.

24 Della Volpe, 'Communismo e democrazia moderna', p. 52.

25 Ibid., p. 53.

26 K. Marx, 'Critique of the Gotha Programme', as quoted in della Volpe, 'Communismo e democrazia moderna', pp. 54–5. For the full text see K. Marx, *The First International and After*, ed. D. Fernbach (Harmondsworth, 1974), pp. 346–7.

27 Della Volpe, 'Communismo e democrazia moderna', pp. 51–2, 56.

28 Bobbio, 'Della libertà dei moderni comparata a quella dei posteri' (1954), in *Politica e Cultura*, pp. 160–7.

29 Ibid., pp. 167–75.

30 Ibid., pp. 175–8. On the problems of relating socialism, liberty and equality see Frank Parkin, *Class Inequality and Political Order* (London, 1972).

31 Della Volpe, 'Communismo e democrazia moderna', pp. 54–5.

32 Bobbio, 'Della libertà dei moderni', pp. 179–91.

33 P. Togliatti, *La Via Italiana al Socialismo* (Rome, 1964).

34 Togliatti, 'Ancora sul tema della libertà', *Rinascita*, nos 7–8 (July–August, 1955), p. 501.

35 Togliatti, 'In tema di libertà', *Rinascita*, nos 11–12 (November–December, 1954), p. 735.

36 Bobbio, 'Libertà e Potere' (1955), *Politica e Cultura*, pp. 272–5, 278–80.

37 See S. Lukes, *Marxism and Morality*, pp. 100–38.

38 Bobbio, 'Libertà e Potere', p. 278.

39 Bobbio's articles, dating from 1973–76, are collected in his book *Quale Socialismo?* (Turin, 1976). Three of these pieces, and the debate they aroused amongst contributors to the socialist journal *Mondoperaio* and the communist review *Rinascita*, can be found in *Il Marxismo e lo Stato*, Quaderni del Mondoperaio, n.s., IV (Rome, 1976).

40 Bobbio, *Quale Socialismo?*, p. 36.

41 Ibid., p. 38.

42 E.g. L. Colletti, 'Stato di diritto e sovranità popolare', *Società*, XVI (1960), pp. 905–29 and 'Stato e Rivoluzione di Lenine', in *Ideologia e Società* (Bari, 1969), pp. 295–304.

43 Colletti, *Intervista Politico-Filosofica* (Bari, 1974), p. 30.
44 E.g. Antonio Negri, 'Esiste una dottrina Marxistica dello Stato', *Aut Aut*, nos. 152–3, (1976), pp. 35–60, and Bobbio's comment, in *Quale Socialismo?*, p. xii.
45 E. Berlinguer *L'Unità*, 18 Sept. 1978, quoted in M. Clark and D. Hine, 'The Italian Communist Party: Between Leninism and Social Democracy?', in D. Childs (ed.), *The Changing Face of Western Communism* (London, 1980), p. 132. See pp. 128–34 for a discussion of the ideological debates between various factions of the left during this period.
46 These articles, written between 1978 and 1984, are collected in Bobbio, *Il Futuro della Democrazia* (Turin, 1984).
47 The most succinct statement of his views on this topic can be found in a number of articles written for the *Enciclopedia Einaudi* between 1978 and 1981, and recently published as Bobbio, *Stato, Governo, Società: Per una teoria generale della politica* (Turin 1985).
48 Bobbio, *Il Futuro della Democrazia* pp. 3–24, 29–31, 38–43.
49 Ibid., pp. 43–54, 72–4.
50 Ibid., pp. 101–24.
51 Ibid., pp. 125–47.
52 Ibid., pp. 8–21, 43–50.
53 Ibid., pp. 22–6, 75–100.
54 Ibid., p. 65.
55 He has developed this argument in *Il Problema della Guerra e le Vie della Pace*, 2nd edn (Bologna, 1984).
56 Bobbio, *Il Futuro della Democrazia*, pp. 8–13.
57 See J. Raz, 'Right-based moralities', J. Waldron, (ed.), *Theories of Rights* (Oxford, 1984), pp. 182–200.
58 Bobbio, *Politica e Cultura*, pp. 280–2.

## 9 Conclusion

1 For a valuable overview of those three schools, to which I am much indebted, see R. J. Bernstein, *The Restructuring of Social and Political Theory* (Oxford, 1976).
2 I found the following discussions of this issue very useful in my own argument: J. Dunn, 'Political obligations and political possibilities', in his *Political Obligation in its Historical Context* (Cambridge, 1980), pp. 243–99; C. Pateman, *The Problem of Political Obligation: a critique of liberal theory* (2nd edn, Cambridge, 1985); C. Taylor, 'Legitimation Crisis?' in his *Philosophy and the Human Sciences: Philosophical Papers 2* (Cambridge, 1985), pp. 248–88; and most particularly, W. Connolly, *Appearance and Reality in Politics* (Cambridge, 1981).
3 For a number of analogous arguments against more recent 'scientific' approaches to politics see C. Taylor, 'Neutrality in Political Science', *Philosophy and the Human Sciences*, pp. 58–90, and W. Connolly, *Appearance and Reality*, chapters 1 and 2.

4 For a full analysis of this topic see C. Taylor, 'Interpretation and the Sciences of Man' and 'Social Theory as Practice' in *Philosophy and the Human Sciences* pp. 15–57, 91–115; A. MacIntyre, *After Virtue* (London, 1981), pp. 84–102; and 'The Indispensability of Political Theory', in D. Miller and L. Siedentop (eds), *The Nature of Political Theory*, pp. 17–33.

5 R. G. Collingwood, *The Idea of History* (Oxford, 1961), p. 213.

6 My argument and examples are taken from MacIntyre, *After Virtue*, pp. 89–96.

7 In formulating my criticisms of this approach and the critical alternative I have found a number of the essays in A. MacIntyre, *Against the Self-Images of the Age: Essays on ideology and philosophy* (London, 1971), very helpful, particularly chapters 11, 18, 19 and 22.

8 V. I. Lenin, *What is to be Done?*, trans. S. V. and P. Utechin (Oxford, 1963).

9 This theme is developed by B. Fay, 'How people change themselves: The Relationship between Critical Theory and its Audience' in T. Ball (ed.), *Political Theory and Praxis: New Perspectives* (Minneapolis, 1977), pp. 200–33 and J. Dunn, 'Social Theory, Social Understanding and Political Action', in C. Lloyd (ed.), *Social Theory and Political Practice* (Oxford, 1983).

10 For a much fuller discussion of this style of politics than I can offer here see H. Arendt, *The Human Condition* (Chicago, 1958), and *On Revolution* (New York, 1963).

11 I take it up in my forthcoming study *Liberalism: an ethical view*.

# Select Bibliography

*1 Introduction*

Ardigo, R. *Opere*, 12 vols (Angelo Draghi: Padua, 1882–1918).
Bobbio, N. *Profilo ideologico del Novecento Italiano*, (Einaudi: Turin, 1986).
De Sanctis, F. *Storia della Letteratura Italiana*, ed. B. Croce, 2 vols (Laterza: Bari, 1954). *Saggi Critici*, ed. L. Russo, 3 vols, (Laterza: Bari, 1979).
Spaventa, B. *Opere*, ed. G. Gentile, 3 vols (Sansoni: Florence, 1982).
Spaventa, S., *La Politica della Destra: Scritti e Discorsi*, ed. B. Croce (Laterza: Bari, 1910).
     *Dal 1845 al 1861. Lettere, Scritti, Documenti*, ed. B. Croce, 2nd edn (Laterza: Bari, 1923).
Villari, P. *Le Lettere Meridionale ed altri scritti sulla questione sociale in Italia* (Le Monnier: Florence, 1878).
Asor Rosa, A., 'La Cultura', in R. Romano and C. Vivanti (eds) *Storia d'Italia*, IV (ii) (Einaudi: Turin, 1975).
Bellamy, R. P. *'Da Metafisico a mercatante* – Antonio Genevesi and the development of a new language of politics' in A. Pagden (ed.)
     *The Languages of Political Theory in Early Modern Europe* (Cambridge University Press: Cambridge, 1986).
Garin, E. *Cronache di Filosofia Italiana*, 2 vols, 2nd edn (Laterza: Bari, 1962).
Oldrini, G., *La Cultura Filosofica Napoletana del' 800* (Laterza: Bari, 1973).
Skinner, Q., 'Meaning and Understanding in the History of Ideas', *History and Theory*, VIII (1969), pp. 3–53.
     ' "Social Meaning" and the Explanation of Social Action', in P. Laslett, W. G. Runciman and Q. Skinner (eds) *Philosophy, Politics and Society*, series IV, (Blackwell: Oxford, 1972), pp. 136–57.
     'Some Problems in the Analysis of Political Thought and Action', *Political Theory*, II (1974), pp. 277–303.
Villari, R., *Mezzogiorno e democrazia* (Laterza: Bari, 1979).

## 2 Pareto

Pareto, V., *Oeuvres Complètes*, ed. G. Busino (Droz: Geneva, 1964–) – some 27 volumes so far. A comprehensive bibliography can be found in volume 20. Some of the Italian works are produced here in French translation, though the Italian originals can mostly be found in vol. 22. The *Trattato* is reproduced in the French edition of 1917–18. Although overseen by Pareto, this was superceded by the second Italian edition of 1923. The standard edition is therefore *Trattato di Sociologia Generale*, ed. N. Bobbio, 2 vols (Edizioni di Comunità: Milan, 1964); the English trans., *The Mind and Society*, trans. A. Livingstone and A. Borgiorno, 4. vols (Jonathon Cape: New York/London, 1935) follows the 2nd Italian edn.

   *Sociological Writings*, trans. D. Mirfin, excellently selected and introduced by S. E. Finer, (Blackwell: Oxford, 1966).

   *The Other Pareto*, ed. P. Bucolo, trans. P. and G. Buccolo, (Scolar Press: London 1980). Reproduces a number of the minor political pieces, but the selections are often curiously and misleadingly edited and translated, suggesting the very reverse of what Pareto said.

Bobbio, N., *Saggi sulla Scienza Politica in Italia* (Laterza: Bari, 1969).

Beetham, D., 'From socialism to fascism: the relation between theory and practice in the work of Robert Michels', *Political Studies*, XXV (1977), pp. 3–24, 161–81.

Burnham, J., *The Machiavellians* (John Day: New York, 1943).

Finer, S., 'Pareto and Pluto-Democracy: The Retreat to Galapagos', *American Political Science Review*, LXII (1968), pp. 440–50.

Meisel, J. H. (ed.), *Pareto and Mosca* (Prentice-Hall: New Jersey, 1965), collects most of the classic articles.

Michels, R., *Political Parties* (Free Press: Glencoe, Illinois, 1958)

Parry, G., *Political Elites* (Allen and Unwin: London, 1969).

Winch, P., *The Idea of a Social Science* (Routledge & Kegan Paul: London 1958), pp. 95–111.

## 3 Mosca

Mosca, G., *Sulla Teorica dei Governi e Sul Governo Rappresentativo: Studi Storici e Sociali* (1884), *Le Costituzioni Moderne* (1887), both in *Ciò Che la Storia Potrebbe Insegnare: Scritti di Scienza Politica*, (Dott. A. Guiffré editore: Milano, 1958).

   *Elementi di Scienza Politica* (1896, 1923), in G. Sola (ed.), *Scritti Politici*, 2 vols (UTET: Turin, 1982), vol. 2, English trans. A. Livingstone (ed.), *The Ruling Class*, trans. H. D. Kahn (McGraw-Hill: New York/London, 1939).

   *Storia delle Dottrine Politiche* (1933) (Laterza: Bari, 1978).

   *Partiti e Sindacati nella Crisi del Regime Parlamentare* (Laterza: Bari, 1949).

A. Lombardo (ed.), *Il Tramonto dello Stato Liberale* (Bonnano editore: Catania, 1971).

E. Albertoni, *Gaetano Mosca Storia di una·Doctrina Politica* (Milan: Dott. A. Giuffrè), 1978.

Bachrach, P., *The Theory of Democratic Elitism: a critique* (University of London Press: London, 1969).

Bobbio, N., *Saggi sulla Scienza Politica in Italia* (Laterza: Bari, 1969).

Hughes, H. Stuart, 'Gaetano Mosca and the Political Lessons of History', in J. H. Meisel (ed.), *Pareto and Mosca* (Prentice-Hall: New Jersey, 1965), pp. 141–60.

Meisel, J. H., *The Myth of the Ruling Class: Gaetano Mosca and the Elite* (University of Michigan: Ann Arbor, 1958).

Parry, G. *Political Elites* (Allen and Unwin: London, 1969).

Sartori, G., *Democratic Theory* (Wayne State University: Detroit, 1962).

Schumpeter, J., *Capitalism, Socialism and Democracy*, 4th edn (George Allen and Unwin: London, 1954).

### 4 Labriola

Labriola, A., *Opere*, 3 vols, ed. L. Dal Pane (Feltrinelli: Milan, 1959). The project for the complete works was never finished, and these volumes contain only his early writings.

*La Concezione Materialistica della Storia*, ed. E. Garin (Laterza: Bari, 1965).

*Scritti vari editi e inediti di filosofia e politica, raccolti e pubblicati da B. Croce* (Laterza:, Bari, 1906).

*Essays on the Materialistic Conception of History*, trans. C. H. Kerr (C. H. Kerr & Co: Chicago, 1903).

*Socialism and Philosophy*, trans. Ernest Untermann (C. H. Kerr & Co: Chicago, 1934).

Dal Pane, L., *Antonio Labriola nella politica e nella cultura italiana*, 2nd edn (Einaudi: Turin, 1975).

Femia, J. V., 'Antonio Labriola: A forgotten marxist thinker', *History of Political Thought*, II (1983), pp. 557–72.

Jacobitti, E. E., 'Labriola, Croce and Italian Marxism (1885–1910)', *Journal of the History of Ideas*, XXX(i) (1975), pp. 297–318.

Kolakowski, L., 'Antonio Labriola: An Attempt at an Open Orthodoxy', in *Main Currents of Marxism*, vol. 2, trans. P. S. Falla Oxford University Press: Oxford, 1982), pp. 175–92.

### 5 Croce

Croce, B., *The Opere Complete* (Laterza: Bari, last ed., 1965) numbering some 67 volumes. A selection made by Croce – *Filosofia – Poesia – Storia* (Ricciardi: Milan/Naples, 1951) is translated by C. Sprigge as *Philosophy, Poetry, History* Oxford University Press: Oxford, 1966). A new critical edition of all his writings and correspondance is in preparation. The official bibliography is S. Borsari, *L'Opera di Benedetto Croce* (Istituto Italiano per gli Studi Storici: Naples, 1964). The best single source for his life and ideas is his *Autobiography* (1915), trans. R. G. Collingwood, (Oxford University Press: Oxford 1927).

Abbate, M., *La Filosofia di Benedetto Croce e la Crisis della Società Italiana*, 2nd edn (Einaudi: Torino, 1966).

Bellamy, R., 'Liberalism and Historicism: Benedetto Croce and the political role of Idealism in Italy c. 1880–1950' in A. Moulakis (ed.), *The Promise of History* (Walter de Gruyter: Berlin/New York, 1985), pp. 69–119.

'Guido de Ruggierio's *History of European Liberalism*', *Historical Journal*, forthcoming.

Bobbio, N., *Politica e Cultura* (Einaudi: Torino, 1955), pp. 100–120, 211–268.

Gramsci, A., *Il Materialismo Storico e la Filosofia di Benedetto Croce* (Einaudi: Turin, 1949).

Hughes, H. Stuart, *Consciousness and Society: The Reorientation of European Social Thought, 1890–1930* (Harvester: Brighton, 1979), pp. 82–90, 200–29.

Jacobbitti, E. E., *Revolutionary Humanism and Historicism in Modern Italy* (Yale University Press: New Haven/London, 1981).

Mautino, A., *La Formazione della Filosofia Politica di Benedetto Croce*, 3rd edn (Laterza: Bari, 1953).

Rossi, P., 'Benedetto Croce e lo storicismo assoluto', *Il Mulino*, VI (1957), pp. 322–54.

Sasso, G., *Benedetto Croce: La ricerca della dialettica* (Morano: Naples, 1967).

## 6 Gentile

Gentile, G., The complete works in 55 volumes is being published by the Foundazione Gentile and Sansoni, Florence, and all the main works have now appeared. The official bibliography is V. A. Bellezza, *Bibliografia degli Scritti di Giovanni Gentile* (Sansoni: Florence, 1950) and is largely reproduced in H. S. Harris, 1960 (i), whilst 1960 (ii) includes a critical survey and bibliography of everything on or by Gentile in English. The most important of the latter are:–

*The Theory of Mind as Pure Act*, trans. from 3rd edn by H. Wildon Carr (Macmillan: London, 1922).

*The Reform of Education*, trans., by D. Bigongiari (Ernest Benn: London, 1922).

Fragments of *Che Cosa è il Fascismo*, trans. H. W. Schneider, in *Making the Fascist State* (Oxford University Press, Oxford, 1928), pp. 321–5, 344–53.

*Origini e Dottrina del Fascismo*, pp. 43–51, trans. D. Parmee, in A. Lyttelton (ed.), *Italian Fascisms: from Pareto to Gentile* (Harper and

Row: New York/London, 1975), pp. 301–15.

    *Genesis and Structure of Society*, trans. with an introduction by H. S. Harris (University of Illinois: Urbana, 1960 (ii) ).

Bellamy, R. P., 'Croce, Gentile and Hegel and the doctrine of the ethical State', *Rivista di Studi Crociani*, XX (1983), pp. 263–81; XXI (1984), pp. 67–73.

    'Hegel's Conception of the State', *Political Science*, forthcoming.

Di Lalla, M., *Vita di Giovanni Gentile* (Sansoni: Firenze, 1975).

Harris, H. S., *The Social Philosophy of Giovanni Gentile* (University of Illinois: Urbana, 1960 (i) ).

Marcuse, H., *Reason and Revolution – Hegel and the rise of social theory*, 2nd edn (Routledge and Kegan Paul: London, 1954), pp. 402–9.

Romano, S., *Giovanni Gentile: La Filosofia al Potere* (Bompiani: Milan, 1984).


## 7 Gramsci

Gramsci, A., *Opere di Antonio Gramsci*, 12 vols (Einaudi: Turin, 1947–72). The first volume contains the prison letters, the next six the notebooks and the other volumes his political writings prior to his imprisonment.

    *Quaderni del Carcere* ed. Valentino Gerratana, 4 vols (Einaudi: Turin, 1975). The new scholarly edition, reproducing the order in which Gramsci wrote them.

    *Lettere dal Carcere*, ed. S. Caprioglio and E. Fubini (Einaudi: Turin, 1965), a new scholarly edition, containing numerous letters omitted for political reasons from the 1947 text.

    *Selections from the Prison Notebooks*, ed. and trans, Q. Hoare and G. Nowell Smith (Lawrence and Wishart: London, 1971).

    *Selections from Political Writings, 1910–20*, ed. Q. Hoare, trans. J. Mathews (Lawrence and Wishart: London, 1977).

    *Selections from Political Writings, 1921–6*, ed. and trans. Q. Hoare (Lawrence and Wishart: London, 1978).

Adamson, W. L., *Hegemony and Revolution: A study of Antonio Gramsci's political and cultural theory* (University of California: Berkeley, 1980).

Anderson, P., 'The Antinomies of Antonio Gramsci', *New Left Review*, 100, (November, 1976–January 1977), pp. 5–78.

Badaloni, N., *Il Marxismo di Gramsci*, (Einaudi: Turin, 1975).

Clark, M., *Antonio Gramsci and the Revolution that Failed* (Yale University Press.: New Haven/London, 1977).

Colletti, L. 'Antonio Gramsci and the Italian Revolution', *New Left Review*, 65, (January 1971) pp. 87–94.

Davidson, A., *Antonio Gramsci: Towards an Intellectual Biography* (Merlin: London, 1977).

Femia, J., *Gramsci's Political Thought* (Clarendon: Oxford, 1981).

Fiori, G., *Antonio Gramsci: Life of a Revolutionary* (New Left Books: London, 1970).

Garosci, A., 'Totalitarismo e storicismo nel pensiero di Antonio Gramsci', in *Pensiero politico e storiografia moderna* (Nistri–Lischi: Pisa, 1954).

Mouffe, C. (ed.), *Gramsci and Marxist Theory* Routledge and Kegan Paul.: London, 1979), Contains Bobbio's classic article.

Sassoon, A. S., *Gramsci's Politics* (Croom Helm: London, 1980).

Tamburrano, G., *Antonio Gramsci, La vita, il pensiero, l'azione* (Laterza: Bari, 1963).

Togliatti, P., *On Gramsci and other writings* (Lawrence and Wishart: London, 1979).

Williams, G. *Proletarian Order: Antonio Gramsci, Factory Councils and the Origins of Italian Communism 1911–21* (Pluto: London, 1975).


## 8 Bobbio, Colletti, Della Volpe

Bobbio, N., *Politica e Cultura* (Einaudi: Turin, 1955).
*Da Hobbes a Marx* (Morano: Naples, 1965).
*Quale Socialismo?* (Einaudi: Turin, 1976).
*Il Futuro della Democrazia* (Einaudi: Turin, 1985).
*Stato, Governo, Societa: Per una teoria generale della politica* (Einaudi: Turin, 1985). The last three works are being translated by Polity Press.

Colletti, L., *Ideologia e Società* (Laterza: Bari, 1969). English trans. J. Herrington and J. White, *From Rousseau to Marx* (New Left Books: London, 1972). *Il Marxismo e Hegel* (Laterza: Bari, 1969) English trans. L. Garner, *Marxism and Hegel* New Left Books: London, 1973). 'Politico-philosophical Interview', *New Left Review*, 83–8, July–August (1974), pp. 3–28.

Della Volpe, G., *Opere*, 6 vols, ed. I. Ambrogio, (Riuniti: Rome, 1972–3). English, trans. J. Fraser, *Rousseau and Marx* (Lawrence and Wishart: London, 1978); M. Ceasar *Critique of Taste* (New Left Books: London, 1978); John Rothschild, *Logic as a Positive Science*: London, 1980).

Buchanan, A. E., *Marx and Justice: The Radical Critique of Liberalism* (Methuen: London, 1982).

Cohen, M., Nagel, T. and Scanlon, T., *Marx, Justice and History* (Princeton University Press: Princeton, 1980).

Lukes, S., *Marxism and Morality* (Oxford University Press: Oxford, 1985).

Parkin, F., *Class Inequality and Political Order* (Paladin: London, 1972).


## 9 Conclusion

Arendt, H., *The Human Condition* (University of Chicago Press: Chicago, 1958). *On Revolution* (The Viking Press: New York, 1963).

Ball, T., *Political Theory and Practice* (University of Minnesota Press: Minneapolis, 1977).

Bernstein. R. J., *The Restructuring of Social and Political Theory* (Blackwell: Oxford, 1976).

Connolly, W. E., *Appearance and Reality in Politics* (Cambridge University Press: Cambridge, 1981).

Dunn, J., *Political Obligation in its Historical Context: Essays in Political Theory* (Cambridge University Press: Cambridge, 1980).

Fay, B. *Social theory and Political Practice* (George Allen and Unwin: London, 1975).

Guess, R., *The Idea of Critical Theory: Habermas and the Frankfurt School* (Cambridge University Press: Cambridge, 1981).

Lloyd, C. *Social Theory and Political Practice* (Clarendon Press: Oxford, 1983).

MacIntyre, A., *Against the Self Images of the Age: Essays on Ideology and Philosophy* (Duckworth: London, 1971).

*After Virtue: a study in moral theory* (Duckworth: London, 1981).

Pateman, C., *The Problem of Political Obligation: a critique of liberal theory*, 2nd edn (Polity Press: Cambridge, 1985).

Taylor, C., *Philosophy and the Human Sciences: Philosophical Papers 2* (Cambridge University Press: Cambridge, 1985).

# INDEX

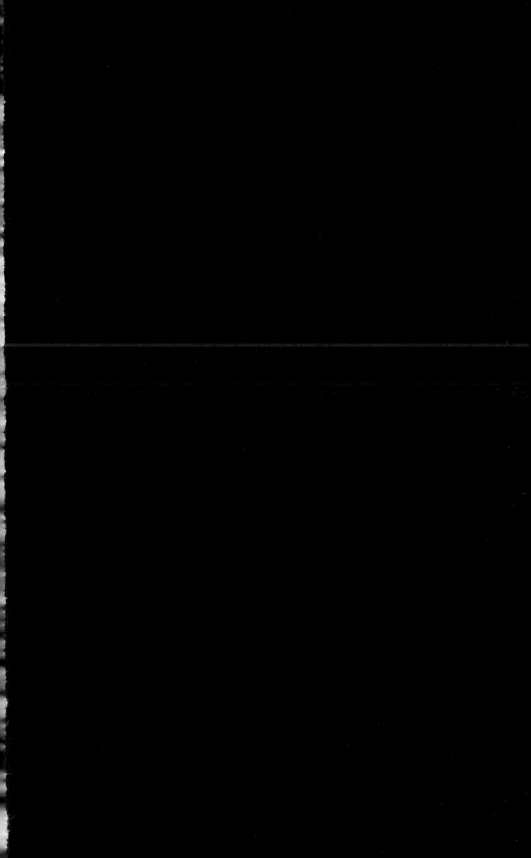